CW00741092

RETURN

OF THE

DOVE

Dedicated to Nikola Tesla, this book provides the
scientific answer to the great spiritual needs of today's
world. Contents: Now and In the Beginning; The Days
Just Ahead; The End of Man's Crucifixion; This Cosmic
Moment; The Nikola Tesla Story; Farewell of the Dove;
The Arthur H. Matthews Story; The Otis T. Carr Story;
Let There Be Light; Suggested Reading List.

Margaret Storm

ISBN 1-56459-975-2

DEDICATED TO

Nikola Tesla and the White Dove

. . . Two understanding hearts, two sustaining
Flames, who still labor faithfully with us, tending the little Lamp of Earth until that nearing
hour when our Illumined Planet will orbit in
glory as Freedom's Star.

"THE TWO HEARTS AND FLAMES" COULD BE REFERRING TO TWO PEOPLE (LIVING BEINGS)

Contents

PART I

Now and in the Beginning

NOW IT is early November, 1957, here on the planet Earth. It is a glad November, a special kind of November, decked with a sparkle and a twinkle and with long tall nights stretching upward to the stars. There are two new pin-pricks of light up there which we call sputniks. Later they will be joined by other little moons and little satellites, all rollicking and frolicking together, round and round the globe, like the gay wooden horses on a merry-go-round. Yes, indeed, it is a glad November!

Then there are those lovely saucers flying about everywhere, their brilliant colors flashing like a peacock's tail. Many of them come to us over great cosmic lightways, winging their way even without wings, traveling about God's great playground, propelled by the sustaining breath of His love for His children—even the foolish ones who now need be foolish no longer. For that is what makes it a glad November here on the planet Earth. We need be foolish no longer!

Now we can awaken, stretch our minds and hearts up, up, up, until we hit a star. We have been prodigals for the last nineteen million years, and the diet of husks has been awful. But the bad dream is over. We can relax and prepare for the feast—a grand and wonderful festival of human victory which will last for two thousand years. By that time we will have long since forgotten about the husks and the nineteen million years of planetary isolation, and we will be out there riding the lightways in spaceships, hopping from star to star on our cosmic assignments, while the great symphony of the spheres plays on and on and the angels sing!

Of course, we still have with us in these latter days the diehards, the spoil-sports, the screwballs, the odd balls, the sad sacks, and a whole assortment of wet blankets in a wide variety of sizes, shapes and shades. They are the ones with the souped-up egos; they do not buy the idea of spaceships, music of the spheres or the singing of angels. They are the foolish ones who want to continue their foolishness.

In the hospital world that we have known for millions of years during our cosmic quarantine, it is correct to say that most of us have been foolish in the majority of our embodiments. We have been dreadful phonies, strictly hams, acting out roles on a stage called the world, a stage like a mixed-up upside-down cake with an animated crazy quilt for a platter. With such a design for living, it is a matter of no wonderment that Whoever-Is-In-Charge had to send flying saucers to rescue us, warn us, cajole us, or to just haul some of us off to a new dumping ground, to a new sort of hospital planet devoted exclusively to drying out wet blankets and removing the sadness from sacks—and that, if you please, just at the very moment when the chemise became high fashion.

But those of us who are left here on the planet Earth, who will continue our evolution here after the saucers have *Flown* (flown) the cracked cups away to a new repair shop—well, we will have a whale of a clean-up job ahead of us because this globe has been lacking in good housekeeping for a long, long time. We will have to step out and keep up with the Joneses, only this time they don't live down the street; they live up there on those gay, sparkling spheres called Venus, Mars, Jupiter and so forth, and in places which sound like a melody—Aquaria, Clarion and a tiny little lighted jewel of a planet called Excelsior.

Excelsior, it has been said, is a delightful little place inhabited by little people, but real little people, very beautiful little men and women of exquisite stature towering two or perhaps even three inches in height. They have perfect forms which move and float in rhythmic dances of breath-taking beauty and grace. They have never known distress of any kind; they are God's dedicated little children; their Fire Dances in honor of the Sacred Flame are all expressions of thanksgiving to their Creator for His gift of Life. That is their way of praying. Dancing is to them synonomous with living, or the expressing of gratitude for limit-less cosmic abundance.

They are extremely artistic, and when they are not danc-ing, they are constantly helping the little nature spirits— the fairies, the elves, the water sprites—to rearrange the decorations on the surface of their planet. Perhaps a min-iature rose tree just there, and a tiny waterfall plunging dizzily down from a sheer drop of one foot would be effective as a backdrop for a new dance. Are ideas such as these pondered by the little men and women who live on Excelsior?

The heavy foot of an earthling may never tread on Excelsior, but it is said that spaceships are equipped with marvelous viewing devices which will bring a planetary surface into a clear focus such as would make all Hollywood's cameras and screens seem like instruments as primitive as a stone arrowhead.

Truly, the cosmos is a place fascinating beyond the imagination of man, and best of all, it is man's heritage. That is where we belong—out there in the playground of the gods—far beyond the silly sputniks, the false moons, the grapefruit-sized satellites: even beyond the moon itself, and beyond the neighboring planets and stars and into the great golden pathway of the Milky Way. We belong far beyond all the rubbish and rubble of this once magnificent planet which we ourselves have turned into a hell. The universe is our heritage and we have but to claim it, to explore it, to revel in its fathomless beauty. It is all ours to use, to improve, and to love.

That is the clue. It is ours to love. But we have forgotten how to love natural things, God-created things. We love only our own grotesque miscreations—our mighty death-dealing weapons, our sculptured monuments marking blood-stained battlefields, our martial music designed to stir the hearts of men as they march forth to kill and to be killed: our guided missiles conceived by unguided men left helpless and bereft without knowledge of their Source: our ungreat bombs that can pulverize a great city at one blow: our unmighty DEW line, known among the hush-hush boys, among the don't-tell-the-taxpayer boys, as the busted bubble.

We love to visit our spacious cemeteries, crowded to overflowing with the silent dead; we love to bedeck the graves with ugly arrangements of withering flowers, piling death upon death. We are sorry we could not give our beloved a more handsome tombstone, but taxes ride beside death on this planet. You know how it is. There was the hospital bill, the doctor bill, the X-ray bill, the bill at the corner drugstore, plus a whopping big bill from the surgeon who cut and carved and sliced and sawed with all his might and main while death just stood there and waited patiently.

It was by no whim of chance that our cosmic Hierarchy designated the earth as Planet D in this solar system. That letter has come to stand for death, destruction, devastation, desperation, deficits, depletion, depressions, devils and the DEW line. It also stands for dainty dancers who have never known distress. But that is on the planet Excelsior.

Somewhere out there in space, somewhere out there where the wind is singing, where the air is fresh and sweet as white daisies laughing in the sun, the little planet spins on its course. A tiny crystal globe is alight with the Sacred Flame, and around it the little men and women circle in their rhythmic dance, their hearts aflame with love of the One. The little waterfall splashes merrily. A brilliant butterfly flits about the miniature rose tree and finds a resting place. The stillness vibrates with rapture. The dance goes on and on—on Excelsior.

And here on this earth death still rides in the saddle, but not for long. Now in this glad November we can live with joy again. Now is the moment of appraisal. Now is the time to catch, to hold, to examine a fleeting cosmic instant covering nineteen million years in the cycle of human

history on this planet earth. For now in these early November days of 1957 we know that the long and terrible
chapter of human struggle has been finished. That is, it
is finished for those who want it that way. For the others
—the diehard skeptics, the sinister secretives, the know-
it-alls, the so-whaters—for all these and others of their
tribe special provision will be made. But elsewhere, somewhere. Not here. Not on this planet. For this planet has
really had it, and far, far beyond the call of duty.

That call first came sounding through the entire galaxy
nineteen million years ago. The universe had assembled a
large number of refugees from evolution. These were the
laggards, the leftovers, the rejected ones from other planets
and stars in this and other solar systems. Using their free
will in a destructive manner, they had made orphans of themselves by refusing the guidance of their own higher natures, their own Divine Selves, and preferred to dally away
their time in experimenting with miscreations of their own
rather than in learning to create according to the Divine
Plan. They contributed nothing constructive to the whole
of which they were an integral part.

They had skipped so many classes in evolution that they
could not hope to catch up. Their miscreations proved so
imperfect and destructive that they were finally refused
further opportunities to incarnate within their own groups.
So the earth people came forward and offered to help the
laggards by receiving them into families here. No other
planet had a classroom for these problem students, or at
least no other planet was willing to tackle the job of trying
to redeem them. But the earth was a young planet, vigorous
and strong, magnificently beautiful, abundant and full of
promise. Disease was unknown. There was no distress in

the sense of strain or pain. Members of the First Root Race were brought to the earth in a natural spaceship, a forcefield formed by their Manu. They were accompanied by their teachers, sages and Hierarchs representing the seven great cosmic Rays, the sacred Flames which contain within their fiery essence all the virtues of the Godhead.

This first group settled down in what is now familiarly known as the Grand Teton area in Wyoming. That country is still beautiful today, but in those days the entire globe was a sphere of unrivalled beauty. It is said that Amaryllis, the Goddess of Spring, so loved the earth that she spent nine hundred years supervising its decoration, preparing it for the first guests. Over the entire globe the climate was always pleasant, neither too warm nor too cold, a land of eternal spring. There were no storms, floods, hurricanes, blizzards or natural catastrophes because there was no discord among the people. Human beings definitely make their own weather conditions.

Moreover, the clear and beautiful lower atmosphere around the earth became steadily more and more radiant as the Hierarchs and sages instructed the people how to draw forth the God-essence of the Rays; how to magnetize and anchor the sacred Fire upon their altars, so that it would be readily available for use for any practical purpose that might arise.

The people had chosen to come into physical embodiment in order to use their thoughts, feelings, spoken words and actions in the material atmosphere of these lower realms, and thereby gain self-mastery within a certain environment. Embodiment was in the nature of a scientific experiment, an opportunity to use the sacred Flame on matter of a low vibration and yet secure a harmonious result. These people

MANU = MANNA OR MANA =
MANU = MAN OR HUMAN, IN SANSKRIT.

knew that matter was spirit slowed down, and that spirit
was matter speeded up.

As more and more energy was drawn forth from the
seven Rays and anchored in matter, the colors in the lower
atmosphere of the earth became beautiful, positive and constructive; the music of the spheres was a natural outpouring
from the earth because of the sustained radiation, and in
those days all the stars and planets sang together in one
vast symphonic paean of praise to the God of Love who
had created a great cosmic paradise for His children.

The earth people, living in this radiant atmosphere, were
constantly bathed in these glorious emanations which flooded
the earth from outer space, and then ascended back to the
Source, for it is in the nature of the Flame, even physical
fire, to rise. As a result, the people felt bouyant, energized
and spiritually attuned at all times. Their vision was un-
clouded and they had not only the visible and tangible evidence of the incoming Rays, and the rising Flames, but
they were in constant association with Cosmic Beings, Masters of the Ageless Wisdom, Archangels, and the Seraphic
and Cherubic hosts.

Each Root Race was supposed to spend 14,000 years on
the planet, permitting the formation of seven sub-races,
each under one of the seven Rays. That arrangement gave
opportunity for a full round of experience under forty-nine
different sets of conditions. The first two Root Races accomplished this with ease, for they had no weight of discord
upon them.

At the close of this type of initiation into self-mastery,
each individual then accomplished the Ascension: that is, he
had attained complete command over matter so that he was
able to raise the vibration of the physical atoms which com-

posed his body and ascend to his home star to await his next evolutionary assignment.

Save for the long drag of time, the initiatory system on this planet remains the same today. At some time, in some embodiment, each individual must make his own Ascension. He must be able to achieve mastery over matter, raise the vibrations of his physical body, form a forcefield or personal spaceship and ascend to his home star. During the present Aquarian Age all death, as we know it today, will cease on this planet. Each individual will be scientifically trained to make his Ascension, exactly as it is done on other planets.

The clue to the Ascension, in olden times as well as now, is the use of Love. If there is any discord shown toward matter, toward a physical atom, it is impossible to raise the vibration in a natural way, but only by the use of brute force such as modern scientists advocate. Discord has the effect of lowering vibrations. The early initiates were trained by Adepts from other planets who came to the earth to assist the first inhabitants. Each individual, in experimenting with matter, was trained to lovingly call forth the God-substance which forms the nucleus of the atom, inviting it to rise and return to the Source. The entire atom responded by increasing the rate of its revolution and rising.

This method is still the one and only method by which the Ascension can be achieved today. Each and every human being must make the Ascension from this earth classroom before he can progress further in evolution elsewhere. Love is the one and only answer. Jesus, the great disciple of Light, demonstrated the Ascension two thousand years ago, but the dark forces working within churchianity perverted the true teachings, and the long-suffering public continued to suffer and pay the bills.

The Third Root Race, under the loving direction of its
Manu, spread its activities out over the globe to the east
and the west, the north and the south. The objective was
always the same—to call forth the God-essence within the
Rays, to anchor that divine energy within matter, thus
spiritualizing the very earth itself so that eventually the
atoms would open like budding flowers, freeing the imprisoned light in the center of the atom, a light which had
gained in brilliance because of its service to the planet. The
light thus set free by the action of the descending cosmic
Rays, joined the great ascending Flame that rose from the
earth on its way back home to the Source.

Meanwhile, as more and more souls incarnated on the
earth, more and more energy was called forth from the cosmic rays; more matter was spiritualized and the area of anchorage extended deeper into the earth. The earth became
more and more perfect in form as the people expended more
and more love upon matter, and attained more mastery in
freeing imprisoned light. Such a high state of harmony
was reached by the Third Root Race that when the call went
forth for a classroom for the laggards, the earth people
responded.

The population agreed to receive the laggards, permitting
them to come in through the natural gates of birth. Birth
in those days was not a physical process, however, but electrical. It was accomplished by the crossing and union of
positive and negative light rays projected forth by the
chosen parents. This system will again be restored on
the planet earth during the present Aquarian Age.

The earth people felt quite confident that the laggards,
being born into such an atmosphere of joy and harmony,
would quickly adapt themselves to the young and progressive

evolutionary procedure on the planet, and forgetting their past would join in developing the Divine Plan on this globe.

The laggards were brought in as souls, but their causal bodies were encased in dense astral bodies of ugly coloration because they were heavily burdened with karma resulting from their misspent lives on other planets and stars. Their mental bodies were beclouded with self-created thoughtforms of monstrous appearance, and they were unable to absorb more than a flicker of light from their individualized God-nature. Therefore, being virtually helpless they had to be brought to the earth in spaceships manned by special teachers, and they were then held in a specially prepared astral atmosphere near the earth until each had a chance to be born in a physical body. These physical bodies were not as dense as they are now, but light and quite ethereal, with a high rate of vibration. The people did not walk, but levitated. There was no physical labor or struggle of any kind, no distress and no disease.

The high hopes which the earth people had for the laggards did not manifest. The laggards, once in physical bodies, continued their old ways. They refused to respond to their new harmonious environment. They insisted on using their own free will to create their own monstrous follies; they declined to assist in unfolding the Divine Plan. Moreover, they polluted and poisoned the radiant atmosphere with their astral emanations. Scorning all cooperative endeavors spiritually, they grew and matured in physical grossness; they mated and produced offspring of their kind; they poisoned their physical bodies with their own misguided emotions and thoughts of hatred; they introduced disease on the planet; they experienced death instead of the glorious Ascension back to the Source; they lost all contact with their Source; they refused to believe in the One; their vision was so beclouded that they could not see the interaction of the descending Rays and the ascending Flame. They doomed themselves to long, wearying cycles of birth, death and re-birth.

For a long while the Third Root Race people, hosts to the laggards, managed to maintain the status quo among themselves. They kept the sacred Flames burning brightly upon their altars; they adored the One; they kept green the memory of those paradisiacal days before the laggards came. But the frightful contamination became worse: the atmosphere around the earth became gloomy and dark: the Rays could no longer penetrate to the vegetation and soil; only the physical sunlight, devoid of the life-giving God-essence of the great universal Virtues, reached the people. No longer did the earth give forth its natural note of harmony: its great vibrant chords were missing from the music of the spheres. No longer did the earth give off light, for the Flame had ceased to rise.

This, in brief, is the story of the Fall of Man.

———— ————

Conditions became so hopeless that the Hierarchy of this solar system, meeting in conclave eighteen and a half million years ago, decided to abandon the evolutionary experiment on the earth and dissolve the planet. But Sanat Kumara, ruler of Venus, asked to be permitted to try to restore harmony on the earth. His wish was granted, and leaving the planet Venus in charge of Lady Venus, Goddess of Beauty in this solar system, Sanat Kumara came to the earth with about a hundred helpers, and set up headquarters on an island in the Gobi Sea, now the Gobi desert. This was called the White Island of Shamballa.

Sanat Kumara, with all his vast powers as one of the greatest Adepts in the galaxy, struggled for eighteen and a half million years to restore order on the earth, and to save the planet from dissolution. Early in His reign as Lord of the World, He submerged the contaminated continent of Lemuria, home of the Third Root Race, in the area now known as the Pacific Ocean. A remaining seed group of Lemurians settled in Africa and became the ancestors of the present negro race. Easter Island was sealed against the ravages of time and preserved as a monument to old Lemuria. Also, the melody of an ancient Lemurian song has been passed down to us and is still sung today— Auld Lang Syne.

Under the direction of Sanat Kumara, a selected group started the Fourth Root Race, the Atlans, in the area now covered by the waters of the Atlantic Ocean. But the contamination of the laggards proved too great: black magicians reigned in high places and the practice of black magic became widespread throughout the populace. Finally Sanat Kumara was forced to order the submerging of Atlantis. Remnants of the population scattered and formed the present Chinese and Japanese races, among others.

The scriptures carry a partial account of this great deluge, together with the significant statement that the world, or worldliness as introduced by the laggards in the form of gross materialism, leading to black magic, would again be destroyed, but by fire from heaven rather than water. This is the Violet Fire of the seventh cosmic Ray which is the Ray that White Magicians use to transmute black magic. It is now in manifestation and will energize the planet for the next 2,000 years of the Aquarian Age. These, then are the latter days.

This brings the history of humanity to the present Fifth Root Race, and to its present turning point as the Sixth Root Race is being formed under the direction of the Christ Forces assisted by thousands of Adepts drawn from all parts of our galaxy. These visitors we have come to know as space people.

Now is the time when the final cleansing is to take place on the earth's surface, within the interior of the planet which had also become contaminated, and in the dense astral atmosphere of the earth, which now extends 10,000 feet above the surface of the globe. It is in this astral area around the earth that all of the contamination has accumulated from the emotional emanations given off by individuals through the ages, and where hover the frightful thought-forms thrown off by the race.

In this astral area, until 1957, were also found all dis-embodied entities known as earthbound spirits. They refused, under their privilege to use their free will in any manner whatsoever, to leave the earth, and mingled freely with the populace, often inciting those in physical bodies to commit deeds of violence.

However, by November, 1957, this sordid and sorry tale of the Fall of Man had ended. Sanat Kumara had completed his work of restoration to a point where He was able to leave the earth and return to His home planet of Venus. With the aid of tens of thousands of individuals from other planets coming to the assistance of the earth at this time, and with renewed help from the Angelic Kingdom which had been forced to virtually withdraw during the isolated years, the interior of the globe has been cleansed; every single earthbound entity has been removed from the astral atmosphere; and all black magicians have been seized and taken from the globe. The forces of darkness are still operating among black disciples and tools in human bodies, but as these individuals die, they will not be permitted to reincarnate unless they agree to serve the Light.

The contaminated astral atmosphere around the earth, although still being constantly poisoned by emanations of hatred, vengeance, greed and lust generated by living human beings, is being bombarded night and day by powerful rays directed from space ships orbiting the earth, by cleansing energies from saucers flying close to the earth, and by fireballs, manufactured on Mars, being exploded near the ground in contaminated areas which cannot be reached by flying saucers.

Although disease and death, and all the old fears of poverty, war, hunger and helplessness, still stalk the earth, these grim spectors are attracted hence only by the unlighted ones—by the diehards, the sinister secretives, the stubborn skeptics—in other words, by the laggards who are still lagging. However, it is now in this brief interval just ahead that death itself will at long last prove to be a cleansing blessing to this globe rather than a curse, for now as soon as an individual is released from his physical body, anywhere on the globe, he is removed immediately from the earth's astral atmosphere. No discarnates are allowed to linger near the earth.

No matter what may be the circumstances surrounding the death of an individual, he is permitted only three months of rest after shedding his physical body. Then he must be up and doing, working on a new assignment. If he is hopelessly enmeshed in karma, he may be removed from the earth entirely and permitted to take rebirth on another hospital planet, with specially prepared vibrations suitable to his condition.

If he is to come back into re-embodiment on this planet, he must prepare by undergoing special purification processes in Temples of the Violet Fire in the etheric realm. This is the time when all worldliness and materialism such as we have known is to be destroyed by the Violet Fire of the Seventh Ray, the fire of transmutation through the divine qualities of Mercy, Forgiveness and Compassion.

On the Inner Planes, the sheep have been separated from the goats in a separation which is final for these times. In other words, the future of nearly ten billion souls associated with this earth evolution at this time, has been decided by the Lords of Karma. Actually, it has been decided by each individual himself, through hundreds of embodiments down through long centuries, but the record for each soul has been submitted for review at this time.

These records clearly show how much light is being used by each individual, for we all use light according to our capacity. If our record shows that in the past we have been able to make use of only a small amount of light, then it is pointless to continue evolution on this planet. These unlighted ones, if they could not keep up with their evolutionary classwork in the past, would be dire misfits in the vastly improved conditions which will unfold on this planet in the immediate future.

These conditions are already causing an extremely increased tempo in mental, emotional and etheric vibrations as well as in material physical aspects.

Material situations will be so greatly improved within a few years that the planet will be unrecognizable according to present low standards. The globe, during the past nineteen million years, became so heavily weighted with discord that it drooped on its bent axis like a weary flower on a stalk.

Now the angelic kingdom, under the supervision of planetary and cosmic Hierarchs, has straightened the axis, a task which was started in its early phase over twenty years ago. The final phase was started on January 1, 1957 and completed late in 1958. Meanwhile, the earth is moving in a sidewise motion as it edges into a new orbit, and at the same time is being lifted up, spiralling into a new spacial region.

In the very near future, the natural action of the cosmic rays will bring about a complete restoration of the planet. It will again become a paradise as it was in the days before the laggards came. What we know as the astral atmosphere will be completely dispelled. Light from the cosmic rays will reach the earth in natural abundance. The climate will change so that the Goddess of Spring, Amaryllis, will again take charge of vegetation the year round, and the little elementals who build the grass and trees, the fruits and flowers, will be able to work without hindrance.

With the incoming light, the atmosphere of the earth will again become brilliant with colors; the sphere will sound forth its great chords in the cosmic symphony. Disease will vanish and its memory be wiped from the minds of men. Death will be vanquished and each individual will make his Ascension in dignity and in peace. In harmony and in love, he will return to his home star, there to await his next evolutionary assignment.

All of this is in the immediate future when the words of the Lord's Prayer shall become manifest: "Thy Kingdom come: Thy Will be done, on earth as it is in Heaven." If there is to be heaven on this earth then it is natural to assume that there will be no place on this planet for the obstructionists, the unlighted ones who are haunted by doubt, fear, hate and greed. This book is therefore of interest only to those who know in their hearts that they really desire to serve the Light; that, as such servers, they truly wish to take part in the unfoldment of the Divine Plan on this planet. We need not waste time and energy trying to convince the unlighted ones that God is a good God. If they have not figured that out in nineteen million years, it is hardly likely that they will learn to lovingly entertain the idea during the next nineteen years—for by 1975, the past dark history of this earth will be scarcely remembered.

Therefore, only those who are interested in taking part in ushering in the new civilization should read this book. Among those bent on vengeance, war, financial profit, and so forth, this book will only arouse further antagonism and jealousy. As these obstructionists are gradually removed from the earth through death, they will not be permitted to incarnate here under present regulations being enforced by the Lords of Karma.

Where their future lies is a matter of no interest to us whatsoever. One of our greatest failures as humans lies in the fact that we have been sentimentalists, and have been so ever ready to sympathize with imperfection. Had we been as eager to admire the Perfection of God and His works, we would never have become bogged down, floundering about, in a sea of imperfection. We cannot have it both ways. Those who are not with God are against Him and that settles the matter.

Our entire energy now must be thrown on the positive side. We must study the situation as of today, find out just where we stand, discover what progress has been made, and what remains to be done. Who are the individuals in embodiment at the moment who are aiding in the unfolding of the Divine Plan? What are they doing? How can we help them today? What positive enterprises, no matter how tiny or how great, can we initiate, not as plodding and weary humans, but as joyous Initiates, on our way to the final triumph of the Ascension?

With this tremendous weight of positive interest in the welfare of our planet, the pendulum-swing between good and evil will soon swing to the side of good, and stand steady in the Light. That moment will bring with it the descent of Peace, the return of the Dove.

Even now, like Noah of old, we gaze expectantly skyward, knowing that the Dove is winging its way from outer space, bearing to us the symbolic olive branch from our planetary neighbors, those good friends we knew and loved so well back in the wonderful days before the laggards came, before we became wandering prodigals, before we became the lost, the bewildered ones. Now let us prepare for the great cosmic festival of reunion, of fellowship, of interplanetary friendship. Let us prepare to welcome the Dove and send forth to all mankind the joyous message that the burning issues of confusion have vanished from the earth.

PART II

The Days Just Ahead

In preparing for the descent of Peace, the return of the Dove, let us examine the seething issues of confusion and controversy so soon to be annihilated by the action of the Violet Fire of the seventh cosmic Ray. This, incidentally, is the Ray discovered by the American scientist, Robert Millikan. Coming to us directly as God's gift, from the great central Sun of our galaxy, Alpha and Omega, it carries the transmuting qualities of Divine Mercy, Compassion and Forgiveness. If called into action by any human being, it will transmute discord, hate, greed, lust and, in fact, all imperfections.

It swung into manifestation in 1675, and has steadily gained in potency as the sixth Ray of the Piscean Age receded. The sixth or Ruby Ray energy, which stimulated world-wide devotion to ideals and ideologies for the past two thousand years, began to wane in 1625. The last of this Piscean energy was withdrawn from physical plane matter in 1954. The new Aquarian Age will be energized by the Violet Fire of the Seventh Ray, during the next two thousand years. Ten billion souls, currently associated with evolution on this earth, will react under the effects of the inflowing Ray.

The earth is being drenched with the Ray coming in from outer space, and focused upon this planet by beamed direction from certain other planets and stars which serve as great reservoirs for this cosmic energy. At the very center of the earth certain Rays carrying certain colors meet, forming the polarities and the axes; this central orb or kingdom formed by the Rays is under the divine rulership of Lord Pelleur. In this central orb, the Rays and colors are blended, and now, during the Aquarian Age, the resultant Violet Fire of the mighty seventh will constantly surge up and through the earth, washing over every single atom that makes up the globe.

At present the process is devoted almost solely to the cleansing of the planet through transmutation of discordant energy. In olden times, before the laggards came, the earth was known to be one of God's many mansions, as are all planets and stars. The center of the earth was regarded as the central altar of the planet, upon which eternally blazed the sacred Flame. The Flame knows only perfection; unlike human beings, it has no sympathy for imperfection; in fact, the Flame of God is not even aware that imperfection exists in the cosmos. That is why it is necessary to have mediators such as Sanat Kumara, the Christ forces, great Adepts and Masters, Initiates and Disciples; in other words, those who can look upon imperfection without taking it unto themselves. In turn these Beings have their human disciples, the trainees, who are still at a point of evolution where they are able to work directly in the dreadful snake pit of human karma and at the same time serve the Light.

The process of cleansing the planet at this time with Violet Fire is directed by the Hierarchy, composed of the Christ Forces, Masters, the Shamballa administration; the Elohim, Archangels and Archaii, Adepts from other planets and stars, and a vast array of White Magicians in cosmic service.

But so far as the human family is concerned, no Adept, no matter how high His evolutionary rank, can force an individual in embodiment to submit to any type of purification unless the individual voluntarily and of his own free will, asks for such assistance. Free will which is being used destructively can be countered to a certain degree if help is requested by others who observe the case of distress. Angels respond instantaneously to all such calls and assistance is rendered, but usually the individual in distress is so bogged down in self-pity that he creates karma faster than the angels can remove the contamination in the amount allowed under karmic law.

The soil, the vegetation and the animals may be cleansed and freed of imperfection within certain karmic limitations which are imposed by humans themselves. For example, the Hierarchy cannot, under Law, cleanse the soil of all strontium poisoning from nuclear test fallouts, although vegetation grown on the poisoned soil may cause animal and human deaths. The strontium was released by stupid and misguided men, dedicated to deeds of violence; but these individuals form part of the human family. Therefore, all humanity must bear the resulting karmic burden, and the soil and vegetation and animals must bear the karmic burden with humanity until enlightened human beings insist that the tests be stopped. This action of insistence immediately lifts some karma even though the tests continue and the karma begins to pile up again.

As of today, the tests are still blasting away, but with every boom-boom more and more people, by the thousands, shout their protests. Each time a protest is made, even as a thought, the light thus released is caught up by the angelic hosts, and the exact same amount of light is used to cleanse the atmosphere.

But it is not enough for us to demand that the tests be stopped, although it is a first step. Human beings are evolving gods and have been endowed with free will. They must, at all times, request help from the Creator, from their own God-Presence, or from a Hierarch if they wish to completely transmute their own imperfections and become free from all distress of body, mind and affairs. But they must also request divine help for the atmosphere, the soil, the vegetation, the elementals, and the animals they have injured. Furthermore, the assistance of the Forces of Light must be requested for all karma created in past embodiments, stretching back through nineteen million years on this earth, and, in the case of laggards who are still lagging, transmutation must be effective for all karma generated by them previously on other planets and stars.

This is a new thought for many, particularly for those dreary, dreamy escapists who insist that Jesus died for them and that they have been saved. Those who prate this frightful doctrine of vicarious atonement are probably among the least saved on the planet. They too, someday, will be called upon to awaken and to stretch their minds and hearts upward to the Light.

It is in this human area of established and reverenced dogmatism that we find the greatest confusion and misunderstanding today. It is in this area that the modern Noah must search the skies for a glimpse of the Dove, winging earthward with the olive leaf. To this area, the Dove must return before these troubled human hearts know Peace.

Instead of considering the One, we find men and women everywhere running helplessly and hopelessly in pursuit of the many things which they think will increase their happiness. Yet they wonder why they continue to suffer; why they are in financial distress; why they are weary and depleted; why they must earn their bread by the sweat of their brow: They wonder why they must endure a twilight existence only to face death as a finality.

The answer is that they judge by appearances. Because the majority of people are troubled, they rashly assume that trouble is inevitable. Because the majority of people die, they rashly assume that death is a normal and natural change. Because the majority of people are often angry, hostile, aggravated people, full of hate and misery, this condition is accepted as the rule for all mankind on this earth. It is, they say, the way the ball bounces.

But, during the next two thousand years, all these delusions will be dispelled. As soon as the people from other planets are received by us in friendship, we will quickly realize that we, as earth people, and as very, very stupid people, are much in the minority in this solar system. We will quickly realize that trouble is not a normal or a natural condition for evolving gods. Trouble is an atheistic condition, brought on by the earth people who have lost contact with their Source, who have lost faith in God, and who have, therefore, lost all knowledge of how to spiritualize matter or transmute distress. They leave themselves helpless and at the mercy of matter which they then feed, inflame and imprison with hate; when all the while they should be loving matter into freedom. They thus poison the soil, the atmosphere and their own bodies with hate, openly inviting disease, disaster and death.

If God is a good God and perfect God, and man is made in His image and likeness even to being endowed with free will, then why should imperfection be accepted? We were told to be perfect, even as our Father in heaven is perfect. We should busy ourselves calling forth perfection, impressing it upon suffering matter so that matter can send forth the radiant energy of love rather than a vibration of pain.

Man has misused his free will, has misspent his God-given energy, and has filled the earth with monstrous miscreations entirely of his own making because he has been willing to accept imperfection. He has not asked for help from his ever-present Source, but has gone ahead on his own, bereft and alone and sorrowful, trying constantly to improve his lot by exchanging one imperfection for another which he hopes will prove slightly less imperfect.

Man has attempted to build entire complex civilizations by using judgment based on appearances. Now science comes forward, following the power-crazed war machine in a frenzied pace to keep up with things as they appear to be. Or as the misguided scientists and politicians think things ought to be. The bewildered public is told that this is progress. Exactly since when has progress been based on fear, the one and only weapon available to the dark forces?

So while the dark forces entrenched in science are busy creating imperfect systems to bolster up already imperfect systems, our hearts need not be troubled. We can turn abruptly from this negative point of view and look upon the positive surge toward perfection which is now rapidly engulfing the human family. We can happily see now how the whole world of appearances will vanish within the transmuting power of the fiery cleansing force which is here upon us—and the fire is the Violet Flame.

This joyous Aquarian Age, in all its glorious fulfillment, has been anticipated for thousands of years; for Those Who guide the cosmos know exactly when certain Rays will swing in and out of manifestation. Of course, all the Rays have been in manifestation many times during the last nineteen million years, but it was only in 1957 that Sanat Kumara had accomplished His great purpose of having humanity ready for the present cleansing, and His preparation was timed to fit in with the waning and waxing of the sixth and seventh Rays.

The entire Piscean Age, ushered in by the birth of Jesus, was but a preparation for the Aquarian Age. It might appear that little was accomplished during the past two thousand years, but that is not correct. Jesus said: "Let not your heart be troubled." This injunction was disobeyed by tens of thousands, and today they are dropping dead from heart trouble. But many, many others did heed the gentle words and turned their hearts to the One. They stood steady in the Light and served the Light during the Piscean Age, participating in the activities planned by the Christ Forces. In this wise manner, the Forces of Light utilized every precious moment in preparing humanity for its present opportunities.

The most outstanding opportunity before us now lies in our acceptance of the hand of friendship extended to us by our neighbors from other planets in our solar system, other solar systems, and from various stars in our galaxy. Because the Lord of Venus, Sanat Kumara, spent eighteen and a half million years on this earth in salvaging humanity, it is to be expected that the Venusians would take a most extraordinary interest in our welfare.

The great message of cosmic import that the Venusians and others wish to convey to us today is identical with the universal Truths demonstrated by Jesus in the west, by Gautama in the east, and by hundreds of other Adepts round the world during thousands of past centuries. The outer world, under the atheistic influence of a global system composed of a mingled mishmash of opportunistic politics, expedient economics, and tyrannical churchianity, has failed to grasp these basic Truths.

But those who, in some embodiment during past centuries, have escaped from the suffocating restraint imposed by so-called authorities and have turned to the kingdom of the untroubled heart within, have discovered their own center of God-consciousness. They have evolved steadily into that consciousness which is the precious and rightful heritage of all men and women and children everywhere in the cosmos. The only difference between the people on this planet and the people on other planets lies in the degree of unfoldment which has taken place in the consciousness of the individuals.

As soon as interplanetary communication is established on a world-wide scale the earth people will quickly realize that they have been very foolish, very foolish indeed, to have wasted their time listening to so-called authorities of church and state, instead of communing with the still, small voice of the One within their own beating hearts.

Since each individual is an evolving god on his way back to his Source, he is never for an instant actually separated from that Source. He only thinks he is alone. In Truth and in fact, he is a complete universe within himself; he need look only to the One for guidance on the path of return to his home star. It is when he looks to his neighbors, his boss, his military leaders, his editors and educators, that he becomes confused—if they are confused. Usually it turns out that they are. Why? Because they, too, have failed to listen to the One; they have lost contact with their Source. They, themselves, listen only to higher authorities so-called, who, in the final analysis, consider themselves authorities simply because they have a stronger capacity to argue and spout double-talk.

Since this planet has now been released from planetary Law, and is to function for the rest of its life span under Cosmic Law, the subject of interplanetary communication has become of paramount importance. We are also learning that the majority of Those Adepts Who have guided us through the tangled maze of years, were not originally earth people. Inasmuch as Sanat Kumara came from Venus, we have perhaps had a greater number of volunteers from that planet than from others.

However, as we begin to learn to identify the various types of individuals in embodiment on the earth, we will find that their origin is fully reflected in their stature, their attitudes, their manner of serving the Light, and in their particular Ray attributes and qualities. We find the same thing true of Adepts. Ascended Master Morya, for example, came to this earth from Mercury. His Mercurian nature is a fiery one that blazes its way like a flaming meteor through all obstacles.

Jesus, so gentle and so full of compassion and love for humanity, was originally a Venusian, although he had many embodiments on this earth, dating from the time of Moses when he emerged into recorded history as Joshua, the son of Nun. It was to Joshua that Moses tossed the flaming torch of freedom, and it was Joshua who carried it through lighted years, and through many human embodiments. These many embodiments among earth people were all in preparation for the great demonstration which He, as Jesus, made before the benighted ones on this globe—the physical demonstration that death was a cruel delusion, and that disease was another delusion, often more cruel.

Jesus demonstrated that He not only did not succumb to any type of disease, but that He could heal any type of disease, even to psychological states resulting from obsession by earthbound spirits. He demonstrated before a jeering, sneering crowd of social hoodlums, mugsters, politicians and militarists, that He could undergo an experience simulating the popular delusion of death, with His body pierced and broken. Yet He lived through the experience in perfect poise and harmony and later completely resuscitated His flesh form. He then spent forty days in that resuscitated flesh body, teaching, writing and working at the old grist-mill in Bethany where His mother and the disciples had assembled. Then, in full view of more than five hundred of His followers, He raised His physical vibrations until His body became a pillar of blazing light that outshone the noonday sun and He made His Ascension.

He did not make use of a mechanical spaceship to enter the etheric realms which encircle the earth many miles above its surface. He created His own forcefield. He was able to do this because He understood the action, interaction and reaction of the cosmic Rays. When He wished to resurrect His broken, physical body from the tomb, He drew energy from the Resurrection Ray, and the resulting Flame, rising back to the Source, carried the physical atoms back into active manifestation. When He wished to make His Ascension, He drew energy from the Ascension Ray, and the resulting Flame, rising back to the Source, raised the atomic vibration from material density to Light, and carried His body upward.

Jesus did not do these things without long years of training in His final embodiments. Nor did He start at the top, for in order to serve the Light and carry a message to the darkened minds of earth men, He had to start down at the bottom of the pit with the unlighted ones. Therefore, He lived on the earth through many, many embodiments in order that he might undergo all human experiences and be exposed to all the popular delusions of the day. He voluntarily took on the darkness that fettered other men.

Yet, in His final embodiments, He realized that He need no longer accept the delusions merely because they were popular, and merely because everyone around Him was battling with illness, trouble and death. In that cosmic hour, He knew that the time had come when He could actually prove these frightful untruths. He refused to accept any surface appearance. He advised others not to judge by such appearances but to go to the Kingdom within each beating heart and there accept in pure love the Reality of the One.

During His childhood years in His final embodiment, when He was forced to flee Herod and remain in Egypt, His training for His great demonstration continued daily. He had His hours of recreation when He played in the sand along the Nile, as any other little boy would do under the circumstances. But He also went with His mother each day to the Temple at Luxor.

Mary had taken on human embodiment as a voluntary task to aid humanity. She had once belonged to the angelic kingdom, and had advanced in evolution until she became an Archaii, the Twin Flame of Archangel Raphael. She trained for thousands of years on the Inner Planes before she was finally offered the great cosmic assignment of becoming the perfect human mother of the perfect human child, Jesus.

So Mother and Son trained together in Egypt for their Ascensions, for Mary was destined to leave the earth and return to Her own angelic kingdom. These two Initiates were supervised by the great Adept, Serapis Bey, Hierarch of the Ascension Flame at Luxor. The training was extremely rigorous for Jesus was to be crucified and Mary had agreed to assist Him by standing at the foot of the Cross and holding for Him the Immaculate Concept of God-Perfection, while He held the suspended breath and at the same time withdrew His consciousness from His body and permitted the flesh to take on an appearance of lifelessness. However, since Jesus had been born without karma, it was not possible for Him to actually suffer in the flesh, for there were no impurities in His nervous system to register a vibration of pain.

Together at Luxor, Mary and Jesus had learned how to suspend the breath for long periods and yet to resume breathing when They willed to do so. They learned how to keep the breathless silent human bodies completely purified by sweeping them through and through constantly with cleansing light from the Ascension Flame.

At this point the reader may say: Ah! yes, probably so,

probably so. But that was long ago. The great Temple at
Luxor is in ruins now. It was fine that Jesus made such a
demonstration. It was wonderful that Mary was interested
enough to join in the training under Serapis Bey. But They
were very important people—important in the cosmic scheme
of things. Today there are no more of Their kind. No more
cosmic VIP's. We are little people, all mediocre nobodies.
To look at us you would think we had all been cut out with
the same cookie cutter. Can you imagine a great Adept like
Serapis Bey bothering with us?

Yes, it can be imagined. It can be imagined, that is, by
all those who are not still lagging with the laggards. It can
be imagined very readily by those who have profited by
nineteen million years of evolution, and who have finally
awakened to the fact that the laggards may lag until the
end of time if they wish, according to their God-given free
will, but that the rest of us can use our free will positively.

We can use our free will to examine carefully this demonstration that Jesus made. We can go to the Temple at Luxor
this very night: we can leave our physical body at home
asleep; we can find the door—the right door amid all the
ruins; we can ask one or more angels to guide us on our
journey, and to show us the door.

We will open the door and step inside: step in from the
hot desert sands to the heavenly cool, green garden that
leads to the vast, magnificent underground Temple. We can
go into the great inner chamber where blazes the sacred
Flame upon the altar—the Ascension Flame of the Fourth
Ray. We can meet the Hierarch there, Serapis Bey, and
talk with Him while we bathe in the pure white light of the
Ray which fills the Temple. This is the blazing white light
which carries the virtue of Purity direct from the Godhead.

The temple room is crowded with visitors. We recognize many of them, our friends and acquaintances who, like us, have left their sleeping bodies at home. Then there are others we knew long ago here on earth, but they have shed their physical bodies and are now in training, preparing to come back into birth in the New Age.

We all bathe in the light of the Flame, just as Jesus and Mary did two thousand years ago. We try to absorb its radiance into our subtle bodies. We try to clear our vision, to purify our bodies so that tomorrow we can remember. The disembodied ones with their subtle etheric brains, will find it easier to remember when tomorrow comes; but will they remember this sublime purity and clarity of existence when they have once again taken a physical earth body? That is their problem, their training task.

Tomorrow when we awaken at home in our physical body, buoyant and refreshed by our visit to Luxor, we can at least make use of the Ascension Flame in a practical way even though we do not remember anything about our travels. The more we can use the Flame in our homes and in our daily work the more familiar it will become; the easier will it be to visualize. More and more of its radiance will penetrate our aura, clearing away all the debris and delusions; all the diabolical accumulations that have weighed us down since the laggards came to the earth.

We can always use it in a practical way by visualizing it sweeping through and through our four lower bodies—physical, etheric, emotional and mental; by visualizing it sweeping through and through our homes, our furniture, our clothes—purifying everything. The underground Temple at Luxor has been there for hundreds of years but there is not ever, ever a speck of dust anywhere. And no one has to

clean anything. The whole place is constantly bathed in the
Flame, and where the Flame of Purity penetrates all imperfections are dissolved.

Serapis Bey wants us to use the Flame for all sorts of
mechanical things, such as tuning a piano or tuning up a
motor. We eventually have to learn to operate everything
on this earth by drawing the energies of the Rays into service. That is how everything was accomplished in the labor-
less days before the laggards came. Those were the days
of genuine God-abundance; when all necessities were drawn
directly from the atmosphere by invocation. There was
no economic system or money exchange of any kind, for
the people used whatever cosmic Ray power they needed,
and then gave thanks to the Creator for providing His children with His own omnipresent Energy.

After the laggards had contaminated the earth's atmosphere with their emanations of selfishness and rebellion, neg-
atively refusing to trust in the God-power of the Flames,
their self-generated poison spread round the earth and
formed a thick blanket of a murky gray sticky substance
which to this day still clings to every object, even to individual atoms. It also penetrates within the shell of the
atom and clogs the space between the electrons, thereby slow-
ing down the revolution of both electrons and atom. This,
in turn, affects the tempo of livingness of everything on
the globe—minerals, vegetation, and animal bodies.

Before the laggards came human brain tissue was sunshine yellow in color—the color of the golden light of illumination. After the laggards infected the atmosphere with
their emotional frenzies of hatred, resentment and spite,
the beautiful yellow brain tissue became contaminated with
this astral debris and gradually, down through the centuries,

as the clogged atoms revolved more and more slowly, human perception became dulled and the brain tissue itself took on the murky gray color of astral maya. Today people pridefully boast of their "gray matter"—certainly a condition . of which no mortal need be proud.

As human brain tissue became more and more clogged, it lost all normal sensitivity and would no longer register the higher vibrations or respond to sights and sounds from the subtle etheric worlds which interpenetrate the physical. Remember that the early Root Races had magnetized and anchored subtle matter within the physical, thus spiritualizing the very soil of the planet and raising the vibrations of sticks and stones, meadows and streams, trees and flowers.

These first people could see and hear on all planes, and for them there was no barrier between the tangible and intangible. But after the laggards came all that sensitivity was gradually lost. As the brain tissue slowly turned from yellow to gray, we all became infected people and we lost even the memory of our Source: the memory of those days of divine glory when we first emerged as White Fire Beings, and individualized as Twin Rays, Sparks of flashing splendor in our robes of Light, glowing with the heart love of Alpha and Omega.

Once the memory of our Source was gone, our capacity to register other subtle contacts vanished. We became helpless, embruted, degenerate, for we had no inherent knowledge of how to accomplish anything without the aid of the Father within. And we could not remember how to invoke His aid.

It was then that the Cosmic Council assembled and decided to dissolve the planet. It was then that Sanat Kumara in His wonderful, magnificent gesture of godly sacrifice, volunteered to come to the earth, to help us and guide us and teach us, and to stay with His self-appointed task until the last weary pilgrim had found his way home.

Sanat Kumara could not overrule our free will and set us back immediately upon the Path. It was by misusing our free will and turning our backs on the Perfection of the Father, that we had plunged ourselves into this evolutionary morass. Therefore, we had to learn to use our free will correctly: that is, we had to learn to make a correct choice through trial and error methods. Sanat Kumara could have told us which was right and which was wrong and we could have followed Him like blind sheep, but that would have made us into robots. Adepts never use such methods in even the smallest instances, for well They know that dictatorship robs people of any opportunities to exert their own strength to extricate themselves from a difficulty.

Yet if we look around us today it can well be seen that much of the karma which lay so heavily upon us in ancient Lemuria is still with us. Some of the simplest lessons we have not learned; we have failed to profit by many of Sanat Kumara's simple examples.

The whole world writhes in agony and responds to vibrations of pain, leading to further pain. Despite what we like to term modern progress, it is in very recent years that virtually the entire world has been engulfed in dictatorship in one form or another. But this could not have happened had petty tyranny not first started in the home, in the school and above all, in the church. And this discordant rhythm, this vibratory response to pain, the desire to inflict pain on others—this sadism has come down to the world over nineteen million years. This is the karma which is still with us and which must now be transmuted within a matter

THE DAYS JUST AHEAD

of a few years before the planet spirals into an orbit of
higher vibrations.

For in the cosmic order of things the planet itself must
now move forward regardless of whether or not the population can stand the high vibratory rate of God's love
for His children. That is the individual test that will come
to each person in the near future. Can you, or can you not,
respond to the love of God? Can you, or can you not, live
in peace and brotherhood with your fellowmen? Can you, or
can you not, free yourself from the desire to inflict pain on
yourself and on others? Can you give up all pain—especially
the pain of death and taxes?

When Sanat Kumara started to prepare us for this day
which is now at its dawning, He could only suggest ways
and means. He could not use coercion. He provided us
with Adept teachers from other planets to show us the way,
and it was up to us to learn the score when and if we could.
Obviously we had to begin at the bottom in our classroom
work, so the training was made as simple as possible. We
were to go out and dig in the soil, much as children playing
in a sandbox. Down through the centuries the dark forces,
working through the limited minds of theologians who tam-
pered with the scriptural writings, have tried to make this
seem like a punishment. They have recorded the event with
an awful pronouncement: You must earn your bread by the
sweat of your brow.

But it was not a punishment. It was the only opportunity
that could be offered to persons so heavily burdened with
karma that they did not know right from wrong. The
teachers were there as group leaders: th.re beside us to
show us how to earn our bread. They taught us agriculture,
architecture, and homemaking tasks such as building fires,

cooking foods, weaving and stitching. They taught us how
to bathe our bodies and bind up our wounds, for now we
were always fighting with each other and hurting each other.
They taught us how to cultivate herbs that would alleviate
the pain in our contaminated bodies.

They could not teach us how to use the beneficient Rays
again and bring about instant manifestation, for we were
slow learners now. We had lost all sensitivity because now
our brains were choked and clogged with that horrible murky
gray astral stuff. Since we could not use the Rays we were
forced to use our muscles instead. It was brutal. And it was
stupid and foolish to pay such a price, and for what? For the
ignominious emotional pleasure of sympathizing with a lot
of lazy, ignorant laggards who could not even keep up with
their evolutionary homework on their own planets.

But now it is over. We have awakened to Truth, or at
least tens of thousands of us have awakened and responded
to the call that is resounding through the galaxy—the call
for servers of the Light to restore the vineyard of the Lord
on planet earth. It is springtime in the vineyard now and
many souls are still sleeping in their accustomed darkness.
But soon, very soon, the Light will reach their inner consciousness. They will stir in their sleep; they will listen to
the message of their own beating hearts beating out the
rhythm of life eternal. Soon, very soon, the vineyard will
be alive and bright and shining with livingness, and the
sleeping ones will unfold like blossoms in the warm summer
sunshine.

Those of us who have already awakened to Truth have
taken a long, long look at our stupidity, our foolishness.
We decided to be foolish no longer. Thousands upon thousands began to serve the Light. Tons upon tons of karma

have been transmuted daily with the aid of the Rays. A sufficient amount of imprisoned energy had been released by 1957 to liberate Sanat Kumara from His voluntary exile on earth and permit Him to return to His home on Venus. At the same time enough karma had been lifted by 1957 to permit the angelic hosts to begin anew their work of straightening the axis of the earth. Before the end of 1958 they had made the final adjustment. Lord Michael, mighty Prince of the Archangels, had stated that an adjustment of 45 degrees was required to bring the earth's axis into the line required by galactic measurement. This bending of the axis and the resultant eccentric orbit of the earth, were caused entirely by the weight of karma on the planet.

So the great task of Sanat Kumara has been successful. He has returned home—to Venus. Although He will still guide us as a cosmic Regent, His position as Lord of the World has now been turned over to Gautama, formerly our Buddha. Gautama will continue the work of arousing our divine sensitivity; of guiding our feet along the Path that leads back to our galactic Source—Alpha and Omega. We are still limping and still weary but we can feel our God-strength stirring within us once more.

We are learning to use the Rays again, though awkwardly. But we must watch ourselves constantly because the old rhythm, so ancient and so wrong, is still extremely powerful. It can so easily pull us back, turn us aside from our one-pointed goal that leads steadily upward—up there, among, the stars.

Constantly we must remind our unaccustomed lower bodies of the new and better way of doing things. We must keep reminding our physical body that it can do nothing of itself; it is the Father within it that doeth the works. It is the Father who lovingly supplies the constant flow of energy that beats our hearts and keeps alive our individual life Flame within each heart—itself a tiny replica of the great sacred three-fold Flame which beats the sun-heart of the solar system, the galaxy, the cosmos.

As White Fire Beings we were given this gift of the Flame straight from the heart of Alpha and Omega. We were made in Their image and likeness for all eternity. Within each beating heart today the image is still clear and perfect as the Father in heaven is perfect. The outer form of the physical body may be ugly or beautiful, diseased or in health, but the inner Flame in the heart remains ever the same as the great Central Sun of the galaxy from whence it came. True, the replica is tiny for it was only a Spark. But in the sight of God the great and the small are equal in potency. God is everywhere and God is all—indivisible. The Spark is equal to the Flame. The Spark is God.

Knowing this, the Flame within our heart becomes the Comfort Flame, the blazing pillar of the Father's strength, forever doing His works within us if we will allow Him to have His way. But if we inject our little free will into the situation and insist upon having our own way, then the Father can do nothing. He cannot even interfere with our foolishness.

But once we become acquainted with the Comfort Flame within us, life takes on a new meaning. Feeling this buoyant sense of livingness flowing through us limitlessly, we need not cringe when we are told that we must all individually transmute the phoney man-made powers we have handed over to a delusion, a spectre called death. We need not tremble with fear when we are told that we must all, individualy, transmute our karma and make our Ascension, not in a spaceship, but in our own forcefield. We need not feel timid or bashful when we are told that we must one and all stand before Serapis Bey, just as Jesus and Mary did two thousand years ago.

Using the Rays, we can obtain straight knowledge. Through straight knowing we will know, without anyone telling us, that we must all voluntarily and of our own free will come to terms with our own recalcitrant natures so that we may freely and gladly participate in the training offered at Luxor. And this Temple is the focus of only the fourth Ray; we must go into all the Temples and learn to use all seven Rays. We must each, individually, make exactly the same demonstration that Jesus made in overcoming death, although it is assuredly not required or desired that we be physically crucified.

But neither can we go on as now, growing old and weary and sick, and then shedding our physical body as a tree sheds its leaves. That process is correct for a tree because it is inherent in the nature of a tree. But it is not correct for an evolving god endowed with free will. Each individual must learn to transmute all his physical, etheric, emotional and mental imperfections, and then make his Ascension in freedom away from the gravitational pull of the earth, into the lightways of space. That is the simple secret of freedom from gravity.

An individual who is burdened with untransmuted karma is a sick person, an infected person who constantly gives off poisonous emantions into the atmosphere. Since virtually every person on this planet has been sick with karma for millions of years, it was a tremendous cosmic gesture of compassion and mercy on the part of the Cosmic Hierarchy to maintain this hospital planet of earth. Here is a spot in the universe where those who vibrate to pain can be visited by wise physicians like Jesus and thousands of other Adepts, and now by the space people.

For in the final analysis each space person, no matter what his role in the liberation of this planet, is basically a physician, ministering to our vibratory rates, raising our frequencies from expressions of hate to expressions of love. The space people, one and all, are here to help us to scientifically transmute our karma and heal ourselves through the use of the Violet Fire. This is not in any sense a mystical process which will lead us into ecstacies of sentimentality and give us that holier-than-thou feeling. These feelings simply indicate the presence of a serious karmic infection. They do not indicate healing of any kind whatsoever. They simply mean that the sufferer is bogged down in pride.

When we are truly healed, scientifically healed through transmutation of karma, we can prove that fact to ourselves by raising the vibrations of our purified physical bodies and ascending from the gravitational pull of the earth. This is not the ordinary levitation of the misguided psychic or medium. Those unfortunate individuals usually have no control over levitation; nor do they have any control over the wagging tongues that love to prattle about the mystical and the psychic.

The space people can move freely from star to star or simply remain in the etheric realms because they have gone through the Ascension Initiation. There is no untransmuted karma within them that can be held by gravity. They do not need to use mechanical spaceships, for they can travel freely, protected by their own forcefields. But when they come into the contaminated atmosphere of the earth for the purpose of working and teaching, they must of necessity protect themselves with certain mechanical devices, just as a diver would prepare to use oxygen if he anticipated an extended stay under water. This does not apply to the higher Adepts, but They rarely mingle with the public, coming only to Shamballa, the Grand Teton, or some similar Retreat.

The value of a mechanical spaceship should not be overestimated, either here on the earth or outside the earth. It is a convenience, a device, but it will not, in itself, give any individual the true freedom of the solar systems or galaxies. Moreover, not all spaceships are mechanical, for even though they may carry dozens of people and are true spaceships they can be formed by a group for a certain purpose and need not contain any mechanisms. They might better be understood as organic in nature, or at least better understood in that sense by our limited earth minds.

During the year of 1957, thousands of earth people gazed at the passage of a magnificent comet as it sailed through the skies and swung close to the earth. It was first sighted by two Belgian astronomers—Arend and Roland—and it became known as the Arend-Roland comet. But the poet Wordsworth, a devotee of the sacred Flame, long ago correctly defined comets as "the diaphanous vestments of some passing plenipotentiary of Heaven's farthest kingdoms".

These efforts to assist us by actually bringing their light to us is the reason why all space people and spaceships visit the earth, or at least the upper spacial regions around the earth. For we cannot, because of our untransmuted karma go to them at the present time.

Now, on this earth, we have at least one man, Otis T. Carr of Baltimore, Maryland, who states that he has solved the problems connected with building spaceships and he is prepared to manufacture them upon order. He claims that these ships will fly safely anywhere in our atmosphere, to the moon, and to Venus, Mars or other planets in our solar system. The ships need no fuel as they generate electricity from the atmosphere as they fly. However, Mr. Carr has discovered that if the ships are to fly into outer space the passengers must be prepared to undergo an instant of transmutation or transition when they go into the etheric realms. Mr. Carr understands that this can be a spiritual experience but he believes that for those who are spiritually unprepared the impact might have a shattering effect upon the physical body.

Mr. Carr is one hundred per cent correct. In fact he is so right that recently no less a person than El Morya, Chohan of the First Ray, stated that no earth person in an unascended body would be permitted the freedom of the cosmic highways. A person with an unascended body is a person who is carrying around in his atoms a heavy load of untransmuted karma. El Morya also stated that an individual with an Ascended body could, of course, travel the cosmic highways freely at any time they are open. But a person with an Ascended body does not need a spaceship for his travels, although it might be convenient in some instances.

This does not mean that Mr. Carr's ships should not be built and used around the earth to replace all present types of aircraft, since they need no fuel. It does not mean that the ships could not be used for outer space travel by those who have made their Ascension, but who have volunteered to work here on earth in an ordinary physical body. Such individuals can instantaneously raise their physical vibrations to meet outer space vibrations, and there will be no discomfort in the process, but only the glory of a heavenly experience.

So now that we can have spaceships built in Baltimore,

Maryland, at any time we wish, we must ask ourselves a few serious questions before we decide to take off for Venus. We must first ask ourselves if the Venusians would welcome us. They most certainly would not permit us to set foot on their planet so long as we are enslaved by karma. When they extend to us the hand of friendship, it only means that they are willing to come here to the earth and teach us how to be free.

In other words, the earth people as a whole now have a cosmic opportunity to reap their reward for the tremendous sacrifice made by our Third Root Race people when they received and welcomed the laggards. From the beginning of the trouble on earth the Venusians have never stopped trying to help us, and they have had unlimited assistance from numberless solar systems and galaxies. Sanat Kumara took the first step toward our eventual liberation, even though it was a giant step which covered eighteen and a half million years of effort.

At this point the Venusians are not going to give up the struggle to liberate us, but neither do they intend to have us running tourist spaceships to their planet, loaded with persons who have not bothered to transmute their karma. The Venusians want no poisonous emanations on their planet, and we are invited to keep our stench of hatred, violence and ugliness right here at home until we have learned the art and science of deodorizing. Remember that Lady Venus is the Goddess of Beauty in this solar system.

When we have learned to utilize the Rays, and when we have become open-minded enough to study the teachings offered by the Chohans of the Rays in the many Retreats right here on this planet, then, and only then, should we start dreaming of transferring our home to Venus. Naturally no one can be blamed for desiring to escape from the earth so long as it is in its present condition. And to get it out of its present condition, and restore it to its original state which existed before the laggards came, we must have help from the space people. They are trained in handling and transmuting troubled conditions. We have not even the faintest notion of where to start. In fact the majority of people think they are living a normal life and are not even aware that they are in difficulty. When we are able to travel the cosmic lightways we will know it, and we can prove it scientifically right here on earth. We do not need to get sensational and start off on some madcap expedition in an attempt to explore outer space. Outer space has been explored thoroughly. If we want to know anything about it, we can ask the people who explored it—the space people themselves, and they are right here among us.

What is this true human freedom which we are seeking? Freedom for man comes to him as a result of his using God-free energy in its natural free way. God-energy in its pure form flows into man heartbeat by heartbeat. As the pure electrons are released by the sacred three-fold Flame within the heart, they enter the bloodstream. As they enter they are immediately qualified or stamped with the pattern of the individual. They can be qualified with love or they can be misqualified with hate.

In other words the electrons, which provide all power, can be used to carry out loving deeds, to think loving thoughts, to speak loving words. Or they can be used in an opposite manner, depending upon the choice we make through the use of our free will.

When man misuses this electronic power in performing hateful acts, he misqualifies the energy. In other words he leaves his stamp of imperfection upon millions of electrons that flow into his bloodstream. This energy is God-energy and as such it must obey the free will of man for man is God-created as a free being. When man chooses to enslave this free and pure energy, so that it will do his bidding and supply him with power to carry out some questionable enterprise, he thereby enslaves himself.

He starts each pure electron on its way through his own bloodstream with a handicap—the weight of his own feeling of discord. The electron itself remains pure, for it is God-energy and can know no impurity. But as it whirls on its course it collects around itself a shell of impure matter; the same murky gray astral matter that the laggards brought to earth. As it takes its appointed place with other electrons and forms an atom, the sticky substance clings, and soon the revolution of the electrons within the atom is slowed by the clogging; then the revolution of the atom itself is slowed, and in addition, the atom collects the same astral substance on its outer shell, adding further weight.

The resulting rate of electronic revolutions, plus atomic revolutions, taken as a whole in a man's physical, etheric, emotional and mental bodies, constitute what is known as his state of consciousness or his vibratory note.

If his electrons and atoms are revolving slowly, he is not only subject to disease, but he is subject to ugly delusions such as death. He begins to feel old age creeping on and in his limited understanding, he assumes that death is not far away. He feels fearful, bereft and alone. He cannot understand who he is or why he is here; he has no purpose in accord with the Divine Plan; he is, in short, a materialist, weighed down by his own burdens of hate which he carries right within his own atoms.

He tends to be separative in relation to his God and his

fellow men because he is usually quite charmed by the
amount of astral debris he has accumulated in his atomic
structure. The weight of the misqualified energy he is using
places him under the delusion that the rioting force within
gives him power. He throws his weight around, as the popular saying goes. He likes to give orders; put people in their
place; clamp down on this situation or that; and in general
act like a big-shot.

If he happens to be a scientist seeking to ferret out the
secrets of atomic power, he can only react according to the
limitations he has imposed upon his own atomic structure.
He, therefore, seeks to enslave the atom, just as he has enslaved his own atoms that he lives with each day. He can
think of atomic power only in terms of fission and fusion. He
wants to split the atom: to tear it apart by brute force: to
strip it bare as one would strip the skin off an orange. His
way is the way of hate, of fear, of snickering smugness.

The individual who is not separated from his Source by
this barrier of astral debris within his four lower bodies,
seeks to become a co-worker with that Source. He daily
works with the Rays and the Flames: he forms a close
friendship with the seven great Elohim who built this planet,
and with the seven mighty Archangels and their angelic hosts
who guard the planet and aid all persons who ask for angelic
assistance.

He reasons that if the Elohim constructed the planet then
he must come to an understanding with these mighty Builders; he must try to learn Their techniques; he must try to
follow Their way. Their way is the way of Love. Therefore,
his way must be the way of Love. If he observes the work of
the fission-fusion scientists, he understands that they have

brought all humanity to the verge of disaster with their way of hate, of fear, of black magic.

He understands that while this planet was yet a paradise, before the laggards came, the light within the atom was released in beauty, in peace, and in all the mighty strength of the One. He knows that this way of Truth must once more shine upon the minds of all men everywhere before man can release himself into freedom, before he can ascend to his home star.

He knows that man can accomplish nothing in his bereft state of loneliness because he feels so far from his Creator. He knows that every individual must someday accept the great gift of God, the Violet Fire of transmutation.

He knows that someday, sometime, some place, each individual must visualize that Flame sweeping through and through each atom in his four lower bodies, transmuting all electronic energy which he himself has misqualified down through countless ages of embodiments. Individual by individual, until ten billion souls have been counted, this transmuting process must go on, atom by atom, electron by electron, until all humans on this planet emerge into freedom's light, and the planet itself enters its new orbit as Freedom's Star. For that is the name written in the Book of Life for planet earth.

This is the program for the Aquarian Age.

PART III

The End of Man's Crucifixion

It has been stated by the Spiritual Hierarchy of this planet that had humanity been wise enough and strong enough and pure enough to have grasped the significance of the Ascension of Jesus two thousand years ago, that millions of souls would have made their Ascension during the Piscean Age.

Our troubles would have been over by now; the earth would have been restored to its pristine beauty; the classroom would have been filled with souls engaged in advanced evolutionary studies; the axis would have been straightened long since; and the globe under its rightful cosmic name—Freedom's Star—would be entering into its new orbit without travail.

We must remember that the cosmic hour that would have

launched all this evolutionary progress occurred not on Good Friday two thousand years ago. That was a public demonstration of the power of the suspended breath wherein a person may appear to die but continues to live, no matter how battered and bruised his physical body may be. That was public proof that pain and death have no power over the higher vibrations emanating from the Source. Jesus had already proved this privately in many instances, He had healed many lepers, many sick persons. He had raised Lazarus from the dead, and also the young daughter of the ruler. In the case of the woman who was healed by touching the hem of His garment, the demonstration was somewhat public but most of the people in the procession were followers and admirers of Jesus.

The event on Good Friday was definitely planned to prove that a human being could so purify the four lower bodies and allow the atoms to function at their maximum efficiency that even crucifixion could not cause death. Jesus did not attempt to do this alone when He was on the Cross and surrounded by jeering enemies. It was necessary that Mary stand at the foot of the Cross and hold inviolate the Immaculate Concept.

Before Mary came into embodiment to give birth to Jesus, She had rehearsed all this before a small council headed up by Lord Maitreya, then occupying the Office of the Christ, and a group of Adepts chosen from His administrative staff. Mary stood steady in the Light for three hours while these Adepts tried in every way possible to intrude upon Her line of thought, to break her pattern of thinking and feeling, to distract Her with all sorts of other ideas, even good ones. But Mary stood and held the Immaculate Concept of Life Eternal within Her consciousness.

Mary passed the test in poise and dignity and sweetness,

but well She knew that in a flesh body, in the physical appearance world, it would be quite a different matter. Standing there on Calvary amid dark clouds of poisonous emanations carrying astral impurity, bigotry, selfishness, greed and lust from the consciousnesses of those around Her, Mary had to hold with every fibre and cell of Her being to that Immaculate Concept of the resurrected, risen, breathing Christ.

But she held to the Immaculate Concept without losing Her poise for even a fraction of a second. She was not alone or without Friends gathered from the entire galaxy and galaxies beyond. There, together, on that windy hilltop the Forces of Light achieved such a mighty victory over darkness that the entire cosmos resounded with glory of the Risen One. For the result depended entirely upon whether or not Mary could hold and steadily visualize without wavering, the risen Christ. Yet She was confronted by Her Son on the Cross for three mortal hours. He was to remain in the tomb for three days, and during that entire time She still had to keep fixed and anchored in Her consciousness the fact that Her Son, in His resuscitated flesh body, would come to Her in the old grist-mill near Bethany when He had risen.

Standing there at the foot of the Cross Mary carried within the folds of Her garment three small packages: one contained gold, another a stick of frankincense, and another of myrrh. She had kept these three packages since that day in the stable at Bethlehem when the three Wise Men of the East had come to see the baby Jesus. These were the especially prepared minerals and spices that were to be used in the annointing of the body of Jesus, so that He could be assisted in the Ascension process. As She left the scene on Calvary, accompanied by John, She gave the packages to the women who were to annoint the body. Incidentally, the three Wise

Men are today serving the Light as Masters of the Wisdom: El Morya, Kuthumi, and Djwal Kul.

Jesus had been born without karma. In his previous embodiment as Appolonius of Tyana, He had transmuted the little karma He had remaining at that time. Nevertheless He had to come back into embodiment as a baby in order to demonstrate that He could be as other men and still achieve the Ascension. He grew up like other little boys, subject to the same childish happenstances. Again it was Mary who had to hold the Immaculate Concept for Her little Son until the full realization of His mission could dawn upon Him. So when He would stumble while playing and running and skin His knees, Mary would call Him to Her and say: Son, let Us not magnify this imperfection. Let Us magnify the Lord. In this way Mary kept from Jesus any stain of fear or vibrations of pain that might mar His perfect atomic purity.

This aspect of the upbringing of the child Jesus and of His crucifixion was not grasped by the multitudes, however. They could not realize that they could refuse to accept pain and imperfection, and that of their own free will they could make a correct choice and magnify the Lord instead.

After the crucifixion not a moment's time was lost by the dark forces who moved swiftly to take advantage of what they sensed might make a good business proposition. Thus was churchianity established and thus it continues down to the present day. Churchianity has dragged humanity on its weary, pain-wracked way for two thousand long years, emphasizing the sufferings of poor Jesus and poor Mary and those poor disciples. Just a bunch of ignorant fishermen, you know. Too bad, too bad, after that poor man Jesus tried so hard, that He did not have a few really intelligent followers.

So they say. And so they have continued to say down

through the centuries. Well, today we can all be grateful to
the Father in Heaven that when the disciples retired to the
old grist-mill at Bethany after the event on Calvary, they were
so simple and direct in their ways that they just spent their
time writing about what they had learned from the teachings
of Jesus. Had they been intelligent scientists they might
have started tinkering around with H-bombs. They might
have thought of taking up the sword and destroying their
enemies, instead of taking up the pen and writing about how
it is not only possible but necessary to love one's enemies.

It is necessary, that is, for anyone who expects to continue
his evolution on this planet or in higher spheres. It is necessary for anyone who would like to transmute his own karmic
burden and stop filling the atmosphere with emanations of
hatred. All of this could have been accomplished during the
past two thousand years had the people taken the trouble to
discriminate between Christianity and churchianity; and had
those same people had the courage to hold to the Immaculate
Concept of oneness with the Source, thereby gaining sufficient divine power and angelic assistance to cast out churchianity and the dark forces—lock, stock and barrel.

But this was not done. Churchianity gained steadily in
power and in greed and in its hold over human minds. It
even pretended to the people that it also had a hold over their
souls, and many of the foolish ones believed this drivel. A
soul, any soul, even the soul of a sparrow, has a direct line
of communication with its Source. A sparrow does not need
to go to church on Sunday morning yet the Father knows
when it falls. Moreover, the fallen sparrow does not require
an expensive funeral and this fact alone has served to keep
the sparrows free from an economic system based on the
doomsday theme of death and taxes.

During the last two thousand years the dark forces have struck again and again at the heart of the people. Jesus said: "Let not your heart be troubled". But the dark forces, especially those who work through churchianity, always utilize such advice as this, twist it around and then proceed to launch a campaign designed to acomplish just the opposite—in this case they set out to trouble the hearts of the people. Since the heart contains the sacred Flame, it must be constructed of special substance with an especially sensitive attunement that will record subtle vibrations. Strictly speaking, the heart is made of universal substance and is considered a universal organ; it is not owned and operated by the individual as is, for example, the liver or kidneys.

Therefore, it is absolutely essential to evolutionary progress that the heart be not troubled by outer things. This fact the dark forces know, and they have taken every advantage of it. As we look about us in the world today it is plain to be seen that virtually everything is so set up as to trouble the heart. This means that as the pure electrons leave the heart and enter the bloodstream they are at once misqualified, and carry the individual through the day in one long, weary, hectic stride.

It can be seen from the foregoing that the Forces of Light must proceed to transmute all of the old order, and it must be accomplished during the Aquarian Age while the seventh Ray is in full power. The Christ Forces, aided by the space people, will not do a patching job. There is no intention of using the old machinery of civilization; all will be swept aside. It will be a world of unlimited abundance for all, and the welfare of all life on the globe has been provided for, down to the last dog and cat. All of these problems are solved and handled on the Inner Planes by Adepts, and then

will be lowered into manifestation on to the physical plane.
A sufficient number of space people and earth people who are
disciples of the Hierarchy will be on hand on the physical
plane to see that the original pattern according to the Divine
Plan is not distorted.

Since the masses did virtually nothing to help themselves
during the Piscean Age, and only got themselves into more
trouble by supporting the forces of darkness back of the H-
bomb development, we are now crowded for time. The New
Age manifestations are ready, the space people are ready; the
disciples are ready; but the masses are still busy with their
endless rounds of eating, drinking, sleeping and procreating,
interspersed by their efforts to make enough money to keep
the other four projects going.

The axis of the earth is straightened—a fact which will
take further karmic burdens off the earth itself and place
them squarely on the backs of the individuals who create
them. The planet is entering its new orbit, and the rapid
vibrations, striking on the four lower bodies of an individual,
will increase his tempo of living enormously. If the individual is making no effort to transmute his karma, and to
keep the atomic structure of his lower bodies clean and free
from astral debris, then he will not be able to cope with the
situation of daily living in the New Age. A bass drum is not
built to handle the vibrations of a violin.

The increased tempo will bring out whatever is within each
individual state of consciousness. If the vibratory note is one
of poise and peace that note will sound and resound with ex-
panding strength and beauty. If the vibratory note is one of
violence and anger the individual, harried by the pressure of
the new tempo and unable to meet the challenge, will express
his state of consciousness as best he can. He may seize a gun

THE END OF MAN'S CRUCIFIXION

and start shooting, or a knife and start slashing; he may jump in his car and drive fast and furiously over the highways, bringing death and destruction in his wake; he may seek out a peddler of dope.

But mostly the average citizen will do none of these things. Mostly he will just sit and sit and sit and watch television, or given a chance he will talk and talk and talk. He may appear to be talking about the state of the world, economically and politically. Actually, he is vocally expressing the confused state of his own consciousness. He is talking about himself and his own troubled heart, even though he speaks about the troubles in the Near East or Russia or the Pentagon. He is sounding his vibratory note. And his vibratory note is always the same doleful moan—the note of crucifixion.

That is why humanity missed the Ascension story two thousand years ago. That is why the Ascension story must now be pushed forward into human consciousness in only a few short years. That is why many will break beneath the forced process of evolutionary growth and will have to be removed to another hospital planet for further long ages of preparation to face the Light, the Truth. There are many, many bigots and skeptics who will have just as little chance to go into New Age evolution as has the camel to go through the eye of a needle.

During the millions of years that have passed since the laggards came men have learned to love the darkness because their atomic structures were filled with shadowed astral substance, the product of their own miscreations. This produced a state of negativity which led not to creativeness, but to a sense of falseness, of artificiality, of melodrama. Finally the whole world turned into a stage, with all the players dis-

guised by phoney masks indicating they had lost their true
identity; they had lost all knowledge of their Source and
knew not the face of the Father. Crucifixion became humanity's keynote; Ascension was regarded as a fable.

Crucifixion has now come to be considered not only normal
but noble on this planet. It has come to be confused with the
purification process. Actually the purification process is always joyous and wholesome; no purification can take place
while the individual feels that he is being crucified, that he is
suffering for some good cause, or while he is busy feeling
sorry for himself and wallowing, simply wallowing, in his
own self-pity. These feelings do not purify the atoms; on
the contrary, they are astral emotions of the most degrading
type and will further clog the atoms with astral debris.

It is correct to say that before we can raise the vibrations
of our atoms to the Ascension frequency, we must let go, let
go, let go, of all our pet peeves. But if this process proves to
be a mental and emotional ordeal then we are right in the
midst of our own crucifixion. And when we let go we are
not to become like a dishrag in the kitchen or a vegetable in
the garden. The letting go must be accomplished through
transmutation; not through shrugging off responsibility. We
are personally responsible for all energy which we have misqualified and which is held imprisoned in darkness. We must
release that energy by transmuting the darkness into light.

We have learned to love the shadowed situation, the
melodramatic touch that will cause the tears to flow. We have
learned to love sorrow so much that churchianity has even
taught little children and strong men to weep over the sorrowful plight of Jesus and Mary. Yet had even a shadow
of sorrow ever touched the atomic structure of either Jesus
or Mary the crown of cosmic victory would not have been
achieved by Them. It was achieved. Both made the Ascen-

sion. Their electronic vibrations were never slowed down for a fraction of a second during Their last embodiment. They lived in a state of constant joy; They did not die: They ascended within Self-generated forcefields of cosmic power.

The only way to redeem a single clogged atom is to visualize the Violet Fire sweeping through it like a blowtorch, transmuting and releasing all misqualified energy within the atom and allowing it to be sent back to the sun for rejuvenation. The only way to redeem an individual whose four lower bodies are made up of clogged atoms is precisely the same. Yet so vast is public ignorance on the subject of human suffering that society is set up to increase crucifying experiences rather that to eliminate them entirely. Tens of thousands of persons are kept in prisons and mental hospitals when a simple explanation of normal evolutionary processes would enable them to transmute the energy they have misqualified, automatically releasing their needless tensions.

On the plane where souls are received after disembodiment they are cared for by the angelic hosts, and now every individual is required to remain for certain periods in Temples of the Violet Fire. Their length of stay depends upon the amount of misqualified energy which must be transmuted.

But on the physical plane proper teaching in transmutation is desperately needed to curb increasing crime, juvenile delinquency, dope addiction, the whole array of nervous, emotional and mental illnesses and, most important of all, the delusion of death. The Hierarchy and space people are waiting in readiness to send us as many teachers as needed to handle this situation but the military powers in every so-called civilized country, backed by a degenerate churchianity, have for several years refused to reveal to the public the truth about flying saucers.

The highest government and church officials on the globe

have been well informed about every angle of the flying
saucer story for many years. But big brass sits back smugly
and issues orders to jet fighter planes to fire on spaceships.
Meanwhile tranquilizer pills may be obtained at the corner
drugstore.

This situation, now world-wide, constitutes the crucifixion
ordeal for humanity at this time. Fashions in crucifixion
methods change. In the day of Jesus it was an officially approved physical act somewhat in the category of arena sports.
In our time the physical aspect is handled by judges, juries
and ku-klux klanners. Mental and emotional crucifixions,
such as most of us are undergoing now, are usually handled
by the neighbors.

This is especially noticeable today in gossipy, insular communities where the natives have not yet felt the impact of the
Aquarian Age. They are the modern laggards, following
exactly in the footsteps of the first refugees from evolution.
They are filled with the same identical resentments, the same
hatreds, the same stupid rebellions against their Creator.
They are as lazy as their predecessors, too, for they are the
ones who are always whining and yak-yakking about why,
why, why doesn't God stop war? Well, He doesn't stop it
because He didn't start it. God never interferes with the free
will of His children, and if war is their idea of fun or intelligence or beauty, then war they must have and will have
until they have had their fill of blood and gore.

Lately though, since the space people have appeared on
the earth scene, the blame tossed out so freely by the whiners
has shifted somewhat from God to interplanetary visitors.
Why don't they stop war? The answer is the same. They
cannot and will not interfere with our free will, our right to
choose the path to destruction or the path to enlightenment—

as individuals. However, at this time a balance has been struck, and the free will of the population as a whole can be considered, for now those on the side of the Forces of Light will soon far outnumber those who are supporting the forces of darkness. Thus it is the weight of world-wide public opinion that is now being balanced in the scales held by Portia, the Goddess of Justice.

The lone individual still has freedom of choice. If he insists upon serving darkness rather than light, he may do so and live out his present embodiment with that decision. But he will not be permitted to incarnate again until he has transmuted his karmic burden sufficiently so that he will be able to see that serving the Light, in fellowship with his earth brothers, is the wisest and most joyous course to pursue.

The space people are here today not to stop war, although war must be stopped, but to asist all those who wish to serve the Light in full freedom, unhampered by a stupid economic system, by conniving political groups, or by competitive churchianity. God, being indivisible, cannot be divided up into little pieces and auctioned off to those with the most money in the collection box.

It was known throughout the galaxy that by the year of 1957, with the Violet Ray in full power, thousands upon thousands of earth people would be ready for the Light. It was known that these informed vocal millions would speak the Word of Power, with their invocative demand for Peace resounding through the cosmos. The entire galaxy, and galaxies beyond, have stood ready and waiting for this cosmic moment; ready to speed assistance to those who had placed their trust in God.

PART IV

This Cosmic Moment

Preparations for this cosmic moment on earth have been so stupendous and far-flung that they are quite beyond the grasp of the finite mind of an earth man, burdened as it is with astral debris. But we can select certain points of light in the human constellation; we can study these points of light, focus our full attention upon them. In this meditative way illumination will come to us, joy will surge within us, gratitude and love will ray forth from us. Then swiftly, silently, the healing wings of Peace will settle over us. In that instant we will know that the Dove has returned.

Before the laggards came to earth every individual rayed forth light like the true sun and Son that he was. Light was his natural heritage which he carried with him when he stepped forth as a Spark, a White Fire Being, from Alpha and Omega. He had never known darkness: he had never known distress or limitation or pain. But as millions of years dragged by on leaden feet after the laggards came, only rarely did an individual on planet earth radiate forth light from his aura.

There have always been a few disciples in the outer world who have caught and held the vision of light, protected and sustained by the Hierarchs of the Rays who constitute the Christ Forces within the Spiritual Hierarchy. Very, very few of these Hierarchs have been earth men. They were all brought in from other planets until quite recently. During the past few hundred years a few earth men and women have graduated and have been appointed to posts as Masters of the Ageless Wisdom and Chohans of the Rays.

Many of these are well known to us historically, but when we examine the records we find that the total number shrinks considerably because the same person had many embodiments. In a world which vibrated to pain and fear, a disciple whose task it was to externalize the Perfection of the Father had a rough time holding his peace and poise and harmony. His state of consciousness had to be held steady in the light without the slightest wavering: he had to reject appearances as untrustworthy; he not only had to raise the vibration of his own atoms to a frequency that would ward off disease and disharmony of all kinds, but he had to dispel the delusion of death. He had to learn these things during many embodiments, and yet live what seemed to be a normal life so far as the neighbors were concerned. That is why the total number of Initiates is small, because we find the same individual back in embodiment again and again.

For an example, El Morya, present Chohan of the first

Ray, was in embodiment as Sir Thomas More, Chancellor of
the Exchequer under Henry VIII of England. Later we find
him back in embodiment as the Irish poet, Thomas Moore.
These were only two of his many incarnations and still later
in history he graduated into the ranks of the Initiates, the
Illumined Ones who serve the Christ Forces. Kuthumi,
Chohan of the second Ray until July, 1958, was known to us
long ago as Pythagoras. Yet in recent times he was in embodiment as St. Francis of Assisi.

So as we look down the great corridors of history we see
many points of light on which we might focus, but the story
of St. Francis, for instance, would not be the complete story.
It would give us but one small clue to the spiritual giant—
Kuthumi as He is today.

We like to think that we know and understand so much, so
very much, about Jesus and Mary and Joseph. Yet there are
few persons today who have even a smattering of correct information about those three Initiates; there are few persons
who realize that back in the days of Atlantis, when Sanat
Kumara was Lord of the World, the man Joseph was a high
priest of the Violet Fire in the Amethyst Temple of Archangel Zadkiel, then located on the physical plane on a high
hill in what is now Cuba. There are few who realize that in
another embodiment as Columbus, this same high priest, this
same man Joseph, sailed across the waters that submerged
Atlantis and landed directly on the island of Cuba, where he
had formerly served in Zadkiel's Temple.

Why, we might ask, is such an intricately woven pattern
of history necesary to sustain the human race on planet
earth? The answer is that the human race has been sustained
here through nineteen million years of darkness, of human
response to pain, distress, ignorance of the basest sort. In

order for Sanat Kumara to carry out His original concept of saving the planet from dissolution, He had to carefully choose and select a few souls who had not lost all memory of their Source. These souls were very rare among earth people: therefore, it was necessary time and again to bring in volunteers from other planets.

In this galaxy the earth is regarded as a beachhead which can be held only by the strongest of commando forces. Yet force in the common military meaning of the word cannot be used: the force must be entirely electronic in nature; it must consist basically of scientifically directed currents of energy or light—penetrating deeper and ever deeper into the darkness of men's minds. The task of bringing light to earth is not an easy one, and when volunteers are requested from other planets to assist in the work they do not snatch up their assignments thoughtlessly.

The Cosmic Hierarchy works on what we could call a time plan which schedules certain events thousands of years ahead. Actually time and space as we understand it on this earth is based entirely on illusion but in order to fit our darkened minds into the cosmic scheme of things, the Hierarchy makes an effort to bring to our attention certain time relationships which we can grasp. Time as it affects us in relation to the galaxy might best be understood if we use the seasonal approach. Spring comes to our land and we are aware that certain changes take place in temperature and in vegetation. In the galaxy similar changes occur as the seven Rays swing in and out of manifestation in major and minor cycles. Here on the earth we are energized by a certain Ray which is extremely powerful for a period of approximately 2,000 years. Certain achievements can take place under certain Ray conditions and cosmic plans are made accordingly.

When the man Joseph was selected as the spouse of Mary, the cosmic appointment was based not so much on events in his past, as on events in his future. The appointment had to fall to a man who was adept in the use of the Violet Fire. Away back in Atlantean times when Joseph had been one of Zadkiel's high priests, he had tended the sacred Flame on the great central altar in the Amethyst Temple. The Temple was actually built entirely of amethyst stones held together by a mortar of pure gold, for the amethyst as found in nature is but crystallized Violet Fire of the seventh Ray.

During the 2,000-year period of the Piscean Age which followed the birth of Jesus, it was the Ruby Fire of the sixth Ray that energized this planet. So Joseph played a somewhat minor role in the Holy Family because his cosmic moment had not yet arrived. Coming back into embodiment again and again, he spent the two thousand years preparing for the greatest role that has ever been played out upon the world stage. As Joseph, as Roger Bacon, as Francis Bacon, as Count Rakoczi and as many other historical figures, the present Lord of Civilization, the Adept who is now guiding our planet into the new Golden Age of Aquarius, has emerged as Sanctus Germanus, the "holy brother", known to millions today at Ascended Master Saint Germain.

At the present point in history, and from now on for the next two thousand years, the very fate of every atom on, in and around the planet earth, will be influenced by the cosmic fact that Saint Germain is now the Lord of Civilization on this globe. It was under His jurisdiction that the axis of the planet was straightened by the angelic kingdom; it is under His jurisdiction that the planet is edging, with a sidewise motion, into its new orbit; it is under His jurisdiction that the planet is spiralling upward into a new spacial region; it is under His jurisdiction that all imprisoned energy on, in and around the earth is now being released and returned to the sun for rejuvenation.

Imprisoned energy is now held captive in virtually all atoms where astral matter clogs the orbital passages provided for the revolution of electrons. This astral matter, man-created, cannot be destroyed under universal Law. It can only be transmuted by the Violet Fire acting upon it under the divine Laws of Mercy, Compassion and Forgiveness. The seventh Ray is also known as the Ray of White Magic because of its instantaneous alchemical action of transmutation. The transmuted energy, freed by divine forgiveness, is usually so weakened by its brutal imprisonment that it must be carried by the angelic kingdom back to the sun for recharging. In recent years, since the fission-fusion boys have roamed the earth, seeking to destroy, the situation has become extremely serious, and that is one reason why hundreds of spaceships regularly fly through the atmosphere, transmuting vast areas of atomic infection.

Beginning in 1957 tens of millions of angels began moving earthward in shining legions. The angels serve throughout the galaxy wherever they are accepted. Only a minimum number have remained in the earth's contaminated atmosphere during the past centuries because they were rejected by the majority of people who could no longer see them. However, by 1957 the calls for angelic assistance had become so urgent that under the direction of the seven great Archangels, each serving on one of the seven Rays, millions upon millions of angels moved into the etheric regions around the earth to stand in readiness to answer any calls. The cherubim are particularly active now and very often their flights through the night skies are observed and they are mistaken for spaceships. The cherubim fly in large groups, in V-formation, and as they fly within their own forcefield they give off a brilliant white light.

The return of the angels to the earth's atmosphere will have a profound effect on the planet as a whole, because no other planet in the system attempts to operate without the aid of angels, with at least five to every member of the human population. Only the arrogant humanity of earth has rejected angelic assistance. Now under the jurisdiction of Saint Germain, Chohan of the Violet Fire, the angels are being encouraged to return to help mankind.

Ascended Master Saint Germain has also supervised the selection of thousands of volunteers from other planets who have been infiltrating into the earth's population in large numbers during the past hundred years. Of course, certain individuals from other planets have been coming to the earth since the days of Sanat Kumara's regime, but during the past hundred years more than ten million volunteers have either embodied here in earth families, or have been brought in as babies and reared as earth children. Within the past decade the space people have used the moon as a space station, and have built tremendous installations there in which adults from other planets are conditioned to live in a simulated earth atmosphere, and then landed here in space ships. These people mingle freely with the population, live as earth people do, and are seldom recognized as interplanetary visitors.

During the past hundred years, Ascended Master Saint Germain has concentrated particularly on the scientific field because this is at once the most dangerous area now being plundered by earth men and also the area most necessary to the spiritual welfare of man. The Ascension process is strictly a scientific one. It is neither mysterious nor mystical.

Certainly it is not religious. Each and every person must learn, in some embodiment, how to raise the atomic vibration of the four lower bodies—mental, emotional, etheric and physical. Each and every person must, in some embodiment, discard that disgusting ancient habit of dying and leaving his physical body lying around for someone to bury. In the New Age, with the tremendous increase in vibratory rates in and around the planet, the entire emphasis of civilization will be placed on living. The habit of dying will be forgotten as soon as the majority of people have cleaned out their etheric bodies by using the Violet Fire.

The etheric body contains all records, all memories of past lives, back to the very beginning of our individualization as White Fire Beings. The etheric body is what modern scientists call the subconscious, which is perhaps as good a name as any other providing its meaning is clearly understood. At the present time the term is used glibly and in a meaningless manner. That situation will have to be changed because a person with a clogged etheric body can make little evolutionary progress. He must understand clearly that the etheric records of bad habits must be transmuted so that the tiny etheric filaments are clean and firmly woven in a perfect pattern of triangles. Wherever the etheric body registers disease or disharmony of any kind the tiny filaments become disarranged and tattered. These records of disharmony remain until transmuted. Meanwhile they are built in, embodiment after embodiment.

A striking example of the horrible after-effects of war memories retained by the etheric body, is now being illustrated on a world-wide scale. It seemed very noble back in 1940 to train young men to march forth and kill the enemy. Now the bewildered public wonders why we have so much

juvenile delinquency. The answer is that many boys who
were killed in World War II are back in embodiment, with
their etheric memories of violence freshly imprinted on their
subtle bodies. The sight of a gun, of a blood-and-thunder
TV show or movie, membership in a street gang, or even a
family argument is sufficient to stir these etheric records into
violent upheavals. Yet the public remains captive to churchianity, militarism and death, resolutely refusing to even in-
vestigate the glorious possibilities of living in a clean and
wholesome world.

In the following chapters are set forth the broad outlines
of Saint Germain's New Age program as it has manifested
in recent years, and as it will affect the immediate future of
every earth person—indeed of every earth atom. Since the
program is in the final analysis a scientific one, designed to
prepare individuals for the Ascension process, we will focus
our attention first upon the vast preparatory work which was
started in 1856 by that great scientific genius, Nikola Tesla.

PART V

The Nikola Tesla Story

Nikola Telsa was not an earth man. The space people have stated that a male child was born on board a space ship which was on a flight from Venus to the earth in July, 1856. The little boy was called Nikola. The ship landed at midnight, between July 9 and 10, in a remote mountain province in what is now Yugoslavia. There, according to arrangements, the child was placed in the care of a good man and his wife, the Rev. Milutin and Djouka Telsa.

The space people released this information in 1947 to Arthur H. Matthews of Quebec, Canada, an electrical engineer who from boyhood was closely associated with Tesla.

In 1944, a year after the death of Tesla, the late John J. O'Neill, then science editor of the *New York Herald Tribune,* wrote an excellent story of Tesla's life and work, en-

71

titled *Prodigal Genius*. As a reporter O'Neill frequently interviewed Tesla and had the greatest respect for the superman. But O'Neill lacked the occult understanding necessary to correctly interpret the extraordinary powers which set Tesla apart from this world. O'Neill made the common error of assuming that Tesla had died as do ordinary mortals: that his work was finished, and that he left no disciples.

O'Neill could not have been more mistaken. In the first place Tesla was not a mortal according to earth standards: being a Venusian he is now able to work on earth in his subtle body with far greater facility than when in his physical body. Tesla carefully trained certain disciples to continue his physical plane work under his supervision after he had shed his physical body.

He entrusted Arthur H. Matthews of Canada with many tasks, at least two of which are of vital current interest — the Tesla interplanetary communications set and the Tesla anti-war machine.

Mr. Matthews built a model Tesla set for interplanetary communications in 1947 and has operated it successfully since. However, he has tuned in only on space ships thus far, for the set has a limited range. He is now engaged in building a more elaborate set, and will be able to speak more freely of it since he is incorporating many of his own inventive ideas in it. The original design was given to him in confidence by Tesla and he naturally does not intend to violate that confidence.

Mr. Matthews has the complete design for the anti-war machine ready and waiting for any nation which has the courage to use it. Tesla designed the anti-war machine in 1935 but Mr. Matthews has worked on it constantly since, incorporating in it many major improvements.

Another disciple who was specially trained by Tesla is
Otis T. Carr of Baltimore, Maryland. Carr has recently invented free-energy devices capable of powering anything
from a hearing aid to a spaceship. Carr was studying art in
New York and working in a hotel package room to support
himself. Tesla, who was not only completely telepathic but
also in touch with the Christ Forces on the Inner Planes,
lived in the hotel where Carr was employed. Telsa came
straight to his young disciple, asked him to buy four pounds
of unsalted peanuts and deliver them to his suite. From this
beginning Carr was trained by Tesla over a period of three
years in almost daily conversations that always started with
the peanut delivery. The peanuts were for the New York
pigeons which Tesla so loved.

The remarkable achievements of both Matthews and Carr
are covered in later chapters of this book. But it may be said
here that Tesla is in no sense a disembodied spirit seeking to
communicate with disciples and guiding them from the astral
plane. Mediums who engage, for profit of course, in receiving messages from the astral plane have tried with vim and
with vigor to drum up trade via the spirit or ghost of Tesla.
But Tesla is not a ghost, nor did he stand a ghost of a
chance of being a ghost. Tesla was an Adept, an Initiate,
a Venusian. He was at all times earth-free; he was never
earthbound.

Naturally Tesla did not go around bragging about these
matters. But when he did meet up with a server of the Light
Tesla lost no time in engaging in a good talkfest. Both
Matthews and Carr have carried out Tesla's work since
1943 without the slightest difficulty. When asked how best
to approach the work of Tesla, how to understand his discoveries, both Matthews and Carr have a standard answer. If

you wish to understand Tesla you must attune your mind
to God.

Tesla and his Twin Ray, the White Dove who was his
constant companion on earth, are now working in the scientific department of Shamballa, and they do overshadow disciples. But it should be clearly understood that this over-
shadowing process, when conducted by an Initiate, is in no
sense related to any type of psychism or mediumship. Every
Initiate overshadows disciples; otherwise there would be no
point in evolution if the higher energies could not in some
manner direct lower energies. Every Initiate must have
disciples in the world of form. Disciples are called upon to
operate typewriters, design machinery and do all the other
chores of the workaday world. A disciple is an outpost of
consciousness for an Adept.

What, the reader might ask, is the oustanding characteristic which distinguishes a Tesla disciple? In every case a
Tesla disciple is, consciously or unconsciously, affiliated with
one or more of the Masters of Wisdom, and is a student
in a Master's Ashram, although this fact may be known
only on the Inner Planes. Every Tesla disciple is working
with the energies from at least five cosmic Rays, and is
usually unconscious of his correct Ray status as knowledge
of this kind can easily become a source of pride and therefore a handicap. Every Tesla disciple extends the hand of
friendship to our interplanetary neighbors. Every Tesla disciple is already firmly oriented in the New Age and has un-
bounded enthusiasm for a free and joyous world.

Many persons who worked for Tesla, or who were associated with him closely as was John J. O'Neill, have expressed
disappointment that Tesla did not leave a heritage of great
scientific secrets which could be explored, and, of course,

exploited. But, Tesla, the Venusian, had no secrets. Only earth people are greedy enough and stupid enough to have secrets.

The Venusians, Martians, and visitors from other planets who fly through the earth's atmosphere daily, have no secrets either. They have a message: Love ye one another. But earth people have successfully ignored that message for at least 2,000 years, and they might go right on ignoring it save for New Age developments based on application of universal Law. Such application was the clue to all of Tesla's achievements. He was a discoverer, not a mere inventor.

There seem to be no records of Tesla revealing his identity as a Venusian during his earth life. But when the announcement of this fact was made to Mr. Matthews by the space people it did not come as a surprise in most quarters, because by then it was generally known that at least ten million people from other planets had been infiltrated into the earth's population. It had long been known that most of the Masters of Wisdom, down through the centuries, were volunteers from other worlds. But it seemed doubtful, for a time, that Tesla himself, had been personally aware of his origin during his physical plane life on earth.

However, it now appears that he did understand his mission which was actually to prepare the planet earth for the space age. The fact that he told Otis T. Carr so much about other planets indicates that he was quite familiar with the subject. He frankly told Carr that he, Carr, was destined to explore space. Tesla also gave Mr. Matthews the design for the interplanetary communications set in 1938, another clear indication that Tesla knew that other planets were inhabited. and he obviously knew they possessed spaceships. He told Mr. Matthews that the set should be built in a few years

after 1938, at which time spaceships from other worlds
would approach the earth.

Tesla never married, and never had any romantic attach-
ments or even close friendships with either men or women,
except in certain cases where the bond was one of discipleship or where some useful purpose would be served for the
benefit of humanity. Tesla not only lived alone in hotels,
but he lived behind locked doors. Only occasionally was a
maid permitted to enter his room to clean it. However, Otis
T. Carr, over a period of three years, was his daily visitor
and Tesla explained to Carr that visitors were not normally
allowed because, coming into his suite from the harsh, outside world, they immediately lowered the vibrations in the
rooms in which Tesla had to live and work and commune
with his Creator.

Mr. Carr has explained that often, when he came to
Tesla's suite, bringing the four pounds of unsalted peanuts,
Tesla would ask him to just sit down and relax for an hour
or more. Not a word would be spoken between the two men.
Yet when Carr rose to leave he would feel refreshed and inspired. The vibrations in the room had done the necessary
work, attuning and purifying his four lower bodies.

Tesla had another trusted friend in the person of Boris
De Tanko, a New York publisher. Mr. De Tanko has related
how, Saturday after Saturday, he used to meet Tesla for
luncheon at the old Hotel Brevoort on lower Fifth Avenue,
a place famous for its fine French cuisine. Mr. De Tanko
always found these luncheon visits highly inspiring, though
unusual in some respects. He said that often the two of
them sat together at the table in complete silence for well
over an hour; finally Tesla would speak and then the illuminating conversation would flow like molten gold.

Both Mr. Matthews and Mr. Carr received from Tesla a great deal of confidential information about future world conditions and developments concerning the emergence of the New Age civilization. Most of this information had to do with space, with space ships, space people, and interplanetary communications.

When Tesla shed his physical body in 1943, it was apparent that he was leaving the physical plane of manifest appearances to enter into more subtle vibrations; vibrations which were invisible to the average man. These vibrations were not invisible to Tesla; he was completely clairvoyant, clairaudient and telepathic, as is any Adept. Again it must be stressed that this type of clarity has nothing whatever to do with mediumship or psychism. The latter belongs to the animal kingdom. Tesla was never really at home on the physical plane, dealing with matter in its harshest state: in the subtle worlds he was completely free. Yet for 87 of the most difficult years ever visited upon this planet Tesla carried on his work like the great gentlemen he was.

In retrospect the pattern of his physical sojourn in the world of form, which seemed so complex to writers like John J. O'Neill, emerges in simple clarity. Tesla had obviously agreed to come to the earth as a volunteer worker to assist in launching the New Age which he knew to be synonymous with the Space Age. It is perfectly apparent that Ascended Master Saint Germain had to bring in people from other planets, people with knowledge of outer space conditions, to handle the major aspects of the planned program.

Tesla was designated to work on the third Ray of Love-in-Action, for that is the Ray which supplies our atmosphere with electricity. The first three major Rays form the three aspects of God as defined by major religions; the four minor

Rays provide what we recognize as God's attributes. Christianity correctly defines the first three Rays as a Trinity, representing the Father, the Son, and the Holy Spirit.

The first or Father aspect is derived from the Ray of Power and Purpose; the second, the Son or sun aspect, is the Ray of Illumination and Wisdom leading to Intelligent Love-in-Action, or the third Ray. Originally, we were all Sons of God or Sparks from the Great Central Sun of the galaxy. From the strictly scientific point of view the first three Rays provide life, light, and electricity to this planet.

The fourth Ray of Purity leads man through conflict to harmony. The fifth Ray is that of concrete science and knowledge and provides the world of form with an understandable functional basis. The sixth Ray energizes all of man's ideals and ideologies, whether wise or foolish. During the Piscean Age it led to the rise of Christianity and churchianity, and to all sorts of experimental economic and political systems. Then follows the seventh Ray, now in manifestation; the Ray which is now being called into action to transmute and release mankind from all past errors accumulated during nineteen million years of struggle since the laggards came.

At the present time, and for centuries past, all individuals who desired so-called occult knowledge have been regularly taken into the various Ray Temples or Retreats for training at night while the physical body lies sleeping. The Temples are open twenty-four hours a day round the globe so their facilities are always available to students. It should not be considered that this training is mystical; it is strictly utilitarian and practical and is designed to make physical plane living easier and more wholesome. It is designed to lead not to death, but to the Ascension for each individual.

For example, every great musical composer down through the ages has been a Temple student. Some composers are able to bring through their memories with greater accuracy than others. Wagner was an outstanding student in the Music Temple, and during his waking hours he was able to bring through musical notations with scarcely a deviation from the original Temple teachings. The story of Lohengrin is one of his finest examples.

It is presumed that Tesla not only had the usual free access to the Temples during his sleeping hours, but that he also had direct communication while in full waking consciousness. This is not unusual for even an advanced student; it is the normal practice for Initiates. In the outer world there is no information available on Tesla's exact evolutionary status on Venus, but it is known that the entire Venusian race is considered adept from our point of view. However, when space people take earth bodies they are often mercifully granted certain mental blockages for their own protection. That is, if a Venusian had a full and complete memory of his life on Venus, he would find it well nigh impossible to cope daily with earth situations. Even the Initiate Jesus did not have a complete mental grasp of His true mission until He was more than twelve years of age. It was then that He was taken to India for personal training under the supervision of His great teacher, the Christ, known in the outer world as Lord Maitreya.

John J. O'Neill has written a most detailed story of Tesla's life and scientific work in *Prodigal Genius*. But for those readers who are just becoming oriented in this field of study, it might be well to pause here for a brief review of the highlights that lighted the path of the man who came to earth to bring electricity to our homes and factories and illumination to our darkened minds.

Historians agree that Nikola Tesla was born at midnight, between July 9 and 10, in the year of 1856. Nikola himself hinted on a few occasions that this was not the date of his birth. These hints were disregarded along with hundreds of other statements made by Tesla, because in most quarters, he was regarded as being a bit impractical. This was not a criticism, for his genius was so highly respected that it was generally conceded that he did not have to measure up to conventional standards. He was to be allowed his little eccentricities, his passing fancies. The space people have now stated that Nikola was born on board their ship on a flight from Venus, and that they landed on the earth at midnight, between July 9 and 10, 1856.

When the space people say that Nikola was *born* on board one of their ships, they do not mean that it was a physical birth. Physical conception and the birthing processes known on this planet are not used elsewhere. A sex system was introduced here after the laggards came, in order to keep the race in manifestation, and to provide for re-embodiment in groups bound by karma. This allowed karmic debts to be paid off in kind under the old law of "an eye for an eye, and a tooth for a tooth." On other planets positive and negative light rays are used to produce a physical form which can be occupied by an evolving lifestream. The form is of full stature. It is only on this planet that tiny, baby forms are utilized.

Djouka Tesla, the earth mother who cared for Nikola
with a rare tenderness, was a most remarkable woman and
assuredly possessed advanced spiritual powers. It has been
said that she, too, was a Venusian, and if this is true, it accounts for her very unusual abilities. She was the eldest child
in a family of seven children. Her father was a minister of
the Serbian Orthodox Church. Her mother had become
blind after the seventh child was born and Djouka unhesita-
tingly took charge of the entire household. She never attended school, nor did she learn even the rudiments of reading and writing at home. Yet she moved with ease in cultured
circles as did her family. Here was a woman who could
neither read nor write, yet she possessed literary abilities far
beyond those of a person of considerable education.

Tesla, himself, never wearied of talking about his remarkable mother, and described how she had absorbed "by
ear" all the cultural riches of her community and her nation.
Like Nikola, she apparently had the power of instant recall.
Nikola said that she could easily recite, without error, long
passages from the Bible; she could repeat. thousands of
versus of the national poetry of her country. It was because
of her great interest in poetry that Nikola, in his busy
American days as a superman, still found time to translate
and have published some of the best examples of Serbian
sagas.

His mother was also famed throughout her home prov-
inces for her artistic ability, often expressed in beautiful
needlework. She possessed remarkable manual dexterity, and
Nikola said her fingers were so sensitive that she could tie
three knots in an eyelash—even when she was past sixty
years of age.

She had an excellent grasp of philosophy and apparently

a practical understanding of mechanical and technical devices. She needed a loom for household weaving, so she designed and built one. She did not think of herself as an inventor, yet she built many labor-saving devices and instruments for her household. In addition she was so skillful in handling business and financial matters that she managed all accounts for her household as well as for her husband's church.

Nikola's earth father was the son of an army officer, and as a young man set out on a military career. But he was soon disillusioned for he was irked by the discipline, and turned to his true calling in the literary field. He wrote poetry, articles on current problems, and philosophical essays. This led, quite naturally, to the ministry, giving him an opportunity to write sermons and to speak from the pulpit. He did not limit himself to the usual church topics, but ranged far and wide, covering subjects of local and national interest concerning labor, social and economic problems. Until Nikola was seven years of age, the father had a parish church at Smiljan, an agricultural community in a high plateau region in that part of the Alps which stretch from Switzerland to Greece.

This then was the childhood environment of the boy from Venus. It was a life filled with joy. He had an ideal home with a loving understanding family. He lived in a magnificent countryside, close to nature. He was a boy like other little boys up to a certain point, the point at which he became the superboy, foreshadowing the superman. And so it was that he lacked human companions, a state, not of loneliness but of aloneness, that was to continue throughout his physical incarnation. The unlighted ones whom he met everywhere through the years felt sorry for him because they assumed

he was lonely. Tesla never tried to explain his position for
he knew he would meet with no understanding from an alien
world. To the end of his time in a physical body he lived
at the very center, the very core, of a magnificent solitude,
listening always to the Voice of the Silence.

As a boy Nikola liked nothing better than to wander in
the woods and over the mountains near his home. His little
friends did not understand or share his boundless enthusiasm
for trees, streams, birds and their nests, sunshine, clouds
and stormy skies. Nor did they enjoy what they considered
the hard work connected with Nikola's many boyhood inventions. He was constantly engaged in experiments that
often failed, a fact which made them all the more fascinating. In reviewing his life in later years, he could look back
upon these many lines of investigation which he had started
as a boy and see how they led directly to some of his major
inventions.

As he grew to maturity he displayed certain characteristics
which might have revealed his Venusian origin had they
been understood. His hands were unusually long, particularly his thumbs, and were extremely sensitive, carrying strong
clean etheric currents. Inasmuch as he was clairvoyant he
could easily see the murky gray astral matter which exudes
from the hands of the ordinary person, an effluvia of filth
so sticky that it will adhere to the etheric structure of
another person—even an individual occupying a body of
high vibrations.

For this reason Tesla always dreaded shaking hands. He
tried to avoid such contacts even at the cost of being thought
inconsiderate or impolite. On occasion, when it was absolutely necessary for him to shake hands with certain visitors
in his New York office, he escaped at the earliest possible

moment to his private washroom where he thoroughly washed his hands, drying them on a clean towel which was handed to him by his secretary and used only once.

He had the deep-set piercing eyes of the Initiate, clear blue in color. He also breathed correctly, something an earth person seldom achieves. This was a natural faculty, for as a small child he discovered that by breathing deeply he was overcome by a feeling of lightness in his body. He felt so weightless that he concluded he would be able to fly if he developed the will to do so. It is said that he did not know he was unusual in this respect while he was still a child. Tesla could leave his body at will when he grew older. He always lived in hotels, and his orders were that he was never to be disturbed in his locked room. Tesla used projected consciousness as do all Initiates, although this is not to be confused with the type of astral projection practiced by the average person. The Initiate uses many types of etheric energies freely and in a manner which is always spiritually correct. The ordinary individual does not have the ability to utilize these energies or even to contact them, and therefore easily falls into the dangerous practice of using astral or lower mental forces. This leads to the next step on the left-hand path—the state of trance mediumship.

When Tesla was a small boy and found that his rhythmic breathing gave him a feeling that he could fly, he quite naturally and normally began to practice levitation. In this is a profound lesson for all of us, and it is the same lesson that Jesus stressed. Jesus warned us that we should not accept appearances, if those appearances might prove limiting to us. We are always imitating that which we see about us. We see people growing old, so we grow old. If everyone thought of growing younger, and youth began to manifest

all about us, we would grow younger in appearance as a matter of course. We see people walking, so we walk. Young
Nikola saw people walking, but he knew in his heart that
it was a cumbersome and laborious method, so he pondered
over it and got the *feeling* that he could fly. Then he followed his own inner *feeling;* not the example set by appearances all about him. He rose from the earth, levitated, and
moved through space freely.

It might have startled unsuspecting New Yorkers to see
Tesla take off like his companion, the White Dove, and fly
over the city. But those who understand levitation and use
it can also throw a cloak of invisibility about themselves.
People jumped to strange conclusions about what they
thought were the eccentricities of a great scientist. Another
great One by the name of Jesus walked on water, and the
curious are still talking about it today. Tesla well knew
that it was the better part of wisdom to remain invisible
when he had his feet off the ground, so to speak.

Some of his close associates knew that he could levitate
and respected the confidence. It might be well to underscore
a point here—the person who levitates by using his Christ
Principle to do so, must have a purpose behind his action,
and it must be a purpose which is in some way furthering
the Divine Plan. It is not spiritually permissible to levitate
merely as a form of entertainment, for oneself or for others.
Levitation is correctly used only if one is definitely going
somewhere for a definite reason in the service of humanity.
The average individual moves according to his own whim
and pleasure, and usually to satisfy some personal objective
which is often unnecessary. The average person moves
about because of restlessness and an inherent inability to
work according to any plan, let alone the Divine Plan.

The limitations of walking have offered certain advantages in the past. Transportation was so difficult that people tended to remain quiet as much as possible, or if they did go on a walking journey they often utilized the time to commune with nature or their fellowmen. But the advent of the automobile, bus, plane, and train, has introduced a method of transportation which adds only noise, confusion and chaos to the general picture; and which constantly exposes the emotional body to jarring impacts of a most distressing sort.

When Nikola was five years of age, he designed and installed a waterwheel across a mountain brook near his home at Smiljan. He utilized a disk cut from a tree trunk by lumber workers, some small branches, sticks and rocks. The device was a wonderful success from the standpoint of the young inventor. It was a bit crude, but it rotated. He had used the methods of antiquity in designing his model and it was only much later that he discovered that waterwheels have paddles, but his wheel operated without paddles.

This waterwheel was his first demonstration of a lesson he never forgot—to utilize free energy which was being constantly and freely replaced by Nature. Later, perhaps as a direct result of this experiment as a five-year-old boy, he developed the smooth-disk turbine. Later, too, he carried his experiments in utilizing the free energy of Nature into the atmosphere, and there he found that electricity in unlimited abundance would give him unlimited power—free energy that would carry mankind itself to freedom from the great curse of grueling labor. This was Tesla's magnificent concept that dominated his every thought as an inventor— free energy for a free world. It was the concept that carried him to the heights of cosmic fellowship, and the one mighty flame of inspiration which he set before his disciples as an eternal beacon—free energy to make and keep the people free.

When he was nine years old, he designed his first motor. It was made from tiny pieces of wood and shaped somewhat like a windmill. But it was not powered by the wind. It was powered by June bugs, flying round and round, trying to detach their feet from the glue which held them fast to their duties.

An incident took place at this time which clearly indicated the clean and wholesome trend of Tesla's thinking. He used June bugs because he needed to somehow capture power from the air although the bugs might have been happier had they not been drafted for this service. But Nikola used bugs just as a plowman would use horses. However, a little companion came in to observe the motor. He spied a reserve supply of June bugs which Nikola had placed in a small jar and the child grabbed a handful of the bugs and ate them. Nikola was so sickened by the event that he set the remaining bugs free and never again utilized bug-power. This was his first direct step toward capturing power from the air without enslavement of animal or human labor.

It was also at this time, when he was finishing his elementary studies and entering the Gymnasium for more advanced school work, that he first came to grips with his occult power of working in the fourth ether. He had only to think of an object, and it would appear before him, exhibiting the normal appearance of mass, solidity and dimensions.

He had discussed this matter in confidence with his mother, for he found the ability to be a nuisance rather than an asset and wished to be rid of it.

Whether or not his mother could explain it was never revealed; now in retrospect it seems that she herself probably possessed the same power and understood it thoroughly. But Nikola was still a child and his mother agreed with him that he should attempt to banish the visions if he wished. From the occult point of view this was the correct thing to do, for no adult person should ever try to influence a child or tamper with a child's efforts to come to grips with spirital realities. This kind of tampering has proved to be the great curse of churchianity and one of the most dangerous of black magic practices.

A little later Nikola confided to his mother that he wished to keep and use the power to envision objects before him, but that he wished to bring it under complete control. Again his mother agreed with him. The power to work in the fourth ether—a psysical substance which forms the plane of density just a little finer than gas—is a power possessed in full by every advanced Initiate. They also work freely in the third, second and first ethers, which together with the lower four—physical, liquid, gaseous and the fourth ether—form the seven ethers which comprise the entire plane of of matter. Scientists have not worked with the ethers because they could not see them, and it is not generally realized that the dense physical plane is only concretized ether. There is nothing mystical about working in the finer ethers; in fact, it is a scientific shortcut. There is actually no reason to dig gold out of the earth and then process it. It is much easier to extract it from the ether and precipitate it on to the physical plane. But in an earlier chapter of this book it was

explained that after the laggards came man lost his power
to precipitate matter, for he lost the use of the Rays. It was
only then that man started digging in the soil and extracting
his needs from the lowest plane of matter.

Today on the Inner Planes where the Lords of Karma
work, the whole plan for re-embodiment has been changed
to bring it into line with needs for the New Age civilization.
Greater selectivity is practiced and many children are now
being born who have the ability to work in the fourth ether
as did Nikola Tesla. Therefore, the whole subject is one
which should be thoroughly explored by scientists, teachers
and parents, if these adults wish to understand New Age
children and participate in the civilization which they will
produce.

It has been stated by the Spiritual Hierarchy that within
300 years the entire race will be telepathic and will possess
etheric vision. These are natural human unfoldments following the normal course of evolution which is now being
guided on the physical plane once again by the Hierarchy.
The race is moving forward in evolution in a manner of
speaking, but at the same time we are striving to get back
to a point at which we stood nineteen million years ago. It
is that point that each of us must attain during the Aquarian Age. Then from that point each will move forward
swiftly toward the Ascension and go on to new evolutionary
assignments on other stars.

At this particular time, it is most essential that the general
public become informed about etheric vision and telepathy,
for there is much dangerous confusion on the subject. This
is planned confusion, engineered down to the last degree
by the forces of darkness. Such confusion does not exist in
the minds of those who are serving the Light. It exists in the

minds of the bewildered masses because of their inability
to exercise discrimination. They listen to the press, the
preachers and the teachers, and swallow whatever happens
to appeal to their basic desire nature. Thus do the dark
forces brainwash the masses into a lethargic state of docil-
ity; the masses follow along like sheep to the slaughter.

The powers possessed by Nikola Tesla were in no sense
psychic powers. The ability to see into the fourth ether, to
mold the etheric substance into machinery as did Tesla, and
then to test that etheric machinery and make any necessary
adjustments as did Tesla—all of this has nothing whatever
to do with the astral plane. The astral plane is man-made.
Astral matter is filthy matter. Tesla struck right through
the astral plane and had no contact with it. As Arthur H.
Matthews has truly stated: When Tesla wanted something
he went straight to God.

In these dangerous times that advice is the best possible—
when we want something we should go straight to God and
talk to Him about it. Today there are hundreds if not millions of people who have responded to ancient decadent Atlantean vibrations. The reason for this is because certain
sections of the submerged continent are to be brought up in
the very near future. When Atlantis went down three cities
were sealed. These cities will soon be brought up to the surface of the Atlantic and will be used as exhibits of Atlantean
culture. This is one of the projects which is being handled
by the angelic kingdom under the direction of Saint Germain
in His capacity as Lord of Civilization.

The response to ancient Atlantean vibrations is a dangerous response. Human beings mistakenly feel that the ability
to see into astral matter is a sign of the advanced Initiate.
An Initiate possesses powers which enable him to stand on

this earth and yet observe incidents on Venus or Mars. He can also look out over the earth and sweep the entire scene with one glance. He can look through the earth and watch activities within the dense physical globe.

Thus it will be realized that the Initiate is completely free. He can see above, as below. The person with astral vision is a prisoner of his own limited and highly questionable power. If he has the ability to see auras, colors, and so forth, what of it? Usually he uses the power merely to satisfy personal curiosity in exactly the same way that he uses the power of speech to indulge in gossip. When an Initiate looks out over the universe you may be certain that He has some excellent reason for doing so. He may carefully inspect the aura of a disciple in order to determine the corrections needed. He may inspect the aura of a great city to determine the spiritual strength of the populace, but along the way He does not stop to watch a football game or look over the latest bargains in the shopping marts. On the other hand, the person with astral vision is not only subject to normal distractions of physical eyesight, but he is subjected to the constant nervous impact of additional colors, movements and so forth.

Peace of mind and serenity of soul do not lie along that route; nor can the Voice of the Silence be heard within the beating heart of the unlighted ones who amuse themselves with such nonsense. Astral vision is more often a sign of regression than of advancement, for it simply denotes the attainment of certain animal characteristics. It must be remembered that all animals in certain advanced groups— dogs, cats, horses and elephants—have astral vision. Many other animals also possess it and most animals are telepathic within certain limits.

In humans, this type of clairvoyance is often associated with solar plexus telepathy, another animal characteristic. Many persons who use solar plexus telepathy are inclined to confuse it with mental telepathy, and those who practice mental telepathy are frequently unaware that the only type of telepathy which can be considered as a spiritual power is from Soul to Soul, or from Ascended-Master to Soul. The Soul referred to here is the I AM Presence Who overshadows us, or the Christ-Self Who abides in the heart Flame.

Individuals who strive to cultivate their astral abilities, even though they may be born with them, are following an extremely dangerous course, and one which can lead easily from psychism to black magic and from black magic to insanity. If an individual is born with psychic powers he should either banish them at all costs, or he should take up the proper study which will enable him to serve the Forces of Light to the limit of his capacity. These astral conditions are karmic, but if properly channeled they can lead to discipleship. If they are not properly channeled, they can and will lead only to mediumship and misery.

Mediumship is the way of retrogression. Discipleship is the way to the path of truth, light, beauty and unlimited cosmic freedom. Every individual has only one rule to follow and this is it: Place yourself at all times under the full power and protection of your own God-Presence, your Christ-Self or Soul, for your own Higher Self is your first and best teacher. There is no need to be running around the Himalayas or elsewhere searching for a guru or Master. When you are ready to be of service to the Hierarchy your own Master, and He will be an Ascended Master, will seek you out—intuitively, of course, not physically—and you will not have to worry about being kept busy in the service of the Light. There is plenty to do."

It is the Soul or Christ-Self that comes into incarnation, not the physical body or the emotions or the lower concrete mind. The Soul builds these lower vehicles for convenience, and in accordance with the pattern of karma carried over from previous embodiments. Therefore, the Soul should at all times be permitted to train and use the lower vehicles according to the purpose designated in the Divine Plan.

The part which Nikola Tesla was to play in the Divine Plan unfolded quickly when he enrolled at the Gymnasium at Gospic, a large town to which his father had been assigned as a minister. He discovered that his favorite subject was mathematics. So intense was his devotion to this study that his teachers had to overlook his loathing for freehand drawing. It was thought that Nikola was unhappy about drawing because he was left-handed at that time. Eventually he became ambidextrous. another mark of the Initiate.

Many years later it was clearly demonstrated that Nikola loathed drawing because he could work in the fourth ether so easily, designing and building his machines in etheric substance, testing them and making necessary adjustments in the ether, and then leaving them "on file" in the ether. For him drawing was utterly unrealistic and an unmitigated nuisance. He did not have to make plans and jot down dimensions, because of his power of instant recall. After designing a machine in etheric substance he might have no occasion to think of it again for a period of five years or so. Yet when he did need the design he could call it up instantly before him, complete with exact dimensions.

In the school at Gospic Nikola first came to desire to keep this power which he had possessed since birth, but he also desired to bring it under full control and use it, rather than allow it to use him and enslave him. Nikola had no wish to be submerged in paper work, even in his schooldays—a thought which might be of value to many business and government executives today.

Nikola found that he did not need to go to the blackboard in the classroom to work out a problem. At the thought of "blackboard" it appeared in the ether before him. As the problem was stated it appeared instantly on the etheric blackboard together with all the symbols and operations required to work out the solution. Each step appeared instantly, and much more rapidly than anyone could possibly work out the problem on paper or slate. Therefore, by the time the whole problem had been stated, Nikola could give the solution immediately.

At first his teachers thought he was just an extremely clever boy who had found some method of cheating. However, in a short time they were forced to admit that no deception could possibly be practiced, so they gladly accepted the glamor shed abroad as the rumor got around that the Gospic classroom was graced by a genius. Nikola never bothered to explain about the etheric blackboard for he intuitively knew that he would be casting pearls. Always through the passing years he guarded his power as the great spiritual treasure he knew it to be.

He used the same power to replace all customary memory functions, and he soon discovered that he could learn foreign languages with little of the usual effort. He became proficient in German, French and Italian in those early years, and this opened up to him entire new worlds that remained closed to other students. His father's library contained hundreds of fine books and by the time Nikola was eleven years old he had read them all. He had little in common with his schoolmates, and, in fact, little in common with his teachers. But they accepted him because he was a lovable lad without a trace of arrogance or pride. But neither did he shroud himself in an exaggerated sense of humility. He was a normal,. natural friendly boy living in a natural, friendly world.

On fine summer days he would often wander over the mountains from Gospic to sit again beside the brook at Smiljin, and watch his little waterwheel in operation—the wheel he had designed and installed at the age of five years. He was constantly working on mechanical devices during the years he was in school at Gospic, but the school offered no courses that could help him—not even a course in manual training.

However, he did bring into focus one decision that foreshadowed the superman. The school on one occasion arranged an exhibit of models of waterwheels. They were not working models but Nikola could easily envision them in full action. In his home hung a picture which he had often carefully studied. His father explained that it was a picture of Niagara Falls in America.

In school, Nikola looked at the model waterwheels. At home he gazed again at the picture of Niagara Falls. Filled with prophetic joy he exultantly turned to his father and said: "Someday I am going to America and harness Niagara Falls for power". Thirty years later he carried out his plan, exactly as he had predicted it at the age of ten years.

Two other experiments which he worked on during these childhood years proved to be starting points for mature inventions. He discovered that air leaking into a vacuum produced a small amount of rotation in a cylinder. This was not the result he had intended, but he accepted it, and many, many years later, it led to his invention of the Tesla turbine, or what he called a "powerhouse in a hat" because it broke all records for horsepower developed per pound of weight.

The other experiment has not been carried out to its final conclusion, but now that Tesla has shed his physical body, he is working on it from the Inner Planes. In some form it will be presented as a New Age development under the general heading of weather control. While wandering in the mountains one day a thunderstorm broke overhead, and Nikola saw the lightning flash and then saw the rain come down in torrents. He reasoned that the lightning had produced the downpour.

Scientists, years later, argued that high up in the air the rain had come first, and the lightning followed. The raindrops fell slowly to earth, while the lightning flash was observed in a fraction of a second. But Tesla somehow knew that if he could produce lightning he could control the the weather.

He never placed any limits on his thinking and even while walking over the mountains, through the downpour, he envisioned the day when rain could be produced when and where needed, thus providing an abundant food supply the world round. He never lost this vision, and thirty years later, in the mountains of Colorado, he produced bolts of lightning. He planned to use such bolts in his rain-making device but was stopped by the United States Patent Office which refused to go along with his invention.

Now it can be readily seen that his invention might have been premature. For both rain and lightning are produced by the activities of the angelic kingdom. The water devas, fire devas and wind devas serve as housekeepers in the atmosphere around the planet. When they wish to wash out a certain section of the atmosphere, they produce as much rain as they need, and shoot bolts of lightning through the skies to counteract poisonous astral accumulations. The amount of rain that happens to fall on the ground depends entirely upon how much scrubbing is being done up yonder. When the scrub pails are emptied the rain stops.

The devas are not charged with duties such as going around with watering pots for the purpose of irrigating gardens. That problem is in the human province. The devas are very responsive and can be called into action by invocation; or when enough water has been sprinkled and floods threaten they can be stopped by invocation. Human beings should be trained to recognize their own karmic results and do something intelligent about it instead of moaning about the weather. All weather conditions can be under human control. Noah tackled that problem and took the steps necessary to deal with it. Then he sent forth the dove from the ark, and the dove returned with a plucked olive leaf, the symbol of peaceful waters subsiding from the flooded lands. But the dove cannot return unless people first send the dove forth.

When Tesla walked through the rainstorm he was witnessing angelic activities, even though he might not have thought of the matter in quite that way. But he knew that somehow his true work belonged up there in space, high above the mountains of earth. He knew that all worthwhile works must start at the Source. He knew that if he could understand the wonders of flashing lightning and streaming rain then weather could be mechanically controlled. He was correct, for while weather can be controlled through human invocation to the angels, it can also be controlled by a mechanical device. This will be another scientific revelation of the New Age: another proof that the old nonsensical concepts concerning mysticism must go, along with the old concepts about floods and droughts.

Nikola had distinguished himself as a scholar at the age of fourteen. That was in the year of 1870, and his school-days at Gospic were over. He was a sensitive lad, highly intuitive, alert to the constancy of angels and the stupidities of men. His strength was actually extraordinary, for he often read and studied the whole night through, attended his classes by day, and completed a vast educational program of his own outside school hours. But because of his extreme sensitivity, his slim build, and his fastidious nature that demanded a degree of cleanliness far beyond the call of duty, his father felt that the boy was in delicate health.

His father was determined to protect him, and as it turned out the protective attitude paid dividends a few years later when Nikola was spared compulsory military duty because his father was convinced that his delicate son would never survive army life. Nikola, in accord with his father's carefully planned arrangements, was forced to hide out in the mountains for more than a year while apparently attempting to recover his health. During this time his father was able to make certain contacts among the military, so that his son's absence was conveniently overlooked.

Nikola himself found military duty a subject so loathsome that he could not even bring himself to think about it. Intuitively he knew he would never serve in the army, so he made the most of his year of mountain solitude, and returned to his home in good health and with his head filled with scientific plans that, if carried out, probably would have proved earth-shaking in a most literal way.

But all this took place when he reached military age. His first serious difficulties started in 1870 when he finished school at Gospic. Because of his sensitive nature, his father felt that he should not continue his studies, but should go directly into the ministry. His scholarship at the age of fourteen was sufficiently outstanding to equip him to serve in the church.

So far as Nikola was concerned the church was as bad as the army, and, in fact, worse, for the army was still some distance in the future but the church was at hand. Moreover, he had already decided on university training in electrical engineering, and was a dedicated disciple anxious to be about his Father's business in the cosmos. When an individual of the spiritual stature of Tesla comes into incarnation nothing is allowed to interfere with the purpose outlined on the Inner Planes. Plans for the embodiment are carefully arranged in accordance with the Divine Plan for the whole project under development. Initiates work with a high degree of spiritual efficiency. Certain universal needs are scheduled which must be met within time limits by certain disciples appointed to the task, and all of these plans must dovetail according to a certain pre-determined pattern.

At this particular point Nikola had to be saved from a career in the church. The point could not be argued, especially between parents and a 14-year-old boy. Moreover, under Law the free will of the family members had to be permitted full sway; between the three of them they had to

come to free will decision, but at the same time the decision
had to be the correct one. Free will is somewhat paradoxical
in any case, but especially so in the case of disciples. That
is why discipleship is always fraught with extreme difficulty. The disciple is called upon to make a decision, and
yet he must make the correct one which stands upon the Inner Planes, and he must meet a time schedule. But happily
a way is always provided, though it may be a way of severe
struggle.

In the case of Nikola it was the way of psychic illness and
was far from pleasant. He lapsed into a lethargic state from
which he could scarcely be roused at times. His parents were
frightened. The doctors admitted they were helpless as they
had no idea what was causing the illness. When it reached a
critical stage they simply gave up all hope of saving his life.

Naturally the doctors in Gospic had no idea whatever
about the true nature of Nikola's illness. Even medical science today knows nothing of "soul sickness" or the diseases
which attack only disciples and not the average person. The
individual himself, however, is usually able to supply the
answer for he is under guidance from the Inner Planes. So
after the Gospic doctors had given up hope for his life, and
his parents had become somewhat resigned, Nikola turned to
his books. He had been working in the local library at Gospic
and had carried home an armful of selections just before his
illness.

Listlessly he looked them over. He found one by Mark
Twain. In it he suddenly discovered a paragraph which
brought instant illumination. His enthusiasm for life was re-
kindled. The crisis passed. His health returned to normal.
Nikola himself understood with profound conviction that it
was the writings of Mark Twain that had saved his life. He

never forgot the incident to the end of his days and often spoke of his heartfelt gratitude to Mark Twain. Many years after the Gospic incident the two men met in New York and became very close friends. When Tesla himself had only a short time left on earth, and Mark Twain had been gone from the mortal scene for years, Tesla spoke of Mark coming to see him in his hotel room, and of their having a long visit together. When Tesla was reminded that Mark Twain had been dead for years, he vigorously denied it, adding that he was very much alive.

As indeed he is, even though invisible to certain people —the very same sort of people who fail to *see through* the humorous philosophy of Mark Twain, and into the supernal Light beyond. What did Mark and Nikola talk about in that memorable conversation which took place on a January day in 1943 in a New York hotel room, where Tesla's physical body lay breathing lightly in almost final readiness for departure?

Mark and Nikola were old friends, companions of ancient days in starry space. Like all such gentle humorists, like all such compassionate observers of human folly, like all old friends, they met on that occasion of joyous reunion, and they talked about the weather.

Standing there together in their magnificent clean bodies of vibrant light, it was only natural that their conversation should turn to that earlier sickroom scene in Gospic, when Nikola, with the vital help of high-frequency energies pouring from Mark's written words, had firmly set his course once again into an uncertain future among foolish mortals. It was Mark who had glimpsed the mortals in a humorous moment when they had reached an ebb point in their foolishness—a point where everybody talked about the weather, but nobody did anything about it.

That vibrant instant with Mark had set Nikola free from
his illness in Gospic. Nobody did anything about the weather,
Mark said. But Nikola joyfully remembered that he had
determined to do something about it years earlier when he
walked through a mountain thunderstorm. He was going to
learn to control lightning, and thereby control the weather.
He was the Somebody whose inventions would liberate and
illumine all the negative nobodies of the world.

Yes, that was what they talked about, the author and the
inventor, on a day in January, 1943.

The Gospic illness over, Nikola was ready to be guided to
his next necessary advancement. His father had been
thoroughly frightened and was now anxious to humor the
boy by permitting him to go to college at Carlstadt in Croa-
tia. Upon arriving in that city Nikola took up residence with
relatives, but his years in their home were unhappy ones. Almost at once he contracted malaria but he insisted upon starting his classes at the college.

His brilliance undimmed by either illness or lack of family
harmony, he completed the four-year college course in three
years. He carried away with him one lasting impression
which was to make everything easier in his life thereafter.
His professor of physics had held him enthralled with demonstrations of feats performed with laboratory apparatus.
Tesla knew beyond a shadow of a doubt that his life was to
be fully and completely dedicated to a study of electricity.

With his life stretching complete before him, he returned
home, only to face up to the demands of the army. Again he
suddenly fell into a psychic illness. Again doctors gave up
all hope of saving his life. A cholera epidemic raged in the
town, and it was presumed that he had cholera in addition to

malaria, plus the nervous strain brought on by his college
work, plus undernourishment resulting from the unhappy
culinary situation in the home of his relatives in Carlstadt.

However, from the occult point of view Nikola suffered
from a psychic illness in order to prevent a greater tragedy—
compulsory military service. During the long illness which
steadily became worse, Nikola's father became more and
more frightened. The space people have not explained how
much Nikola's father knew about the boy's origin. Of
course, his mother had to know the details: but it is fairly
clear that she herself was originally a Venusian. Perhaps
the father was not, and it is even possible that Nikola was
placed in the care of the mother without the father knowing
of his origin. This all happened long ago in a remote mountain province. Women gave birth to children, often alone,
or with only a midwife or neighbor in attendance. There are
many possible explanations.

At any rate, whatever his understanding about his son,
the Rev. Milutin Tesla was ready to accept anything to save
the life of Nikola at a moment when the boy was drifting off
into unconsciousness from which it seemed apparent he
would not emerge. His father, in a firm, clear voice, commanded him not to die. In exchange, Nikola used his few
remaining breaths to gasp out the news that he would remain if his father would let him become an electrical engineer. The bargain was struck on the instant, and within a
matter of seconds vital energy began pouring through the
tired body. In a few days Nikola was up and about and life
was glorious once more.

The shadow of death had hovered close and then withdrawn. The shadow of the army loomed directly ahead. But
Nikola's father had given his promise. Nikola was to be an

electrical engineer and the army was to be minus one recruit. It was then that Nikola's father realized that his son needed at least a year's vacation in the mountains in order to regain not only his health but his freedom. Hurriedly Nikola was provided with a hunting outfit, some books and papers. He was gone before anyone in Gospic knew he had risen from his deathbed.

In 1873 Nikola went to Gratz to study electrical engineering. He knew that the forces of destiny were shaping him for a great purpose, and during his first year at Gratz he did more than twice the amount of work required. passing all examinations with the highest marks that could be awarded. He hoped in this way to express his appreciation to his parents for saving him from army service and for permitting him to study electrical engineering, but because they feared he was again undermining his health they did not receive the news of his high marks with joy.

During the second year he limited his studies to physics, mathematics and mechanics in order to placate his parents. Actually, however, he was guided in this decision by higher forces, for it was important that he have plenty of leisure time to devote to the next step in his unfoldment.

A piece of electrical equipment, a Gramme machine, that could be used as either a dynamo or motor, had been acquired by the Institute. It was a direct-current machine, and was demonstrated to the class. It did not please Tesla because a great deal of sparking took place at the commutator.

The professor explained that as long as electricity flowed

in one direction, a commutator would be necessary to change the direction, and the sparking could, therefore, not be avoided. Tesla replied that by using alternating current the commutator could be eliminated.

The professor was waiting for this suggestion and let loose a storm of criticism. He informed Tesla, in an abrupt and lofty professorial manner, that many men had already experimented with alternating current, and it was simply not feasible. In that instant Tesla had an intuitive flash. He knew the professor was wrong; he knew alternating current was possible; he knew that he would and could demonstrate it. The argument between the student and teacher went on during the remainder of the term, and although Tesla was unable to bring his vision down to practical results, he was by no means discouraged. The professor stated that Tesla's theories were contradicted by Nature and that settled the matter. It was far from settled in Tesla's mind.

The following year Tesla was to go to the University of Prague, but a lucrative position was offered him, so he saved his earnings, and enrolled at the university a year later. He extended his studies in physics and mathematics, but the vision of alternating current remained ever before him. In his heart he knew that he would make the great discovery that would elevate the infant science of electricity to the maturity of a great power.

Just after his graduation from the University of Prague his father died, and then Tesla set about to become self-supporting. The telephone invented by Alexander Graham Bell was making its advent in Europe at this time and in 1881 he was placed in charge of the new telephone exchange in Budapest. While there he developed an amplifier, which led to the present amplifiers on radio sets. He never patented the device, however, as his sole interest was still the problem of alternating current.

At this time, he underwent another severe psychic illness, during which his sense organs were affected by acute sensitivity. Apparently his vibrations were raised for some occult reason, and although doctors despaired of saving his life, he came through the period of suffering and his vibrations were restored to normal. But during the illness his dedication to the problem of alternating current had fully crystallized. He could scarcely think of anything else, and he knew that if he stopped working on it he would die; if he failed he would likewise perish.

He was a man without a choice, and on a late afternoon in February, 1882, he had recovered sufficiently to take a walk in a park in Budapest. His companion was a former classmate by the name of Szigeti. The two young men walked toward the setting sun. The skies ahead were painted with colors of high brilliance. Tesla was reciting aloud Goethe's *Faust*. It was a cosmic moment and Tesla was at one with the angels. Suddenly he stopped in a rigid pose. "Watch me," he cried out. "Watch me reverse it."

His startled companion was thrown into a state of panic, for Tesla seemed to be gazing at the sunset, and Szigeti feared that Tesla thought he could reverse the sun.

Szigeti suggested that they rest a moment, but Tesla talked on excitedly, looking steadily at something directly in front of him. Szigeti could see nothing, but Tesla was calling out in an exultant voice: "See how smoothly it runs. Now watch me stop it. Then start it. It goes just as smoothly in the opposite direction!"

Eventually Tesla became somewhat more composed and explained to his companion that he had just solved the problem of alternating current. He also revealed to Szigeti that he could see the motor before him, in full operation, and that he would not need to make drawings. But for the benefit of his friend who could see nothing but clear air in the spot where Tesla was operating his motor, they returned home together and talked far into the hours of the night, discussing every detail of the discovery.

Shortly thereafter Tesla was recommended for a job in Paris, and he was pleased to go to that city because it meant many contacts with Americans who were interested in all sorts of mechanical developments. Meanwhile he had mentally built a complete alternating-current system, both two-phase and three or more. His famous polyphase power system was a reality. As usual, he designed his dynamos, motors, transformers and all other devices in the fourth ether, performing his mathematical calculations on the etheric "blackboard" just as in his schooldays. He could test these mental constructs by leaving the machines in the ether to run for weeks. He would then examine them for signs of wear.

When he arrived in Paris he formulated a certain living pattern to which he adhered for the rest of his life, insofar as possible, or insofar as money would permit. He was always meticulously neat in dress, full of self-confidence, and carried himself with a poised, quiet attitude. For many years he had never rested more than five hours at night, and he claimed that he never slept more than two hours out of the five.

In Paris he would rise at five, swim in the Seine for half an hour, then dress and walk briskly for more than an hour to his place of work. He then ate a hearty breakfast, and by half-past eight he was ready for his duties. In the evening he would return to the center of Paris, dine at the best cafes, and contact any companions who were willing to listen to him describe his polyphase alternating current system.

At this point Tesla demonstrated that he was a world disciple, pledged to serve humanity and not a privileged group, for he never developed a secretive attitude about his inventions. He would gladly talk to anyone who would listen. He wanted only one thing—to give his invention to the human race so that all might benefit from it. He knew there was a fortune in it, but he was never concerned about the process of extracting fortunes from his machines.

He did not understand anything about money-making. This was due to the fact that he was a Venusian, and had not had any previous training in handling money. Money as we know it does not exist on Venus or anywhere in this solar system. The solar system operates on a basis of spiritual economy in which God's unlimited abundance and supply is accepted as Divine Law. A man-made money system such as exists on this planet is a direct contradiction of that Law. Further, the money system was created here as an instrument to serve the forces of darkness and has been used for the enslavement of humanity. Paul knew exactly what he was talking about when he stated that love of money was the root of all evil.

Tesla may have known nothing about money-making in the commercial shopping sense, but he had a deep understanding of the evils of the money system on this planet: In fact, his understanding in this regard was so profound that he never made the slightest attempt to come to terms with banking interests, because he realized that in doing so he would be coming to terms with the dark forces themselves. However, he was not going to take time out from his work to attempt to explain his attitude to anyone, so he just went ahead with his job of serving humanity and the Forces of

Light, and left others to serve the devil if they wished. Tesla was not a reformer. He was a transformer. His job was to transform the world from darkness to light. from enslavement to freedom.

Tesla made every effort to break down any secrecy surrounding his inventions. He was ready and willing to explain to all who would listen. There was no danger of his inventions being stolen at that time. In fact he could not even give them away. The forces of darkness were already securely entrenched in the electrical field. They wanted no part of any invention designed by a White Magician. Well they knew that if Tesla ever invaded the electrical field in global fashion it would mark the end of the old way of life with all its international complexities—its evil money system, its corrupt political delusions, its churchianity, its educational inadequacies.

There remained nearly twenty years until the turn of the century, and yet Tesla stood as the great colossus, the mighty genius who, working hand-in-hand with his Creator, might have saved the world from further violence of clashing forces of evil. Years later, when alternating current was finally adopted in America through the good offices of George Westinghouse. the dark forces still fought to turn the tide against Tesla. Finally they capitulated and took the opposite stand. They supported the adoption of alternating current and its widespread use, but only when they found that Tesla had outwitted them by obsoleting his own invention. He abandoned the whole system set up around the distribution of electricity by wires and developed a World Wireless System whereby everyone could have all the electricity they wished by merely attaching a small antenna to home, shop or office building.

The forces of darkness would have none of this and to this day, in· 1958, they have been successful in preventing the wireless system from reaching the attention of the public which would demand its use. But now Tesla, working in the scientific department of Shamballa, has again had the last word to say through his disciple, Otis T. Carr of Baltimore. As the New Age advances it is quite likely that Tesla's wireless system for electrical distribution may be obsoleted by Carr's free-energy devices. And so it is that the Legions of Light move steadily on to Victory.

As the new civilization takes shape it will be clearly seen that Tesla had access to no secrets at any time. He had direct contact with Universal Truth. Tesla worked out ways and means to anchor Truth on the physical plane through using physical matter. The early Root Races on the·planet worked in exactly the same manner. They brought down and anchored in physical matter the higher vibrations direct from the Godhead. Matter is spirit slowed down; spirit is matter speeded up. All is One.

The anchoring of Truth, or the lowering of vibrations, has never been a secret process. It has always been part of the teachings of the Ageless Wisdom. But it is a well-known fact that you can't get Truth out of a man if he has no available Truth in him. Truth is Light. Light which is imprisoned or obscured cannot illumine a person. Only the individual with a clean atomic structure, or one who understands and practices transmutation, can hope to anchor Truth in physical matter. The average scientists, especially those contaminated by working with military weapons, are in no position to embark on a search for Truth. It will not be found in an H-bomb.

When Tesla agreed to undertake the task of bringing light

to the earth he envisioned this globe as one vast terrestrial lamp spiralling through the skies toward its God-ordained destiny of perfected evolution: bearing upon its lighted body a race of Illumined Initiates, freed from the cycle of rebirth, journeying back to their Source, to their appointed mansion in the Father's House.

This was Tesla's great secret, if secret he had. Let those who feel overlooked because they were not called upon to share it, ask themselves at this point if they are sure they are quite ready, even now, to share it. Or are they like those disciples of Jesus who had to listen to the Master tell them they were not ready to share the knowledge of certain things: that to speak of such Truths would place upon them a greater burden of Light than they could bear.

Tesla's life in Paris went on smoothly. He enjoyed robust health. But he was employed by the Continental Edison Company, working all day on direct-current machines, and this proved to be an irksome point. His superior alternating-current inventions, although still in the fourth ether, were tauntingly close at hand.

Finally the situation was changed abruptly by an accident in the railway station at Strassburg in Alsace, where an Edison powerhouse and electric lights had been installed. Alsace then belonged to Germany and the electrical installation was formally opened with Emperor William I present. Unfortunately, when the lights were turned on the glory was indeed brief, for a short circuit caused an entire wall of the railway station to be blown to bits.

Tesla was sent from Paris to Strassburg to survey the damage and proceed with repairs. Once the work got under way and he could serve in a supervisory capacity, he arranged for space and tools in a nearby machine shop, and there he proceeded to transfer his dream of alternating current from the fourth ether to the physical plane.

He was an amateur machinist but a meticulous worker, and gradually a large collection of miscellaneous parts of a two-phase alternating-current motor took shape in the machine shop. Tesla not only made each part exact to a thousandth of an inch but he carefully polished it to make it more exact. He had no working drawings or blueprints. He formed each part from metal to exactly match the etheric part which he saw before him.

He did not have to test the parts because he knew they would fit. When he had finished the entire collection he quickly assembled the machine and started up his power generator. The cosmic moment had struck. He closed the switch. The armature of his motor turned, built up speed. He closed the reversing switch. The armature stood still, then instantly started turning in the opposite direction.

Alternating current had been transferred from the invisible to the visible, from the fourth ether to the dense physical plane, from a substance lighter than gas to metal.

So there in the noisy machine shop in Strassburg stood the very motor which Tesla had first discovered in the sunset glow in the park at Budapest, walking with his friend, Szigeti. Even the beautiful lines from Goethe's *Faust*, which he had been proclaiming aloud as he walked, were still appropriate:

> The glow retreats, done is the day of toil:
> It yonder hastes, new fields of life exploring:
> Ah, that no wing can lift me from the soil,
> Upon its track to follow, follow soaring. . . .

Tesla's unique method of constructing his first motor gives an excellent clue to the manner in which all Initiates consciously work, although they usually precipitate the etheric form instantly into physical matter, without intermediary construction work. They can externalize whatever they need by first visualizing it in the ethers, then calling it forth into physical density.

That is why spaceships are described as being constructed without rivets, welding, seams, or cracks around doors. They are not constructed but precipitated direct from the ether.

Since the laggards came and human beings forgot how to precipitate what they need, all man-made forms are first created in mental matter by a designer thinking through his problem and creating a thoughtform. Mental matter is on the same plane as gas, and is, therefore, one density lower than the fourth ether. But mental matter is all that the average person can manipulate, and is not by any means pure but is heavily weighted with astral accumulations. It is virtually impossible for the average person to create a clear, precise thoughtform, free from personal emotional distortions. Since he cannot control his mental constructs with any degree of success, his matrix or thoughtform is often composed more of fantasy than of fact. When it is lowered into form the physical plane result is often useless, ugly, and a spiritual monstrosity.

In the summer of 1884, shortly after Tesla returned from Strassburg to Paris, he arrived in New York City with exactly four cents in his pocket, and a book of his poems. In addition, he had a letter of introduction to Thomas A. Edison.

In a few brief weeks in Europe many things had happened to force this hurried and unplanned voyage to America. While Tesla was still in Strassburg he tried to interest business men there in his new alternating-current motor which he had built from the parts he had made by hand. He could not stir up a spark of enthusiasm for the machine which was later to revolutionize the electrical industry of the world. Then, when he returned to Paris to collect the substantial fee which he had been promised for getting the Strassburg installation in operation, the company conveniently failed to remember anything about the arrangement. One official however, did suggest to Tesla that he go direct to Mr. Edison in America.

Within a few days Tesla sold his personal belongings, packed his bags, and bought his railroad and steamship tickets. However, just as he was about to board the train to take him from Paris to the ship he discovered he had been robbed. He ran along the moving train and boarded it, paying his fare with loose change and notes he had in his pockets after his wallet was stolen. He also boarded the ship, explaining that his ticket had been stolen. Fortunately, no one showed up to claim his reservations, so he was allowed to continue on his way to the United States. Without luggage and with only a few cents in change, he finally landed in New York.

He lacked fare for either cab or trolley, so he set out to walk from the pier to the home of a friend, for he had fortunately retained his address book. He walked past an electrical repair shop and inside he saw a weary and obviously harrassed workman struggling to repair a machine.

He entered the shop. "Let me repair it," he said to the mechanic. The workman, without further inquiry, permitted Tesla to set to work. Although the task was difficult Tesla finally had the machine operating. The grateful mechanic handed him twenty dollars and offered him a steady job. But

Tesla thanked him, explaining that he was on his way to another job, and could not accept his offer.

He continued on his way, found his friend, and remained at his home overnight. The next morning he set out to call on Mr. Edison who then had headquarters in New York on South Fifth Avenue, a street which later became known as West Broadway.

The meeting between the two men was not auspicious. Edison belonged to the direct-current school of thought, and Tesla was not only in opposition to direct current, but was actually the inventor of alternating current. Furthermore, Edison was lacking in technical education. He was totally unable to understand Tesla's ability to visualize a problem in its entirety without doing any mechanical work on it or following the usual trial-and-error method.

Yet Edison was conscious of Tesla's great value, and while he could not afford to hire him as a competitor of the direct-current method, yet he could not afford to let it be known that he had not hired him. Rather grudgingly he employed Tesla, and almost at once Edison was placed in a position from which only the incomparable Tesla could rescue him.

The finest passenger ship of the day was called the Oregon. Edison had installed one of his electric light plants on the steamship and the vessel was ready to set sail. However, the lighting plant failed completely, and Edison was unable to find the cause of the difficulty. Tesla was dispatched to the ship late one afternoon and by the following morning had the dynamos functioning perfectly.

This incident served to advance his prestige with Edison. When he later approached Edison with a plan to improve the design of the Edison dynamos and at the same time lower the

operating cost, Edison not only agreed but offered Tesla a
fee of $50,000 if the work came up to expectations.

Tesla labored at the task for many months, putting in
many hours of overtime daily. He completed designs for
twenty-four types of dynamos.

Some of the machines were built and tested and proved to
be very satisfactory. Patents were taken out by Edison.
When the entire job was finished, Tesla requested the $50,-
000 which he had been promised. Edison, however, claimed
that the agreement had been merely a "joke", whereupon
Tesla resigned his job immediately. The Strassburg incident
had been repeated.

It was the year of 1885. Had Tesla known the heartaches
that lay ahead he might not have had the courage to continue
his efforts to provide alternating current for a world that
seemed to offer him nothing but scorn. Looking back over
Tesla's entire life it can be seen that he never capitulated to
the evil money system which prevails on this planet. Again
and again, just as he was about to grasp and use the contaminated medium of exchange, it was snatched from him.
This left Tesla free, but the karma engendered descended
upon humanity.

Even today, fifteen years after Tesla's death, humanity
still awaits the superman's great inventions which could give
untold comfort to physical plane existence. And the reason?
—a lack of funds adequate to develop the inventions on a
world-wide scale. Tesla would settle for nothing short of
global operations, bringing help to all the peoples of the

earth. It is very significant that he wished to encompass the planet with his work, and in the case of the interplanetary communications set, the solar-system. Being a Venusian he could not produce inventions that would remain earthbound. The superman was restless to grasp the extended hand of interplanetary friendship; to prepare the Dark Star of earth for its great cosmic initiation into solar freedom.

But in 1885. the financial world was not ready to give up its evil interests in the Dark Star. It perhaps is even less ready today, but today the Christ Forces have all dark manipulators on the run, and happily for humanity, it will be the last run. The Forces of Light are now able to stand firmly on the side of humanity and fight evil to a finish.

In 1885 financial matters were handled with shrewdness and cunning. Honesty was easily set aside by the fortune-makers of the day. At this time a group of promoters offered to finance a small company to promote Tesla. They were to pay him a modest salary and were to reward him on a grand scale with stock in the company. He thought he saw an opportunity to develop alternating current, but once the company had been formed Tesla was obliged to develop an arc light for street and factory illumination. It was to be a type of light which the promoters could use to further certain schemes of expansion.

The light was developed and Tesla took out patents on his design. However, the company had been organized in such a tricky manner that when Tesla was awarded his stock he soon found it to be worthless. The promoters prospered and Tesla was left without funds.

He then struck bottom in his American venture, for by the year of 1887 he was actually forced to dig ditches and take other laboring jobs at $2 a day. But even this provided the ladder on which he climbed to success, for the foreman in charge of the ditch digging recognized Tesla as a man of genius. He introduced him to Mr. A. K. Brown of the Western Union Telegraph Company. Mr. Brown, in turn, interested a friend in Tesla. The two men put up sufficient money to finance the Tesla Electric Company.

In April of 1887, Tesla opened his own laboratory and workshop on South Fifth Avenue, now West Broadway, and found himself a neighbor of Edison. Edison had turned down Tesla's idea for alternating current, striving to boost the prestige of direct current. Yet, in the end, Tesla won the competitive fight, despite the fact that he was backed by limited funds while Edison was financed by J. P. Morgan.

Tesla's hour had struck and ever thereafter the Dark Star was to be illumined by his incomparable genius.

It is impossible, even today, to evaluate the virgin field of electrical science which Tesla explored within a few months after his new laboratory was opened. The United States Patent Office could not easily grasp the scope of his work. They considered his inventions so original and so basic that they simply started issuing a succession of patents that brought the new age of power to birth in one mighty surge of advancement.

The entire electrical world of 1887 was engulfed by the sweeping new advance. It can now be seen in retrospect that in the seventy years which have since elapsed, civilization has not yet absorbed even the basic fundamental scientific achievements produced by Tesla. As for the philosophy of Tesla, it is hardly known that he had anything to offer in that field, as perhaps he did not—for his philosophy had already been presented by Jesus. Since western minds had failed to grasp even the basic teachings offered down through the countless centuries by the Hierarchy, and then had ignored the true meanings underlying the work of Jesus, it is abundantly clear why Tesla did not bother to waste his time tossing pearls.

Within six months after Tesla opened his laboratory in 1887, he applied to the Patent Office for a single patent covering his entire electrical system which he had designed at that time. The Patent Office was overwhelmed by this "package deal" and insisted that Tesla break his single patent down into seven parts. This was done and in April of 1888 he applied for five more patents which were granted. Toward the end of 1888 he was issued eighteen additional patents.

By this time the entire scientific world was not only amazed, but completely baffled by the sudden manner in which their cherished concepts were swept away over night. It was not easy to make such a quick and monumental adjustment to new values, especially in view of the fact that many of the scientists and technicians of the day, then as now, prided themselves on being strong-minded, free-thinking men who were capable of standing on their two feet and meeting the issues of the day.

They also prided themselves on being God-fearing men, independent men, who, if they wished to invent a machine, could do so without calling upon the aid of the Creator. But in some mysterious fashion the Creator had somehow got back on the job through Tesla. So these God-fearing men looked everywhere for the answer except in the right place. For a man who fears God can never love Him, and a man who places God on a pedestal high in the sky is most certainly in fear of Him. The only way to love God is to bring His energy down into dense matter by lowering the

vibration, and then anchor it there. The early Root Races
had the answer as did Tesla.

The social gossips of the day back in 1888 also had their
word to say about Tesla. To them he was at once the most
fascinating and the most aggravating of men. He did not
share their interests, and they could not seem to find a way
of sharing his. It was incomprehensible to them that a man
of such cosmopolitan tastes could overlook them so completely, so utterly. So far as women were concerned Tesla
was considered to be the world's most eligible bachelor.
Ambitious mothers and anxious daughters hovered close,
or at least let us say they tried. But no one ever got close
to Tesla. So far as men were concerned, Tesla was constantly inventing machines which could be manufactured and
sold. This stamped the sign of the dollar indelibly upon
him. Over the years the Tesla-marriage-money subject became a topic of international conversation.

The next momentous Tesla development came on May
16, 1888 when, in response to an invitation, he gave a
lecture and demonstration before the American Institute
of Electrical Engineers. This lecture served notice upon
the entire world that the greatest genius of the age had
brought his discoveries to fruition, presenting civilization with alternating current, and thus setting electricity
geographically free. Under Edison's direct current system
it was necessary to have a powerhouse in the center of
every square-mile, or even closer in large cities. This presented an impossible situation if electricity was to become
a planetary source of power as Tesla visualized.

Tesla had no desire to develop his inventions commercially, for he preferred to spend his time in research. He
knew that the very inventions which he was in the process

of patenting would become obsolete in a short time if he could continue his research. Edison fought resolutely to maintain the prestige of direct current, for he had invented the incandescent electric lamp, and in order to sell the lamps he had to make electricity available so that the lamps could be used. Moreover, Edison's financial interests were tied completely to those of J. P. Morgan, and Edison was not free to pursue any course except the strictly commercial one.

When Tesla gave his famous lecture on May 16, 1888, George Westinghouse of Pittsburgh was in the audience. Westinghouse was already well known as the inventor of an air brake for trains and of many other electrical devices. He had made a fortune in exploiting his own inventions. He was a man of tremendous vision and he immediately recognized the vast possibilities, commercially and geographically, of Tesla's alternating current system. Shortly thereafter he contacted Tesla for an interview. In a matter of minutes Westinghouse agreed to pay Tesla one million dollars outright for the alternating current patents, plus a royalty of one dollar per horsepower.

It was Westinghouse, therefore, who seized the opportunity to develop Tesla's patents which would supply electricity to the entire world. In the few moments required to negotiate the deal, a friendship was formed between the two men which, in its magnificence and trust, was of transcendent beauty. As things worked out, the friendship was almost the only happy development that resulted from the meeting, but as the years passed Tesla never betrayed the slightest bitterness or regret over misfortunes that came to both of them as a result of their cooperation.

Tesla spent a useless, weary year in Pittsburgh attempting

to get Westinghouse launched in his manufacturing efforts, but finally refused to remain longer. The Westinghouse engineers, accustomed to their own way of doing things, were baffled and confused by Tesla's magic. Tesla in turn had no way of communicating with the men since he could not get down to their level of understanding. Tesla was a great teacher of philosophy to certain individuals. He was also a great teacher of what might be called cosmic engineering— again to certain individuals. But he selected these individuals personally. They were disciples, but they were already active disciples for the Forces of Light.

To expect Tesla to go into a manufacturing plant and teach a group of American engineers at all stages of evolutionary development was, of course, ridiculous. But perhaps even Tesla did not realize the scope of his own greatness, and the intellectual gap which existed as a barrier between him and those of earth who had not yet attained discipleship. At any rate, after his departure from the Pittsburgh plant, the Westinghouse engineers worked out their own problems, and eventually the manufacturing process got under way.

Tesla returned to his own laboratory in New York, to his beloved research—a wealthy man, free from the need for commercialism. This freedom was for him the greatest triumph that might come to a human soul. Working again on research for his polyphase power system, he was granted forty-five patents in this country during the next four years, in addition to more than a hundred in foreign countries.

Edison had long been busy aiming competitive lances in all directions. He was strictly a commercial money-making man. He was untrained in the science of electrical engineering and, therefore, had to depend upon those whose services he could get for hire. He was tied, hand and foot, to the value of the dollar and was thereby forced into the role of a huckster. He could never shake himself free from the clutches of the monkey on his back in the form of the J. P. Morgan interests, although there is no evidence to show that he desired to do so. Some men are destined to play the role of the organ-grinder. It does not lie within the karmic patterns of all men to compose great music.

Edison had tangled with Westinghouse on many occasions. But when it was discovered that Westinghouse, capable and far-visioned, a successful inventor and a successful business man, had taken on the task of developing Tesla's alternating current, the battle took on a new and fiercer phase. It was at this time that the New York State Prison authorities stepped openly into the White Magic field of electricity, and turned it into a field of black magic almost overnight. They adopted alternating current as developed by Tesla for the electrocution of condemned prisoners.

Tesla claimed that the Edison interests had engineered the project to discredit alternating current. There was more than a little truth in this, although that was probably not the original purpose. For the Edison interests, anxious to make a dollar even one jump ahead of the undertaker, had tried to provide direct current to power the electric chair. But they had failed, because the plain fact of the matter was that direct current could not be produced at the high voltages required. All this was lost on the public, however, as the

Edison interests proclaimed from the housetops that the prison's choice of current was proof of the deadly danger of Tesla's invention.

Now we can look back and realize that this victory of the ' forces of darkness, operating from the astral plane directly through the prison authorities, touched off a retro-gressive movement which has since carried certain aspects of civilization back to evil days which have not been known on this planet since the sinking of Atlantis.

Now people like to look back to the pre-atomic age, and blame the nuclear scientists for the present destructive threat to humanity. But nuclear scientists would not have had a ghost of a chance of exercising their black magic, had not the road to darkness been well paved already by black magicians long in control on the astral plane. The New York State Prison authorities cooperated to the hilt in as-sisting the black magicians to take over control of the alter-nating-current invention and all humanity has suffered by being robbed, and robbed, and robbed of the true advantages of the invention since that dreadful day.

The control by black magicians and their tools has since been broken on the Inner Planes, and even the tools will soon be eliminated from the physical plane. The Christ Forces. assisted by the angelic kingdom, have seized and removed all black magicians from the planet. Their human tools still exist on the physical plane, by the thousands, but their nefarious endeavors will be smashed down as soon as the seventh Ray has done a bit more of its beneficent work of transmutation.

While New York State Prison authorities were busying themselves in an all-out effort to lower the planetary vibra-tions by using electricity, the Third Aspect of God, or the

Holy Spirit, to electrocute condemned prisoners, George Westinghouse prepared to use the Tesla invention of alternating current to put the entire United States on an electrical power basis. Tesla, meanwhile, back at his research, set about to make obsolete his earlier inventions, and place the entire world on one simple electrical system which would enable all of God's children, from the Arctic to the Antarctic, to have light—more abundant light and living advantages.

The year had turned to 1891. Tesla and Westinghouse were firmly aligned with the Divine Plan and their combined energies were enabling a tiny portion of this Plan to manifest. But where there is Light-in-Action on this Dark Star, it is always consuming darkness. In other words, there has not yet come a time when we could say that we had a safe dividend of light left over for intelligent, constructive uses. Every unit of light released by disciples on this planet must still be used to illumine the suffering atoms wherein evil is bottled up in the form of astral debris.

In 1891 the karma that was being engendered by the New York State Prison authorities alone, was so dense in its accumulation that the forces of darkness were enabled to sweep into the alternating-current field without hindrance. The black leaders were reinforced by a vast horde of disembodied criminals from the astral plane, bent on vengeance. They struck savagely at Westinghouse, for his company alone would supply the nation with alternating current, providing great wealth to Tesla for years to come in the form of horsepower royalties.

The dense overshadowing of the Westinghouse financial advisors commenced. In those days little was known about astral influences, and when the deluded, bewitched money-men went into a panic, they merely thought they were being astute financial wizards. Here was a picture of little big-shots, utterly dazzled by the mocking brilliance of their own arrogance.

A number of quick mergers with smaller companies took place and a new unit was formed, known as the Westing-house Electric and Manufacturing Company. But before this deal was finalized, the financial group put George Westing-house on the spot, and told him that he was to destroy his contract with Tesla. The alternative? The money-men would destroy the Weshinghouse organization as it existed at that time.

The financial wizards were crazed by their astral over-shadowing, and goaded into a greedy desire to consume all. They were adamant in their determination to share no profits with anyone—not even with the goose Tesla, who had laid the golden egg. Against this mighty army of darkness, George Westinghouse stood out like a giant pillar of light—but a lone giant. The financial interests were set to see the company destroyed rather than yield a single dollar in horse-power royalty to Tesla.

But even one on the side of the Forces of Light is in itself a victorious majority against evil. Westinghouse firmly grasped the scales of justice, and he went direct to Tesla and humbly told the story of his seeming defeat. Tesla quick-ly turned it into a spiritual triumph that will ring down through the years as a cosmic moment in which two men touched divinity.

Standing there before Westinghouse, Tesla smiled serenely and tore up his contract without a trace of bitterness. At that moment he was entitled to at least twelve million dol-lars in royalties, but he tossed the scraps of his contract into the wastebasket. He had saved the Westinghouse organization, and Westinghouse would give his polyphase system to the world. The bankers could satisfy their love for money. Today this unfortunate planet is still reaping the black harvest from the seeds scattered far and wide by the bewitched money-men.

It has been said often that failure to pay horsepower royalties to Tesla proved to be the greatest handicap to scientific and industrial progress which the human race has ever experienced on this globe. In this year of 1958 the United States and all allied nations of the world are wondering why scientific superiority has been lost in recent years. The answer is simple. The pattern of events is not difficult to trace.

Karmic law was set in motion by the New York State Prison using Tesla's alternating-current invention to electrocute condemned prisoners. The karmic debt thus incurred precipitated at the point where alternating-current development was centered. Tesla was a White Magician and was protected against direct attack by the dark forces. He could be reached only indirectly. But the Westinghouse organization, through its money system, was wide open. The dark forces were able to attack freely through that open channel. This imperiled the work of Tesla. But since it was society that connived to support the prison authorities in their nefarious work, it is society that has had to suffer the karmic results. America allowed the Tesla inventions to be mis-used. It is America that must pay the karmic debt through a decline in scientific achievement.

A very few years after Tesla and Westinghouse made their historic decision, Tesla was a global intellectual giant of such stature that he could easily, with the use of his inventions and discoveries, have swung this planet from evil to goodness, from darkness to light, from ignorance to illumination. But society, in its utter complacency, preferred prison methods to the methods of a Venusian Initiate. And so the mills of the gods continued to grind slowly, awaiting the incoming seventh Ray which would bring the cleansing Violet Fire of transmutation to the Dark Star.

After the financial setback engineered by the Westinghouse money-men, Tesla never again had sufficent funds to develop his inventions. On many occasions his co-workers begged him to develop some small aspect of his inventions in order to make money to support his greater discoveries, but Tesla always refused to spend his time on what he termed small stuff. He had no desire to benefit a few people. He desired only to benefit humanity. Some of his co-workers felt that he was just being stubborn, but Tesla wisely knew his proper course.

It must be remembered that another great Initiate by the name of Jesus also tried to sell society on the idea of a better world. In this year of 1958 Jesus is still patiently waiting for the majority to join the minority in the support of His efforts. Tesla was well acquainted with the work of Jesus, and with the work of hundreds of other Initiates who had made supreme sacrifices for a belligerent and ungrateful humanity. Sanat Kumara waited nineteen million years for the prodigal sons of earth to grow weary of consuming their husks. Intuitively Tesla knew that he, too, could await the day of man's great awakening.

When Tesla was nearly eighty years of age he was asked to give a speech before the Institute of Immigrant Welfare which, at a dinner meeting at the Hotel Biltmore on May 12, 1938, was to present the great inventor with an honorary citation. Tesla wrote out a speech which was read at the dinner because he did not feel equal to attending in person. He had not only survived through many, many years of extreme poverty, but he had been ridiculed for failing to commercialize his inventions. He was often unable to pay his hotel bills, and was forced to move frequently, leaving his luggage until friends could assist him to get settled in another lodging place.

Yet with this spectre of poverty always dogging at his heels, he gazed without rancor at a world which had waxed wealthy out of the power he had made available. And so on the occasion of the Biltmore dinner he paid tribute to Westinghouse in a magnificent testimonial to the heartfelt friendship which had always existed between the two men: .

"George Westinghouse was, in my opinion, the only man on this globe who could take my alternating-current system under the circumstances then existing and win the battle against prejudice and money power. He was a pioneer of imposing stature, one of the world's true noblemen of whom America may well be proud and to whom humanity owes an immense debt of gratitude."

So it was at the age of 80 years that Tesla, the only man on the globe who could have invented alternating current, cited George Westinghouse as the only man on the Dark Star who could have developed it in spite of the pitiless and ruthless attacks by the forces of darkness, entrenched behind the money screen within his own company. Tesla declared his position as an Initiate in this statement about his friend, just as surely as did another Initiate who entered into the Temple and flayed the money-lenders with a whip.

As a Venusian Tesla was not karmically obliged to deal with money-lenders. His magnificent gesture of tearing up his own contract with Westinghouse showed that as a

Venusian he was willing to go to any length to help his friend, knowing full well that Westinghouse was shouldering for all humanity a karmic burden so great that he could scarcely bear up under it. With the aid of Tesla's warm and enduring friendship he did bear up, giving Tesla's polyphase system to the world, thus eliminating a vast part of society's karmic debt. Tesla voiced a divine pronouncement when he stated that George Westinghouse was one of the world's true noblemen.

During the final years of his life, as he neared the age of 80, Tesla was aided by a $7,200 annual honorarium paid to him by the Yugoslav Government on behalf of the Tesla Institute at Belgrade. As the hour of Tesla's birth approached, the spaceship on which he was born neared the earth in a mountain province that is now part of Yugoslavia. As the hour of his death approached, it was Yugoslavia that honored him and supported him financially.

The Tesla Institute was opened in Belgrade in 1936, in commemoration of Tesla's eightieth birthday. Formal celebrations were held throughout the country over a period of a week, honoring the greatest national hero the Yugoslavs had ever known. The Tesla Institute, endowed by both government and private sources, was equipped with a splendid research laboratory and library. Every bit of writing or information that had any bearing on Tesla and his inventions was collected and made available to research students at the Institute. American students have been deprived of any opportunity to learn about Tesla because his name is seldom mentioned in school books, even science textbooks.

In the United States, the nation which Tesla had honored with his citizenship, and the point from which his great in-

THE NIKOLA TESLA STORY

ventions had rayed forth like light from a central sun. Tesla passed his eightieth birthday quietly. He was interviewed and questioned about his World Wireless System for electrical distribution, a system which he had perfected many years before, and which rendered his polyphase system obsolete. He showed not the slightest sign of resentment over the fact that billions upon billions of dollars had been wasted by promoters in a greedy effort to extract the last penny of profit from an electrical system that was as outmoded as a dinosaur.

Tesla was comforted by his own inner joyous knowledge that he had not been called to share in commercial exploitations that needlessly sapped the wealth of the world. His philosophy of brotherhood, of friendship toward humanity, of gratitude toward his Creator, never wavered. And so he said, when questioned about his World Wireless Power System:

"Perhaps I was a little premature. We can get along without it as long as my polyphase system continues to meet our needs. Just as soon as the need arises, however, I have the system ready to be used with complete success."

It is still ready and it is still waiting to be used. Promoters are still withholding from the public the knowledge that such a system exists as an invention, waiting to be used. Promoters are still seeking to expand Tesla's obsolete polyphase system throughout the world, burdening the earth with miles upon miles of needless cables, conduits, wires and posts, providing dangerous playthings for high winds and blizzards. But this is the greedy method by which fortunes are made at the expense of the public.

In the New Age only new age methods will be utilized. Very soon now will come the big planetary housecleaning.

Then down will come all the cables, conduits, wires and posts, which the public is now paying to have installed. What fools these mortals be!

Since Otis T. Carr has now come forth with his free-energy devices it is quite probable that Tesla, working from Shamballa, has in mind a system that will obsolete the World Wireless System. But at any rate, as Tesla said on his eightieth birthday, the system is there, waiting to be used with complete success if needed.

It calls for a small antenna device to be attached atop every house, office building, shop and factory. This device will enable the occupants of the building to have all the electricity they need without meters or wirings. The antenna will pick up a beamed supply of current, just as a radio picks up a broadcasted program. Inside the home or building the electrical service units such as lights, irons, stoves, adding machines, typewriters, and so forth, will be free from wires and plugs for wall outlets. The units will pick up the necessary current beamed from the antenna.

Even when Tesla had his old laboratories on South Main Street (now West Broadway) in New York, he had lights which could be picked up and placed in any position anywhere in the laboratory, wherever light happened to be needed at the moment. His lights were merely glass tubes, free from wires and wall fixtures.

So the inventor, for many years, enjoyed the fruits of his own inventions, while the public has paid and paid and paid the pipers who ever pipe for more money profits from their outmoded merchandise.

The Tesla wireless method for electrical distribution is a gift which the world might have utilized for the past half century had the public demanded it. But an uninformed public is a silent public. The public gets its information largely from newspapers and magazines, radio and TV. These sources are, in turn, controlled and censored by their advertisers and government secret-guarders. This conditioned public then dictates to its teachers and its preachers, telling them what to teach and what pulpit topics would be most uplifting to the community spirit. Thus the vicious circle whirls round and round like a sputnik.

Even Tesla himself was told off by J. P. Morgan when he explained his world wireless system to the financier. Morgan listened to Tesla describe the glories of his invention, and then the money baron dismissed the whole subject as impractical because, as he pointed out, there would be no way of making money off the people if the people could have as much electricity as they wished by merely putting up a little antenna on their homes, or factories or office buildings.

Morgan further reminded Tesla that under the present system the manufacturers of wires, poles, and electrical installation equipment of all kinds, could make fortunes, and in addition, the electricity could be metered and everybody could be charged for every kilowat they used. Tesla pointed out that electricity was free in the atmosphere, a free gift of God to His people, but such idealism naturally could not penetrate the thinking of a financier.

Early in the years when Tesla was training Otis T. Carr, he called Carr's attention to the same fact—electricity is free in the atmosphere, a gift of God to His people. Carr agreed with Tesla instantly. But Carr was not a financier. He was merely working as a clerk in a hotel package room. Perhaps therein lies the answer.

PART VI

Farewell of the Dove

When Tesla left his sleeping body on the night of January 7, 1943, he did not return to it. The three-fold Flame which had blazed so brightly in his physical heart for 87 years was withdrawn into his subtle structure. The flowing line of electronic light known as the silver cord, which enters the body at the top of the head and is anchored in the heart, with another branch anchored in the brain, was broken.

At once the flow of electronic light ceased; no more pure God-substance carrying the energies of the Rays entered the physical body through the silver cord. The power which beats the heart of a man, the heart of a solar system, and the heart of a cosmos, was withdrawn from the physical. Tesla stood free to enter in full consciousness the realms of unlimited lighted awareness that he had left 87 years earlier, in order that he might walk and talk with men on the plane earth.

During his years in America Tesla had mentioned to certain persons, among them John J. O'Neill, that he planned to live 130 years. This statement was privately regarded as another bit of eccentricity that could come only from the lips of the genius Tesla. It was understood that Tesla had earlier fixed the period of his stay on earth at 150 years. He changed the figure shortly after World War I when prohibition was adopted. Because of his paradoxical statements about the matter at that time, and the unusual circumstances surrounding his pronouncement, his words were interpreted in the usual earth manner, and it was generally believed that the prohibition amendment had somehow shortened his life.

However, Tesla was not in any sense a "drinking man", as the term is generally used. Neither was Tesla a hearty eater. It was true that for years and years, immaculately groomed and attired in full dress, he entered the Hotel Waldorf dining room promptly each evening at 8 o'clock. sitting quietly alone at his reserved table, and dining while he read through several newspapers. until 10 P. M.

It was true that in his early days in New York he often gave lavish dinner parties for many guests, taking them afterwards to his laboratories on South Fifth Avenue for an evening's entertainment. There he demonstrated to his guests thrilling electrical feats of such magnitude that men literally felt their hair rising straight up on their astonished heads. Women squealed and giggled and would have swooned except that they did not want to miss an instant of the magic.

But Tesla, while the very core and center of these dinner

parties, magic evenings, and conversation fests, actually ate little food. As the years passed, he was seldom observed eating. Otis T. Carr said that during the three years that he was being trained by Tesla he never saw him consume any food.

However, prior to prohibition days, Tesla would occasionally, and after due ceremony, drink a tiny glass of whiskey. He said that it gave him a special type of energy that he could use. Then when prohibition came, he ordered his last glass of whiskey and made the astonishing statement that prohibition would shorten his life by twenty years, reducing his time on earth from 150 to 130 years.

In retrospect, it is clear that he was making a direct reference to the future political situation in the United States and to the world situation in general. Prohibition was an early symptom that a sick world was growing sicker. A man of Tesla's caliber was certainly not vitally concerned with a glass of whiskey, *per se*. In the final analysis, it is also clear that Tesla was using the whiskey as a focus for some sort of transmutation. It is doubtless quite true that the tiny glass of liquid would supply him with a special sort of energy, but only after he had called certain energies into action within the liquid.

Tesla's atomic structure was relatively clean, at least during the first seventy or seventy-five years of his life, or perhaps even longer. Apparently at the close, as he was nearing 87 years, the atoms may have slowed their revolutions somewhat. But at no time did he permit himself to take on an accumulation of astral debris, for remember, Tesla could see the astral filth all about him and took special precautions to avoid it. For many, many years he passed currents of tremendously high voltage and high frequency through his body. His associates and friends were astonished that these experiments proved not only harmless but healthful, and most people thought it was merely a feat of showmanship. It was not, however, but rather something which Tesla had extracted from the ether as a definite construct for his own protection.

His atomic structure was normally vibrating at a very high rate, and the vibrations were raised even higher by passing the electric currents through his body tissues. He could not burden such a body with quantities of food intended for the ordinary earth man. Moreover, the process of transmuting food, already cooked and prepared, would have been too laborious. It would require a useless expenditure of time and energy. But a small glass of distilled alcohol could probably have been acted upon instantly by forces summoned into action by Tesla.

The little contemplative ceremony in which Tesla engaged before he finally raised the glass to his lips was probably the transmuting ceremony. It could be performed in public, in any bar, without attracting any attention whatsoever.

A better understanding of this action can be arrived at by reading the accounts of experiences which various earth men have had while visiting on board space craft. All of these contacts agree on one point. When they board the craft they are handed a beautiful crystal goblet containing a liquid of such delightful flavor and fragrance that it is said to be utterly indescribable. It is non-alcoholic but when it is consumed it provides the body with a buoyant, refreshing type of energy which clears the brain and gives the individual a subtle sense of serene awareness, freeing him from any feeling of fear or hostility.

Those contacts who have been invited to dine aboard space-

ships have had some interesting experiences along similar
lines. George Van Tassel of Giant Rock, California, author
of several books on spaceships and space people, said that
he was offered small cubes of substance that resembled
ordinary cubes of sugar. But before eating them, he was
asked to qualify them with any flavor he desired. If he
thought of ice cream while gazing at the cube it tasted like
the most delicious ice cream. If he thought of a juicy steak,
it tasted like a juicy steak, and so on.

George Adamski, in his book *Inside the Space Ships* tells
about dining on board a space craft and enjoying a wonderful meal of fabulous foods that tasted like the finest meats
and vegetables and desserts, but actually the dishes did not
seem to fall into any of these categories. Adamski was also
treated to a preliminary crystal goblet of the marvelous
liquid which has been known down through the ages as
"elixir of the gods".

But all of this food and drink served aboard space craft
is precipitated direct from Universal Supply. All Adepts
must be able to practice precipitation. Moreover, during the
Aquarian Age, we must all re-learn this method which we
knew at one time, but which was blotted from our racial
memory by the contamination brought in by the laggards.

Ascended Master Saint Germain, the Adept in charge
of our present era, became a man of mystery all through
Europe during the hundred years He served humanity after
His Ascension on May 1, 1684, because no one could understand His powers of precipitation. In His high-frequency
Ascension body Saint Germain was permitted by Law to
mingle with His disciples on the physical plane for an entire
century prior to His appointment as Chohan of the seventh
Ray. During this time He was constantly supplied with

every good thing; an abundance of money, fabulous jewels, fine clothes, and a whole century of leisure hours in which to teach and train His disciples for the present age. Virtually every disciple who is working with Saint Germain now was called into embodiment during that century to prepare for the present incarnation. It is these disciples who will be able to restore and again anchor the precipitation process on the physical earth plane.

Back in the early Lemurian days before the laggards came, and before the world fell into its present state of atheistic materialism, human greed was unknown. In those days, men had never heard of such a preposterous thing as earning a living by the sweat of one's brow. In fact, they were totally unacquainted with sweat. They enjoyed a perfect climate. They did not live in huts or hovels: they lived in the most exquisite surroundings amid an endless globe-encircling garden of trees and grass and flowers prepared under the direction of Amaryllis Herself, the Goddess of Spring.

When a family group sat down to dine, the family head, the father, presided at the communion ceremony, for that is what it was. The group prepared to eat of the body of God-substance; to drink of the elixir of His circulating energies. In a degraded manner the communion service practiced by churchianity today is an attempt to produce this ancient Lemurian custom of precipitation.

The Lemurian family group, their minds held steady in the light of Universal Light, joined in the thanksgiving and acceptance ceremony for that which they were about to receive. Instantaneous precipitation followed, with the table bedecked with the finest linens, silver and dishes, and laden with an abundance of food and drink which met the exact nutritive requirements of that particular family.

At the close of the meal the mother performed the next necessary ceremony of etherialization, or returning to Universal Supply all unused food and drink and all table accessories. This is the key step in the precipitation process. If the etherialization process is not performed in love, and faith and confidence, then the ability to precipitate further supply is withdrawn. In other words, as children of God we are entitled to as much of His abundance as we can use to serve Life constructively. If we precipitate food then we are not privileged to toss the left-overs into the garbage can or store them in the refrigerator. They must be returned to the universal storehouse where the molecules are broken up and the atoms freed for use elsewhere.

The depths of depravity reached by the human race can easily be estimated by our one great product—waste. Only earth people are so arrogant as to speak of waste matter, let alone produce it. There is no waste in the universe. The Father not only knows when the sparrow falls; He also keeps a strict account of each atom, for an atom is a tiny life. The only way to handle so-called waste is to permit it to be returned to the universal storehouse. This storehouse is a reservoir of unqualified electronic substance. In that state it is ready for use by anyone who wishes to qualify it.

In recent years the space people have pointed out again and again that it is our excessive waste matter from nuclear fission and fusion that constitues the greatest threat to our destruction. The bomb explosions are much less harmful than the resulting fallout, and the fallout is even less destructive than the waste accumulated during the manufacturing process.

During the last quarter of a century, Ascended Master

Saint Germain has been working actively among his disciples, particularly those in the United States, because North America is now the physical beating heart of the world and as such it requires the most subtle protection. Without the full functioning of North, Central and South America the sixth and seventh Root Races could not come into existence; the Divine Plan could not continue its unfoldment according to Universal Law.

Inasmuch as the ancient karmic fiat which man brought upon himself—to earn one's bread by the sweat of one's brow—was active under planetary Law, it was automatically set aside in recent years when the earth came under Cosmic Law. As soon as the knowledge of this liberating change penetrates the consciousness of the people, and they can accept the fact that they are free from the curse of drudgery, then they will desire to draw forth free Ray energies to accomplish all things. Therefore, it is obvious that during the Aquarian cycle every person will be required to study the process of precipitation and etherialization. Recently the seven Elohim, the Builders of this planet, have come forth with a dictated book which outlines precise instructions for precipitation. This volume now serves as a textbook for disciples who are studying the process. (See *Suggested Reading* section.)

From time to time Saint Germain lowers the vibrations of His subtle bodies so that He may be seen visually, and mingles with groups of disciples. In the United States in recent years He has given actual demonstrations of the precipitation of food, complete with exquisite linens, silver and dishes. He has even made an exception in many cases and retained the linens, silver and dishes in manifestation, presenting them to His dinner guests.

It is noteworthy that the linens need never be laundered as no effects of soil cling to them. While the linens appear to be of cloth, and apparently are precipitated as cloth, they are probably charged with fourth Ray energies and, therefore, vibrate at such a high frequency that imperfect matter is cast off.

This is the Ray of Purity which Serapis Bey has urged us to use for such practical matters as cleaning our homes; tuning pianos and tuning up motors. It is apparently the Ray which is used by space people who visit the earth and who can walk through dusty deserts, muddy roads, and under rainy skies, and yet appear at the homes of earth people without a trace of soil on their clothing or shoes. Several contacts have observed and commented on this feat.

Although no hint has been given that Tesla and Ascended Master Saint Germain actually met and conferred on the physical plane, there is abundant evidence to indicate that they were in close communication. Nearly all Adepts, from Noah down to Saint Germain and Tesla, have been associated with angelic messengers who take embodiment as white doves. This is a subject which is difficult for the earth mind to understand because we know so little about the angelic kingdom.

Angels themselves sometimes take human embodiment in order to perform some special service, but little is known nowadays about these cases. However, we can gain considerable knowledge from the story of Mary, the mother of Jesus. (See *Suggested Reading* section.) She not only belonged to the angelic kingdom, but was originally an Archaii, or Twin-Flame of Archangel Raphael.

She also spent untold centuries in working with the Elohim, assisting in the training of elementals. The Elohim design and build planets, but like all good architects and contractors, They have an army of helpers. These are the little elementals or nature spirits. According to the design made by the Elohim, the little elementals carefully fashion each blade of grass, each flower, each tree, and even each tiny, lima bean or apple or orange that we eat. When we say that the little elementals build the fruit and flowers we mean precisely that. They build out of the substance of their own bodies just as a spider spins a web.

After the Ascension of Jesus, while Mary was living with the disciples at the old grist-mill outside Bethany, She spent considerable time training groups of little elementals. She taught them how to make a certain type of fern among other things—a fern which we still have in abundance today, commonly called maiden's hair.

When Mary made Her Ascension, She returned to Her place in the angelic kingdom, but with the added ability to work freely with humans after spending long years among them. Inasmuch as Ascended Master Saint Germain was Joseph in a former embodiment, Mary and Her angelic group will play a major role in assisting human beings to orient themselves in New Age activities. It is very easy to contact Mary mentally and there is always instant angelic response to every call from a human being.

Aside from the cases where angels have taken human embodiment in order to render assistance to humanity, the white doves, which are Initiate birds, have served down through centuries of time, as angelic messengers. Angelic entities occupy the bodies of Initiate doves in order to get close to the earth and close to human companions, serving them in a thousand subtle ways, radiating forth peace and joy and healing. How often, walking in Central Park, have we felt electrified with sudden joy as a pigeon wheeled through the bright air before us. It is in those moments of flashing splendor that we know the Paraclete is nigh!

Like humans, not all doves are graduates, or Initiates. Many are undergoing discipleship and the majority are just ordinary aspirants to higher initiations. It is from the ranks of disciple doves that carrier pigeons are drawn forth and trained by humans. Also, like humans, doves vary considerably in appearance. Our rock doves and wood doves which have moved into the big cities of Europe and America have become known as pigeons. Like so many city folks, with all the comforts of urban living at hand, the pigeons have grown somewhat fat and lazy for the most part; so much so that their brethren in the wilderness would not even recognize them.

When Tesla volunteered to take an embodiment on earth, he did not come to the planet alone. He was accompanied by his Twin-Ray, an entity so highly evolved that she did not take a human body, but instead manifested through a beautiful white dove. Naturally, living in New York the dove could not appear too beautiful, or too exceptional, or she would have attracted too much attention. So Tesla's pigeon, as she was called, looked much like any other pigeon and mingled freely with her bird companions in the New York parks. But Tesla knew her well, and could spot her instantly among hundreds of other pigeons.

"A white female, with a touch of gray in her wings," he used to say. "I would know that pigeon anywhere!"

Naturally Tesla never gave the slightest hint as to the actual identity of the bird. In many quarters he was considered just a little over-touched by genius, and his remarks from time to time left his listeners with their heads fairly spinning. Assuredly he had no way to reveal that the white dove, with a touch of gray in her wings, was his Twin-Ray.

It is only in recent years, since Ascended Master Saint Germain began His major activities in connection with the New Age, that even disciples have known a few facts about Twin-Rays. But one of Saint Germain's projects is to bring together the pairs of Twin Rays in embodiment at the present time, and thus far He has united a considerable number. This is of tremendous value to His Aquarian program, because the average disciple, working alone, accomplishes very little at best. But if a disciple can be reunited with his or her Twin-Ray, the spiritual efficiency of the two, working as a team, is increased about a millionfold.

The Ray divides into positive and negative White Fire Beings after the original divine Spark leaves the Great Central Sun of the galaxy. That Sun is composed of two Twin Flames, Alpha and Omega. The White Fire Beings, individualized into positive and negative polarities, are completely free. They also have all the attributes of the Godhead. They are endowed with free will and may do exactly as they wish. They need not leave Alpha and Omega if they wish to remain. On the other hand, they may pursue an evolutionary course if they so desire. Those of us who are here on earth today are accountable only to ourselves for getting involved in what seems to be a somewhat hazardous ordeal. We were once White Fire Beings but we wanted to go out and explore the cosmos and we were for some reason attracted to this planet.

Usually Twin-Rays do not remain together during their evolutionary explorations. Sometimes one remains with Alpha and Omega and one goes forth to wrestle with the world of matter. But at no time are they ever separated so far as their higher Presence is concerned.

When Tesla volunteered to come to the earth his Twin-Ray, exercising her free will, decided to accompany him, not only because it would be more pleasant for them to be together, but because her presence would enormously increase his efficiency in the job he had to do. She wished to remain in the background, however, so she chose to manifest as a white dove. She was always somewhere fairly near Tesla, and they were in telepathic communication. Frequently, she flew into the open window of his hotel room at night and they would have long talks together. But she was an advanced Initiate in her own right, and made herself as useful as possible in service to the Light.

Between twenty-five and thirty years ago in the United States, Saint Germain arranged for the reunion of several pairs of Twin-Rays. At that time He frequently used a white dove as a messenger, and although this may not have been Tesla's dove, still it serves as an example of the type of work that she would do for the Hierarchy.

If Saint Germain wished to send a message to a disciple who was not telepathic, He would write the message on a small white card and have it delivered by a dove. In these cases the doves are always Initiates: they are completely intelligent and never make a mistake. The dove, card in beak, would tap at a window or otherwise call attention to his presence. Upon admittance, he would deliver the card, pause for a loving caress, and then fly away. After the message on the card had been noted by the recipient, the card would vanish into thin air. In other words, after the purpose had been served in physical matter, the imprisoned energy was released and returned to Universal Supply.

FAREWELL OF THE DOVE

Reference has already been made to imprisoned energy which is so weakened by its long and brutal confinement in matter that it must, when transmuted and released by action of the Violet Fire, be sent back to the sun for re-charging. This burden of imprisoned energy constitutes man's karmic burden today. A great part of this confined energy is stored away in attics, cellars, old buildings, slums, abandoned debris, junkyards, crowded clothes closets, the bottom drawer of the dresser, and especially in cemeteries where burial has replaced the clean, swift, releasing process of cremation.

Man will never have access to Universal Supply until he learns to get rid of junk—not for the sake of getting rid of it—but with the specific mental injunction that it is to be returned to Universal Supply: Then he must get rid of his magpie-like tendency to hoard, hoard, hoard. The person who hoards does not have faith and trust in God, no matter what he may say to the contrary. Some of the greatest hoarders, and, therefore, some of those who trust God the least, are often found up in the pulpit telling other people how to live.

Persons like Mary and Saint Germain and Jesus set the correct example. Mary wished to leave the planet richer and more beautiful, even on the physical plane. So she precipitated the design for maidenhair fern and taught the elementals how to build it. Saint Germain lowers His vibration so that He is visible to the ordinary human eye, and then demonstrates to His disciples how to precipitate food, dishes, linens and silver. Jesus, during His last embodiment, also precipitated food in a similar lesson for the benefit of His disciples. He supplied enough precipitated loaves and fishes, or what appeared to be genuine earth food, to feed five thousand hungry and weary people who had been good enough to give their attention to His discourse. Then, remember that He instructed His disciples to secure baskets and gather up the fragments of the food lest they be lost. In other words, He was obligated to etherialize the leftovers and return them to Universal Supply.

Later, at the wedding feast of Cana, Jesus demonstrated another form of supply through qualification. For two thousand years the scriptural account of changing water into wine has seemed to be a somewhat useless piece of information. Now we have vital need of this account in order to better understand how and why the space people qualify substance, and how we can qualify all things by thought, molding them to meet our desire. A thought is a thing.

The scriptural story tells how Jesus commanded that the wine jars be filled with water. Then in a simple silent ceremony He transmuted the water into electronic substance with a high frequency, ridding it of all impurities or qualifications. When the purified and unqualified water was poured into the wine glasses, the assembled guests naturally thought they were to taste a delicious wine. They had been drinking wine and expected to drink more wine. They fully qualified the water with their own thoughts. When they drank the water they declared it to be the finest wine they had ever tasted. Thoughts are things and, in this case, the thing was transmuted water qualified to taste like wine.

When Van Tassell was offered tiny cubes of substance by the space people he was told to qualify the cubes before eating them. He did so and enjoyed a meal of his favorite foods. This bit of White Magic was identical with that demonstrated at the wedding feast of Cana.

Those demonstrations also lead us to an understanding of

the One. The One is actually the universal sum-total of unqualified energy. The One is no-thing. The instant the energy is qualified its vibratory action is lowered and it becomes something. When Jesus raised the vibration of the water in the wine jars it became no-thing. When qualified by the thoughts of the wedding guests the vibratory action was lowered in conformity, and it became some-thing which tasted like wine.

For untold centuries the Masters of the Ageless Wisdom have tried to explain to retarded humanity that they could secure any desired results in their lives by properly qualifying the electronic energy which flows constantly from the Higher Self to the four lower bodies. Finally, after nineteen million years people are beginning to grasp the idea. Since thoughts are things, the time to create something or anything according to a certain pre-determined pattern is at the time the pure unqualified electronic substance enters the bloodstream with each heartbeat.

Each electron that enters the bloodstream with each heartbeat is necessarily qualified in any event, but usually in an uncontrolled manner. The average individual does not understand the proper method of working with pure Godsubstance, and, therefore, the electrons, undirected by human thought, are forced to take on whatever qualities the bloodstream carries. If an individual is angry the bloodstream reflects that fact, and the pure electrons, whirling on their course, are surrounded with murky gray astral matter carrying the vibrations of anger.

On the other hand, if a man is in the act of composing a symphony, the electrons, leaving the heart, enter into a bloodstream that is vibrating at an inspirational level. The shell of astral matter which collects around the electrons will, therefore, carry a great deal of light and brilliant color patterns which reflect the exact intensity of sincerity and love which the individual has for his creative effort. If he is a composer of the caliber of Wagner, the magnetic qualities of the light will attract memories from the subconscious or etheric body; memories of melodies heard in the Music Temple while the physical body was asleep.

The memories will come surging back; consuming all darkness which may impede their path, and magnetically anchor themselves to the atomic structure within the bloodstream which is forming around a common center. As the blood is pumped back to the heart and circulated again hundreds of fresh, pure electrons of God-substance are attracted to the atomic center which is to produce a great symphony.

The atomic structure is vibrating at high speed; the message is carried by the blood to the entire body; the composer brings the entire focus of his attention to his task; he is filled with exultant joy for like the Father, he looks upon his work and finds it good. Thus is a symphony born. Thus is a great poem written! Thus are more humble tasks accomplished in glory—the tending of a home, the tilling of a field, the feeding and loving care of a little child.

This is controlled precipitation. It is controlled entirely by the attention of the individual, and in the normal course of events, from day to day, we become that upon which we focus our attention. The majority of people focus their attention upon becoming older, and they look about them at others who have likewise focussed their attention upon old age. They find that these individuals have become aged in appearance. They say to themselves: Yes, that is normal; one does grow older, that's for sure. They are falling right into that ancient human booby-trap of judging by appearances. They, therefore, precipitate old age.

It is wholly unnecessary, because thoughts are things, and the pure electrons. if qualified with thoughts of youth and beauty when they enter the bloodstream, will produce youth and beauty as surely as an apple tree produces apples. not grapes.

Adepts and Masters who work behind the scenes or only among understanding disciples, never seem to be more than about 30 years old in appearance, although they may be hundreds or even thousands of years old. But if they are working among ordinary people who observe them each day, they voluntarily take on the appearance of age so as not to attract undue attention and even jealousy.

Tesla did not need to grow old in face and form with his ability to apply Inner knowledge. But he attracted so much attention by his outstanding genius and was the focus of so much jealousy, that had he remained youthful besides it would simply have been too much for the hostile public to swallow.

Tesla was highly prophetic but he seldom demonstrated his gift, for he was seldom in the presence of an understanding human being. Thus his prophecy that prohibition would shorten his life by twenty years was misinterpreted. Tesla. after World War I, could already foresee the political situations that were in the making. He knew that out of the particular piece of stupidity known as prohibition would develop certain activities of the dark forces that would necessitate his leaving his physical body sooner than originally planned.

A little dictatorship leads to more dictatorship. A little

government leads to a lot of government. Goodness cannot
be legislated into the hearts of men. The withdrawal of the
freedom of man to make a choice, even in his brand of
whiskey, is bound to have a weakening influence and a bad
karmic effect on both parties—in this case the government
and the governed. No Master ever achieved mastery over
matter by having the matter removed from His reach—especially if the removal was carried out by politicians seeking
to satisfy their lust for power over people.

Many years ago a gentleman by the name of C. A.
Wragg came to New York from Australia. Mr. Wragg was
and is associated with aircraft development. Upon arrival
he sought out Tesla for an interview on certain patents designed to improve the speed of aircraft.

When Mr. Wragg arrived at Tesla's office, he sat in the
reception room waiting for Tesla to finish talking with
another visitor. The door into Tesla's office stood open and
his conversation could be heard clearly in both rooms. Tesla
was speaking to his visitor about the plane he had designed
in 1917 and given to the United States government to assist in World War I. The government officials at that time
were merely amused when they looked at the design and
promptly buried it in their files.

The design showed a circular craft which looks very
much like the flying saucers observed in the skies today.
The craft carried no power plant but was to be operated
from a central power station on the ground which would
broadcast a beam of energy that could be picked up at any
distance around the earth by suitable receiving devices. Tesla
told his visitor that an airplane of this type in the skies
over Australia, for example, would be able to fly with power
drawn from a generating-projecting plant in America.

At this point the visitor left and Mr. Wragg then entered into a long discussion with Tesla on various subjects, including his aeronautical devices. Tesla was animated by Wragg's theories which he heartily approved. Suddenly Tesla became silent and appeared to be looking into space directly over Wragg's head, with a fixed gaze. Then his eyes filled with tears which streamed freely down his face. and he said: "They'll steal it—they'll steal it!"

Well, the end of this story is that they stole it, just as Tesla predicted, and Wragg, to this day, wonders at Tesla's great gift of prophecy. The two men never met again and Wragg often speculated on what had happened to the aircraft design which Tesla had described to the other visitor.

When Mr. Wragg chatted with the author recently we were able to bring him up-to-date on the plane which was known in 1917 as the Tesla Sphere. After the government of Yugoslavia established the Tesla Research Institute in Belgrade during the '30's the design for the Tesla Sphere was turned over to the Institute library, together with all other information which Tesla had released. After Tito rose to power the papers in the Institute were available to Soviet scientists.

By 1957 the Russians had discovered the secret of the Tesla Sphere, and had placed the plane in production. It is still probably the most advanced aircraft in the skies today, although the United States had the design in its possession for forty years and had not bothered to develop it. The Russians have given Tesla full credit for the design.

The Tesla Sphere, as has been said, is earthbound, but is highly maneuverable and can fly at tremendous speeds, drawing power beamed to it from a single power plant located on the ground. However, Otis T. Carr now has his new circular-foil aircraft design ready for production, and, undoubtedly, it will supplant all present planes including the Tesla Sphere. Carr's craft is not earthbound because it draws fuel directly from the atmosphere in the form of electrical charges. The Tesla Sphere, if seen during daylight hours, can easily be mistaken for a flying saucer. But the Carr craft glows at night and actually is a flying saucer although designed on this planet.

Although Tesla had announced his own prophecy about his life span being reduced from 150 to 130 years, the very political situation which he had envisioned at the time of prohibition, turned out to be even worse than he had anticipated. Tesla was fully conscious that he alone was responsible for the power age which had made World War I possible. No earth man would have been able to invent alternating current. Tesla was brought to the earth to rescue the electrical age from the limitations of direct current and to set power geographically free, in order to prepare the people of the planet for the space age. Without alternating current a vast, global war, even on the relatively small scale of World War I, would not have been possible.

Tesla accepted full responsibility for his inventions, however, and knowing that World War II was just over the horizon, he perfected and offered to the world in 1935 an anti-war machine. This mechanism, electrical in operation, is capable of setting up an invisible and impenetrable curtain of polarized light which can be directed along national borders, thus making a nation safe within its own boundaries. Tesla offered this protection to the governments of the United States and Great Britain. The offer was flatly rejected.

Tesla's vision of the future had been perfectly clear.

He knew that the dark forces were driving into the very heart of American civilization, and that a world blood-bath had been scheduled. He knew that it had been planned as a preliminary effort to set up a world dictatorship under a leader of the dark forces. The dark forces were well aware that Ascended Master Saint Germain was breathing down their necks, so close was His pursuit. They also knew that the American nation was of vital importance in the Aquarian Age, and that many of Saint Germain's most stalwart disciples were Americans. Under a world dictatorship these disciples could be so hampered in their efforts that little could be accomplished for the Forces of Light. Further, under a world dictatorship America could be so merged with all other nations that it might even cease to exist as a separate entity.

Tesla knew all this, and he knew that his alternating current had made it possible by making the power age possible. But he knew, too, that the Forces of Light would do whatever could be done for the American people short of interfering with their own free will. That They could not do. They could not exert any pressure to get newspapers, magazines or radio to place the issue of Tesla's anti-war machine before the people. The government, having already rejected it, would naturally not make it a public issue. .

The anti-war machine was described in many newspaper and magazine articles back in 1935 and the years that followed, but at no time were the people told that the Tesla invention was absolutely necessary to protect this nation against a world war which was even then in the making. Those in high places in many nations were fully aware of this fact, but it was carefully concealed from the public.

So the days passed with complacency on all sides. People

everywhere were talking about the depression. Little did
they know that the depression had been carefully staged so
as to give them something to talk about: something to distract their attention from the fact that they were about to
be sold down the river. Finally, after years on the dole and
years on various boondoggling jobs, the American people
were in a mood for war. They were in a mood for anything
that would open up factories and get Tesla's alternating
current humming, although they were not even aware that
he existed or that his invention had supplied the power they
were so eager to use. But they wanted jobs, jobs, jobs. Anything to make some real money for a change.

Meanwhile the forces of darkness were driving deeper
and ever deeper into the heart of the nation. The people
were completely in their grip. Disciples who had been in
incarnation back in 1776 and remembered Valley Forge
could hardly believe their eyes and ears. The seventh Ray
was growing stronger and the sixth Ray power was waning, but the Aquarian Age was not yet in full control. Ascended Master Saint Germain, Chohan of the seventh Ray,
took up His work, however, and His disciples in the United
States struggled valiantly to carry out His instructions.

While the governments were busy turning down Tesla's
offer of an anti-war machine, a polarized light mechanism
that would protect the nation's boundaries, Saint Germain's
disciples themselves proceeded to mentally qualify energy
and with it build a wall of light around North America;
they later extended it around Central and South America.
It stands today, more firm than ever before, about three
miles out from the mainland. While it is invisible to the
majority of people, it is sometimes seen by travelers at sea
who are mystified by it, and who attribute it to all sorts of

things such as atmospheric disturbances. There is nothing unusual about it, however, because similar walls, built by Adepts, have been used down through countless ages to protect certain sacred spots on the earth, such as the Wesak Valley in the Himalayas.

The wall of light built by disciples of Saint Germain through the power of directing electronic substance by human thought, can be constructed to meet many human protective needs, personal or national, but it cannot be built for any selfish reasons. Therefore, it can be said the wall of light can be built only by Adepts, or by disciples in training and affiliated with Hierachial interests. It is always a product of the Forces of Light acting directly or through disciples. This is a protection, because it would be extremely inconvenient and impractical if persons with less than honest intent, could build a wall of light which might be detrimental to the constructive interests of others. On the other hand, the tube of Light, described in a later chapter, can and should be built by everyone for self-protection.

The Tesla anti-war machine is a stepped-down utilitarian version of the wall of light as constructed by Adepts and disciples. The light which is utilized in the Tesla invention is related to certain Ray frequencies, but since the curtain of light is produced by an electrical mechanism, it can be used without the understanding or even the support of the people within the nation which is being protected.

The wall of light built by Adepts and disciples without the use of any mechanical devices, but only by controlled and directed thought power, must be maintained. It must be strengthened almost hourly by feeding into it visualized energies. It demands focussed attention from groups of disciples, for it must be kept firmly anchored to earth and must be kept free from rents or weak spots. The wall is actually anchored Ray energy, and since it is in the nature of all flame to rise, the wall would simply disappear and return to the Source if the attention of the disciples was removed for any length of time.

Saint Germain requested the American disciples to construct this wall of light in order to protect this nation from direct attack by the forces of darkness operating in other nations, and also to lessen the activities of the dark forces within the United States. The wall of light served the desired purpose during the years of the so-called phoney war in Europe which finally exploded in World War II. But the black magicians opposing Saint Germain finally took their activities away from the mainland of the United States and concentrated on Hawaii, where they succeeded in conniving with black magicians in Japan to arrange the attack on Pearl Harbor. Neither the dark forces within the United States nor those working outside the country were able to break the wall of light and stage a direct attack. Therefore, the sneak attack on Pearl Harbor was devised in order to draw this nation into World War II.

Had the Tesla anti-war machine been used as Tesla planned, the entire question of attack would have been brought out in the open, on the physical plane. The American people could have been assured of their safety and could have remained within the protected borders of the country until the European storm blew over. Moreover, England had been offered the Tesla anti-war machine and could have utilized it in the same protective manner. There was no reason whatsoever for either Britain or America to have been drawn into this challenging activity of the forces of darkness.

There was no reason except stupidity, that is. The American people, had they heard of the so-called mystical activities of Master Saint Germain's disciples and of the wall of light, would have laughed out loud. The very people who would have laughed then, are the ones who are laughing today at the idea of space ships. They are the people who would like to laugh at Tesla if they dared. Not daring to come out openly against Tesla they have managed to keep his name out of school books, and his theories out of university science courses.

The actual reason that Tesla's scientific methods are not taught is because colleges cannot find professors who understand Tesla. Why do they not train them? Because the adoption of Tesla's inventions will disturb the status quo; they will offer a whole new way of life; they will upset churchianity, and, in fact, abolish it; they will make the establishment of Christianity possible and desirable; they will cast political conniving into oblivion; they will make the present economic system look exactly like the silly thing it is.

Darkness never wins out over light in the long run, and if there is a seeming victory it is but temporary. So the forces of darkness, conniving with their colleagues within the United States, smashed at Pearl Harbor on December 7, 1941. The attack was carefully planned but not by the Japanese people. They stood only to lose, not to gain. How much they have lost the world now knows, and perhaps some day the Japanese people will have the courage to probe the depths of their side of the story—the story of how they flew into Hawaii with a gun at their backs, and with everything all set and prepared in advance for swift destruction.

Out through Saint Germain's great wall of light American battleships then sailed forth to their destiny. American aircraft flew through the wall and out upon their unknown missions. The great Tesla, the incomparable genius whose inventions might have prevented this world tragedy, sat in his hotel suite preparing to wind up details of his physical plane work and take up his new activities in Shamballa.

The Dove had returned to him for a final farewell. She told him she was going to shed her physical body, but that when the appointed hour came she would return for him, and together they would go to Sanat Kumara's headquarters at the White Island of Shamballa, now located in the etheric realms over the Gobi desert.

Even in those last days, in the little time left to him on earth, Tesla did not forget the hundreds of companions of his Twin-Ray, the White Dove. Over a long period of years Tesla had fed thousands and thousands of pigeons in New York, our wood doves and rock doves. In constant care and tenderness, he had ministered to birds that were sick or injured. During the years that Otis Carr was in training, he assisted Tesla daily with the feeding of the pigeons in Bryant Park, around the Cathedral, and in other areas. Carr often went out into the parks and gathered up ailing or injured birds, bringing them back to Tesla's hotel suite. Tesla fabricated splints for their broken wings or broken legs, ministered to their various ailments, and kept them in his room until they were ready to fly again.

It was around the year of 1940 when Tesla, in the presence of a witness, told John J. O'Neill the beautiful and magnificent love story of his life—his love for the White Dove. Tesla described her last farewell.

She flew into his room in the dark of the night when he was deep in meditation. They had a long conversation, and it was then that she told him she was going to die, and that she would not come to him again. Then she flew to the windowsill and stood there gazing at Tesla sitting alone in the darkened room.

"Suddenly," said Tesla, "from her eyes came great sweeping rays of light. Powerful, dazzling, blinding light—light more intense than had ever been produced in my laboratories."

His listeners remained utterly silent as he paused to remember.

"I loved that Dove," he said softly. "She was a white female with a touch of gray in her wings. I loved her as a man loves a woman."

In speaking to O'Neill about the farewell, Tesla omitted all references to the actual identity of the dove, and to their plans to go to Shamballa, for O'Neill would not have understood. He did tell O'Neill that after the dove's last visit he knew that he would not remain long on earth.

O'Neill's esoteric knowledge was so limited that he completely missed the significance of the dove's farewell. He was utterly confused, as he stated later when he related the incident to friends, about the phrase which Tesla used in describing the depths of his love: "I loved her as a man loves a woman." But in the light of later revelations as to the identity of the White Dove, it is clear that Tesla was using the only words he could use to describe his Twin-Ray.

So it was O'Neill's great privilege to hear the story of the dove from Tesla's lips. Yet later O'Neill stated that he would have regarded it as a dream experience had a witness not been present. He included the story of the dove's farewell in his book *Prodigal Genius*, but unfortunately, he tried to interpret it and completely missed the point which Tesla had attempted to get across to him. Tesla assuredly had some special reason for telling the story to O'Neill, although he must have known it would not be understood. Perhaps Tesla knew that O'Neill was also living out his final years in a physical body, and perhaps the story of the dove was told in order to provide some future link on the subtle planes.

O'Neill was a great admirer of the genius of Tesla, and he sensed the fact that Tesla had profound esoteric depths to his nature. But O'Neill was caught between two opposing forces—his longing to plunge deeply into esoteric studies, and his need to serve the forces of materialistic science in his capacity as science editor of the *New York Herald Tribune*.

His job prevented him from freely and openly exploring esoteric subjects. He carefully avoided being seen in public places with certain well-known occultists. He regularly had occult books brought to him by friends so that he would not be observed entering or leaving occult libraries. He lived in constant fear of making a slip in his newspaper writing: of putting something esoteric into print that would make him the laughing-stock of the materialistic scientists to whom he had to cater in order to earn a living.

Moreover, O'Neill was glamored by esotericism; it was all so new and so wonderful to him. Down through the years Tesla often had discussions with him about various subjects that touched on the mystical and the occult—or so O'Neill thought. Actually they were scientific discussions but O'Neill did not grasp that point. He wanted to keep the two entirely separate, and yet sip the honey from both. Tesla repeatedly pulled O'Neill down abruptly from his mystical clouds of glamour, pinning him firmly to earth.

One of their most heated arguments was touched off by

O'Neill's sentimental concern for imperfections of the human body. Tesla, who had no time for imperfection in anything, stated without qualification that the human body was a meat-machine. O'Neill was horrified to hear such a bold statement come from the superman. But Tesla was perfectly correct for the human body is, in itself, without value: it can become a servant of God only when it is powered by God-substance that will beat the physical heart, pouring free and pure electrons into the bloodstream.

In *Prodigal Genius*, O'Neill relates some extremely revealing points which were covered in his discussions with Tesla on the meat-machine topic. As a rule, persons who are glamored emotionally, but who are at the same time intellectuals, have the good taste and the judgment to refrain from obvious negativity in their statements. O'Neill did not dwell unduly on the negative aspect of the meat-machine theory. He insisted, rather, that Tesla, in his consistent and unremitting demonstration of genius, was a living contradiction to the very meat-machine idea which he advanced.

O'Neill held that under the meat-machine theory we would all have to be geniuses like Tesla, or all mediocrities, since we would all be living inside similar meat-machines, all responding in the same way to uniform external forces. This was not the situation, so O'Neill flatly regarded the meat-machine theory as disproved, and went on to his next point.

He rather chided Tesla for failing to be frank with him, claiming that Tesla was afraid to discuss certain strange and supernormal experiences for fear of being misunderstood and ridiculed. Then he went further and challenged Tesla to some day open up and talk about these cloistered experiences to one who would not fail to understand him—

namely, John J. O'Neill. As one reads O'Neill's recounting of this conversation between a great genius and a neophyte, memories crowd close—memories of another similar moment when Jesus turned to His disciples and closed a discussion with the gentle words: There are other things which I cannot tell you, because the Light would be more than you could bear.

Tesla knew that a great unquenchable thirst for Truth was physically consuming O'Neill because his atomic structure, clogged with astral debris, could not stand the Light. The meat-machine in which O'Neill was living stubbornly refused the concentrated diet of illumination that Tesla was able and willing to offer. Tesla could not get his lighted words through the coarse vibrations of the meat-machine, and thereby release the inner splendor of the three-fold Flame imprisoned within O'Neill's heart. Had he been able to do so, the Flame from within would have provided O'Neill with Its eternal sustenance. The greatest gift of compassion that Tesla could offer to his beleaguered pupil was withdrawal of the tremendous stimulation induced by these verbal discussions.

O'Neill says that he did not see Tesla for a long time after the meat-machine episode, but when they did talk together again Tesla made a statement which, had it not been so subtle, so carefully couched in vibrant words of compassionate, loving understanding, pulsing with the very essence of Truth, might have filled O'Neill with overwhelming discouragement. But the gentle Tesla knew the innermost heart of his earnest, striving chela, athirst for Truth in a barren wasteland of materialistic science. Confidingly, Tesla said: "Mr. O'Neill, you understand me better than anyone else in the world."

O'Neill grasped this crumb of comfort and cherished it
in sheer ecstacy. He never even suspected that he had been
tested and had failed. He did not catch even a hint of the
correct meaning of Tesla's pronouncement. He lived out
the last glamored years of his life without ever knowing
that Tesla had finalized an evaluation of a pupil who, after
long personal exposure to some of the highest teachings
ever offered in the outer world, had in the end turned from
the powerful brilliance of an Illumination he could not bear.
Like so many others who stand in the valley of decision,
gazing at the distant peaks, O'Neill turned back once again,
back toward the familiar shadows, vainly seeking in outer
darkness to discover and to understand the Light that lighted
the loving heart of his great Teacher.

O'Neill, like all materialists who dread to face facts, had
a way of reversing higher truths. He claimed that he was
the one with occult understanding, and that Tesla was the
materialist, thus freeing himself from any obligation to
listen to Tesla with serious intent and an open mind. When
Tesla told him the story of the dove, O'Neill jumped to the
conclusion that Tesla was a frustrated romanticist. O'Neill
could not find any suitable explanation for the great beams
of dazzling light that came from the eyes of the dove during the farewell, so he just mentioned the incident and
ignored its meaning. Later, when he wrote *Prodigal Genius*
he related the story in a manner which indicated he had entirely missed its profundity. He even went so far as to state it
was Tesla who did not understand the symbolism of the
Dove.

As the years passed and as O'Neill's book was read more
and more widely, the story of the dove's farewell became
almost a source of embarrassment in many quarters. Many

of the more materialistic scientists privately expressed the opinion that Tesla should have stuck to his laboratory and not messed around with pigeons, especially one certain pigeon. It was even suggested that Tesla had fabricated the story and was just having fun in relating it to O'Neill.

But in 1956 many electrical engineering groups in the United States prepared to honor Tesla by observing the hundredth anniversary of his birth. The White Dove chose this occasion to prove Herself. One evening an anniversary committee member was in his home preparing some publicity for the forthcoming Tesla observance. Suddenly he was startled by an object alighting on a windowsill near him. As he looked at it he realized that it was Tesla's Dove. At that instant great dazzling rays of light came from the eyes of the Dove; powerful, blinding light: light more intense than Tesla had ever produced in a laboratory.

For a few minutes at least, on this evening in 1956, Tesla's White Dove returned into manifestation. Who knows what great and special work is being performed by this messenger from a far kingdom? Tesla knows. And perhaps the White Dove will return again and again, until all humanity becomes aware of the sacred Presence of Peace on earth.

PART VII

The Arthur H. Matthews Story

It was in October, 1956, that Mr. and Mrs. George Van Tassel, accompanied by Art Aho, arrived in New York for a series of lectures on spaceships. According to our usual custom, we arranged an informal gathering for them, with About thirty guests invited to share the evening.

As usual, more than thirty showed up, and it was around 2 o'clock in the morning when the last guests reluctantly said farewell. They had listened for hours in spellbound attention to the ready conversation of George Van Tassel about his contacts with space people who had landed their craft on Giant Rock Airport, a landing spot located on the edge of the California desert for the service of private planes.

George Van Tassel, a former pilot and flight test technician, had leased the lonely spot shortly after World War II. He was settled there when Kenneth Arnold made his famous sighting of nine flying saucers skimming over mountains in the state of Washington, a sighting which brought the subject of spaceships to the attention of the entire world.

The Van Tassel family had moved to Giant Rock and lived on the desert nearly eight years before the space people finally landed a craft late one night on the airport strip. They awakened Mr. Van Tassel, invited him aboard the craft to inspect it, and then arranged for additional contacts via beamed facilities. Over a period of months he learned to use the beam, recording their messages and publishing the material received in a little magazine called *Proceedings*.

The space people, in addition to giving a digest of their philosophy, also gave practical instructions for the building of equipment which they said could be used in the Aquarian Age.

They told him how to construct a small metal antenna device in the center of a dry desert spot of sand near his living quarters. Although no rain falls during many months and the desert sun beats down without respite, the little metal post keeps a large circular area sufficiently damp for a vegetable garden to flourish.

The main piece of equipment suggested to Van Tassel by the space people is to be used for health purposes, and its design is now almost completed. Each part must be made by hand, and the entire unit is to be housed in a domed wooden structure built without the use of any metal. Even wooden pegs must be utilized in place of nails. A person may sit comfortably within the unit for a few minutes, permitting the vibrations to act upon the atoms of the body. This action raises the vibrations of the four lower bodies of an individual, freeing the atomic structure of astral debris, and permitting electrons to return to their proper orbits, and atoms to increase their rate of revolution.

Van Tassel first built a small model and found that an injured lizard, its head smashed, returned to normal and crawled away completely healed, after a brief period in the unit. From the description, this mechanism seems to be another piece of New Age machinery designed to push forward Ascended Master Saint Germain's program to abolish the concept of sickness and death from this planet. A unit of this sort could be utilized by anyone from time to time, and would gradually accustom the individual to live in a high-frequency body.

In the July, 1956, issue of *Proceedings,* published by Van Tassel, he carried a remarkable story of some trips he had made in projected consciousness to an Air Force base located in the far north. There he found a mountain, surrounded by barbed wire and armed guards, and inside the mountain he found great caverns filled with a vast amount of machinery, together with a modern workshop that was humming with activity.

Van Tassel said that many of the machines were stored there by earlier civilizations, some dating back to Lemuria and Atlantis. It is a well-known fact among occultists that when Sanat Kumara ordered the submerging of Lemuria and Atlantis, He directed that those lands first be stripped of all valuable machinery, gold, gems, and all records and these items were stored in mountain caverns in various parts of the world.

Several of these storage caves exist in the United States: many are in South America. All of them are carefully

guarded by the Hierarchy and protected with a wall of light.
It is utterly impossible for anyone to gain entrance to one
of these caverns unless the Hierarchy wishes that to happen in order to serve some phase of the Divine Plan. If the
cavern in the far north was discovered by our government
forces, it was a planned discovery, arranged by the Hierarchy. In this case, it was arranged in order to cast the
burden of guilt on those government authorities who insist
that flying saucers do not exist; that they are weather balloons, or as one brainy scientist claims—temperature inversions.

Some day it will be revealed that during the years when
the government tried to maintain this phoney screen of
secrecy around flying saucers, that high brass within the
military forces, supported by American taxpayers, were in
full possession of complete information on flying saucers
from outer space and on flying saucers stored in caverns
by earlier civilizations. All of this information was withheld
from the public because from the beginning of the present
flying saucer era, the space people made it abundantly clear
to all government leaders throughout the world that they had
come to the earth to abolish war first, and to establish a new
way of life after the housecleaning.

Naturally if there is to be no war there will be no need
for a military machine. Militarists and allied bureaucrats, supported by captive taxpayers under constant threat of pen-
alties for non-payment of taxes, have known for years that
the space people plan to eliminate the military at the first
opportunity. The space people have been most considerate
about the whole matter. They said bluntly, but firmly: If you
cannot see your way clear to peaceful living without some
sort of national defense then use the Tesla anti-war machine

during this interim period when new international and interplanetary relationships are being adjusted. You men of earth have no time to waste in fighting and building of weapons. You must live abundantly, and have plenty of leisure time in which to study and prepare yourselves for the higher path of evolution which you must pursue. Use machines such as the Tesla anti-war machine to automatically serve you. Do not use human bodies and souls for defense, for you are only adding to your already overwhelming load of karma by so doing.

Many years ago the disciples of Master Saint Germain were informed by the great Adept Himself that large numbers of space ships were stored away in various caverns, dating back to Lemurian and Atlantean manufacture, and that these ships could be reconditioned and put into service as soon as the general public could grasp the significance of Aquarian Age plans. Let the reader not think for one instant that news of this sort did not reach the ears of the military in a quick flash. Saint Germain was well aware, even when He gave the information, that the dark forces had their spies right within the group of disciples of the Light. The modern Judas type is extremely active.

Every military group in the world today is riddled with members of the dark forces, pledged to serve the cause of ignorance, savagery, war and confusion. Originally churchianity was the center for dark force activity, and later the political and economic arenas served as a focus for evil. These three centers still serve, and another is coming up to a strong second lead right behind the military—and that is the whole field of medicine and associated interests such as pharmaceuticals. The military is still in the lead because since the invention of the printing press the more astute black disciples have concentrated on building a global propaganda machine. They have need of strong military backing to keep the machine running and to keep the unfree press under strict control and censorship.

The dark forces work only by inspiring fear; in the final analysis fear is their only weapon. Of necessity they must always work secretly or at least they must think they are harboring secrets. Actually, however, the Hierarchy has complete and instantaneous accounts of their every activity and even of their every thought and plan. But even those who serve the cause of evil, degraded as they are, still have free wills which must be respected. They are still children of God, even though benighted children.

When Van Tassel visited the cavern in the far north, he found that secrecy shrouded every movement in the area. Or so these deluded people thought. It is high time that every individual who has reached the age of reason and is of sound mind, should learn to think correctly about that which is not directly in front of his nose. Tesla would never have been able to invent alternating current had he not been able to work in the fourth ether.

There is nothing mystical about working with gas which may be invisible to the average human eye. Therefore, why should anyone hesitate to work with physical matter which is one grade finer than gas? And why should anyone be considered lunatic who can project his consciousness into areas where he cannot conveniently take his physical body?

The guards in the cavern, according to Van Tassel, were psychically aware of his presence in that they sensed something unusual. They were extremely tense and suspicious. He said the people working in the cavern had the finest equipment including the latest electronic and magnetic devices. The cavern was well lighted, heated and ventilated. All machine parts were covered so that no person could see any assembly except the one he was working on. In one supersecret area Van Tassel came across what appeared to be a flying saucer under construction. It stood on a large base. and across the base were stencilled words—Tesla Sphere—P-A.

On that October night in 1956 when the Van Tassels visited us, very little was known by any of us about Tesla's current activities. Therefore, after the last guests had gone the conversation turned to Tesla, and the fascinating trip which Van Tassel had made to the northern Air Force base was discussed in detail. Van Tassel was of the opinion that perhaps Tesla did not die. He also thought that the Tesla Sphere was a flying saucer.

It was out of this early morning conversation that this book began to take shape. A magnetic focus had been formed and suddenly a flood of information on Tesla came pouring in, much of it from strange and unexpected sources. Over in Paris a spacecraft convention was held for interested Europeans. Arthur H. Matthews of Canada submitted a paper on the Tesla set for interplanetary communication, which he had built and operated since 1947. A report on this paper reached New York and a contact between Mr. Matthews and the present author was established by correspondence.

Mr. Matthews frequently contacts spaceships on the Tesla set, and has had numerous personal conversations with the crews as well. His property in the Province of Quebec is quite secluded and the spaceships can easily land at night without being observed by the merely curious. Over the years since he first built the Tesla set and since the space people first came to visit him, he has cleared up many points about Tesla, such as those discussed by Van Tassel.

Mr. Matthews had never been uncertain about the death of Tesla, although many persons are of the opinion that he did not die. Probably this doubt is stimulated by the fact that both Tesla and the White Dove have continued their work in Shamballa in their subtle bodies, and many people intuitively feel that they are still here. Apparently the White Dove does manifest from time to time. Recently there was an interesting experience reported where two white doves— not pigeons—flew into a tree and perched there for a brief period where they were observed by persons who had just completed some work on a Tesla project. This happened in an area where doves had not been seen for more than a quarter of a century.

If Tesla cares to use the methods followed by Adepts who are members of the Spiritual Hierarchy of this planet, he could lower his vibrations if necessary, and his body would appear to be physical. The Masters use this method, as do Adepts among space people. By lowering his vibrations he could engage in normal physical plane activity, but since he has trained disciples in embodiment it is not likely that he would find it necessary to perform physical plane work.

Another reason why many people think that Tesla is still alive and active in a physical body, is because of an unexplained incident which happened at his funeral; an incident which was extremely puzzling to the press. The funeral service was held at St. John the Divine Cathedral in New York, and a special Yugoslav honor guard, resplendent in their uniforms, stood around the casket, which was draped with the American flag. Many reporters and press photo-

graphers were present and during the service made a large
number of pictures.

However, not a single negative turned out successfully.
The cameras were focussed on the casket, of course, and
this entire area on each picture was blurred with what appeared to be currents of oscillating energy. Around the
edges of each picture the background of the cathedral itself was clear and in perfect focus, but not a single picture
was obtained of the casket, the honor guard, nor even of
the people who sat in the pews near the casket. After the
service the body was cremated.

There was a rumor that the body in the casket was
not that of Tesla; or that the body of Tesla had been resuscitated and possibly removed from the casket before the
funeral. But there is a more likely explanation. There have
been cases where bodies of advanced disciples have been
removed from the casket with angelic assistance, after the
casket was closed, but this was done in order to prevent
the body from being buried. Since Tesla's body was cremated this precaution against the barbarous practice of
burial was unnecesary. Moreover, Tesla's body had been
used for a long time and was quite worn, so it is not likely
that resuscitation would have been considered. It would be
far easier to simply get a new body for him if he needs one.

The probable explanation is in line with a New Age
practice now being used by disciples who are ready to make
their Ascension, but who are tied to families and social
groups whose members are less advanced in evolution and
unable to understand the Ascension process.

If one individual in an average othodox family is ready
for his Ascension, he cannot under ordinary circumstances
raise the vibratory action of his body and disappear. The

shock would be too great to those left behind, and besides a disappearance of this sort would result in police action and a search for the missing person. Consequently, the individual follows custom and sheds his physical body. Then he remains with the body for a few hours and with angelic assistance he withdraws every electron, leaving only empty atomic shells. All the electrons are then recharged and returned to Universal Supply to be used over again.

There have been many instances of this type of withdrawal in recent years since so many disciples are completing their earth experience and leaving this planetary classroom. In these cases the body structure that remains after the withdrawal of the electrons is a source of puzzlement to undertakers. They cannot understand what has taken place, although they quickly realize something unusual has happened.

It is probable that this process was used by Tesla. Intense angelic activity was centered around the casket while all living electronic substance was being removed from the body, resulting in the peculiar oscillations recorded on the photographic negative. The camera is not sensitive enough to handle high frequencies. That is why an actual photograph of a Master of the Ageless Wisdom is seldom seen, unless it is made by certain photographers in India who have special equipment. A Master's body is vibrating at such high speed that the camera cannot record the image. That is also why space people are seldom photographed. The camera will catch them only if they have lowered their vibrations to an earth level.

Arthur Matthews learned last year that the Russians were manufacturing the Tesla Sphere, the powerless aircraft which Tesla designed late in 1917, and which the

United States government rejected at that time. It is probable that the craft which Van Tassel saw in the cavern represented a belated and recent attempt to utilize the old design for the American military machine. Whether or not the attempt was successful is not known, and, of course, is no longer of interest. Russia is already producing the ship, and even now it is already completely outmoded by the new craft designed by Otis T. Carr.

It becomes more and more clear as we follow events in recent months that it is Ascended Master Saint Germain Who is riding in the saddle these days. Steadily, inexorably, the Forces of Light are moving forward, transmuting all darkness as They advance. Always the message is the same: Abolish sickness and death on the planet earth. Use the Violet Flame to transmute your destructive human creations. Set your four lower worlds in order. Prepare to make your own Ascension, but meanwhile prepare all humanity for the same eternal glory of evolutionary progress through God's many mansions.

Fantastic new mechanisms are now being brought forth by many inventors, unheard of until now. Some of these inventors are completely lacking in scientific or even technological training in the outer world, proving that they are actually outpicturing that which they understand and develop on the inner planes. This does not mean that they are necessarily considered spiritually advanced in the outer world, or that they are working in Higher Realms while in their physical bodies in a waking state. In full waking consciousness many of these inventors and discoverers of methods of applying universal principles, are working in the fourth ether, just as Tesla worked. The fourth, third, second and first ethers are part of the physical plane; they are merely finer grades of what we can visualize as gaseous substance.

However, even though inventors like Arthur H. Matthews, Otis T. Carr, Nikola Tesla and many others, are able to work in the fourth ether, the full understanding of the free-energy concept as visualized by these men involves the utilization of power drawn forth from the highest galactic realms—even the Cosmic Light from the Great Central Sun of Alpha and Omega. It matters little about the outer garb, or physical body, worn by these men. An understanding of the great power Sources from which they draw forth energy, can be obtained only by removing the attention from the outer or human forms, and focussing it steadily upon the Light which illumines their efforts.

A disciple is an individual who has voluntarily surrendered his human control of his human free will, and who has asked that he be guided at all times to merge his creative efforts with the unfoldment of the Divine Plan. Inasmuch as the average person is not aware that there is a Divine Plan, and knows absolutely nothing about surrendering self-will, the tendency is to emphasize the human side of an inventor, and forget the magnificent ability that makes a creative genius who serves the Light, at one with the Cosmos.

Today the average person who knows something of the work of Tesla, Matthews and Carr, is impatient that this work is not brought into actual manifestation right now. They expect Matthews and Carr to leap forward over all human obstacles, and give to humanity a war-free world protected by the Tesla anti-war machine, and a spaceship in which to spend leisure hours sightseeing around the solar system.

A disciple cannot do such things, for a disciple is serving the Light. A disciple is such because he conforms to real discipline. Real discipline does not mean that he must rise with the sun in the morning, sit cross-legged on the floor, eat raw carrots, or commune with invisibles. A disciple refrains from all tyranny, however gentle, which would thwart innate progress. A disciple holds in check the urge to exhibit human qualities, and instead gives the inner or Real Self an opportunity for expression.

Matthews cannot give the Tesla anti-war machine to a public which still nourishes the viper of hostility within its own heart. The public, or at least a majority of people within one nation, must use the Violet Fire to transmute their own discord. Then this same nation can demand the Tesla anti-war machine to protect its borders from hostile advances by other nations. It would not be the first time in history that a single nation stood firmly on the side of the Light and won victory through total pacifism.

The inner core of the earth is populated today by such a nation. These people originally lived on the surface of the planet, and they served the Light at all times, completely surrendering their human free will to the Divine Plan. At one point they were threatened with immediate extinction as they stood and watched invading hordes approach. Suddenly the earth opened and they were gently lowered into a magnificent region at the globe's center—the kingdom presided over by Lord Pelleur.

There they live today, still serving the Light, and helping to maintain the balance of the planet while its surface is torn asunder by plunderers and wastrels, descendents of the hostile hordes they once faced. The interior of the earth provides living conditions so magnificent in every phase that the mind of surface man cannot conceive of such wonders. The air is pure and vital at all times, with a soft white light illuminating the whole scene. The climate is perfect. The vegetation is basically a soft rose pink shade varied with golden tones, and with gem colors of the seven Rays. Not a single vibration of pain penetrates to this great Core of Harmony. The last vibration of distress which touched these people was on that day long ago when they stood valiantly in the Light, watching the hostile hordes advance, and the good earth opened to offer them the hospitality of its innermost heart.

Long aeons of time have since passed upon the surface of this earth and within its pulsing heart, where abide those blessed with the unique joy of serving the Light under the leadership of the great Lord Pelleur. Even though they abide within the earth, they are still part of the human race, and are one with us in all harmonious things. They constantly work to bring about greater balance in conditions on the surface of the earth, and many lifestreams who are able and willing to free themselves from discordant karma, take embodiment in Lord Pelleur's kingdom rather than return into incarnation in the disturbed atmosphere on the globe's surface.

Until recently the outer world had heard little about the activities within the heart of the earth. However, when Tesla was brought here from Venus it was decided to re-establish communication and acquaintanceship with these lovely people who have labored ceaselessly to restore harmony on the surface of the planet. Tesla was charged with the task of bringing wireless or radio communication to the attention of a forgetful humanity, as well as television. He then confided to Arthur H. Matthews precise instructions for the building of the interplanetary communications set. Beyond that point it was not necessary or even prudent for Tesla to reveal the ultimate plans for communication.

There was a reason for this, and it is explained by a well-known statement that is a truism in esoteric teachings: Take a single step toward the Light, and the Light will advance two steps toward you. Tesla came into embodiment to take a single giant step on behalf of humanity. In the matter of communications he discovered radio waves and then invented a machine to use them—the wireless set which was later developed to transfer pictures as well as words. He discovered cosmic waves from rays and then invented a machine to use them—the interplanetary communications set which will make Venus as close as a neighbor on a telephone.

It was not necessary for Tesla to build a machine to communicate with the folks at the center of the earth because such a machine had already been provided. It was invented by a woman known to us today only as Leonora. She is now an Ascended Being. Leonora was among Saint Germain's disciples who were in embodiment in France at the time of the French Revolution. She knew Lafayette well. and through his assistance left France and went to the land of Wyoming where she had the protection of Saint Germain's Retreat—the Cave of the Symbols.

There she completed her work on an instrument which she called a radio. In Volume II of *Law of Life*, a new book by A. D. K. Luk, will be found a biographical sketch of Leonora, and a description of the room in the Cave of the Symbols in Wyoming, where the machine now stands on a table, awaiting the moment when man's inhumanity to man will cease, and he can enjoy the full abundance of cosmic fellowship.

A. D. K. Luk tells us that Leonora spent seven embodiments perfecting this machine. Four of these embodiments were masculine and three feminine, and She carried the memory of Her technological work over from one incarnation to the next, without interruption. Her machine can be tuned in to the center of the earth; in another operation it can tune in to any spot on the surface of the earth or anywhere above the earth in any etheric realm; and in a third operation it can tune in, on any planet in this solar system, and some planets in adjacent systems.

Thus it can be seen that Tesla was working in accord with the Divine Plan when he brought to the attention of the public the fact of radio waves in the atmosphere, and then invented a machine to use them. This was Tesla's quiet way of taking a step toward the Light for an ignorant humanity. Tesla was well acquainted with Leonora's machine, but he also knew that humanity would never even suspect that this instrument, complete and ready for instant operation, has stood for many years in a room in a cave in Wyoming. So he invented a radio. He got the public interested in radio and television.

Then to Arthur H. Matthews he gave a design for an interplanetary communications set. He left to Matthews the task of getting the public interested in communicating with the inhabitants of other planets. He took the young Otis Carr under his guidance and into his confidence, and told him that he was to explore space. He left to Carr the task of getting the public interested in actual mechanical spaceships, and the task of building such spaceships.

Now comes the next phase of the unfoldment. To Saint Germain's disciples have been entrusted the task of actually publicizing the Divine Plan and urging the people to cooperate with the Aquarian Age program of restoring the planet Earth to its rightful place as Freedom's Star. In the Cosmic Records the name of our great Aquarian Light-bearer is not Sanctus Germanus. Our "holy brother" is known as Freedom. The earth is known as His Star, or Freedom's Star, for He has labored steadily for more than 70,000 years, without respite, to bring this planet to its present point of evolutionary unfoldment.

This planet has a pulsing heart center at the core of the earth, but it likewise has a pulsing heart upon the surface— the United States of America. Surrounding this power source are the great American continents—north, central and south. Saint Germain might have had His Ascension over seventy thousand years ago, but He refused in order to re-main in embodiment, close to his people, and guide them to Freedom. His active work for freedom on Freedom's Star now stems from the American heart center. He has worked through thousands of years in close association with the Ascended Being known as Lady Nada, Who was recently appointed Chohan of the Sixth Ray. Saint Germain and Lady Nada have brought civilization after civilization into the Light, despite every obstacle presented by the dark forces. They will bring our civilization into the Light, and it is the great privilege of humanity to assist Them in this phase of the Divine Plan.

These are the things it is necessary to review when we consider such a concept as free energy, and such mechan-isms as those presented by Tesla, Matthews and Carr. These men are pioneers, but there will be many, many others, all working toward the Light, until all humanity will be illumined. The mechanisms already described, all based on the free-energy concept, whether invented by strug-gling disciples, or Beings already Ascended, like Tesla and

Leonora, all point to one thing—the hour of freedom is here. It is not some dreamy, metaphysical concept: it is a reality. It is the freedom that leads to man's Ascension: it is freedom from the curse of drudgery.

No longer will coal, petroleum and gas hold humanity in enslavement. Existence limited by that type of primitive power will shortly come to an end, and with the changeover to free energy will come an entirely new way of life: an economic system based on unlimited abundance instead of scarcity, maximum leisure and a work schedule devoted only to those constructive creative efforts designed to produce heaven on earth in accordance with the Divine Plan for this planet.

Tesla held this vision for humanity as a sacred and inviolate trust. Even when the dark forces, entrenched behind the world money racket, made it impossible for him to develop his world wireless system for power distribution, and when the same forces of evil, entrenched behind the world political racket, made it impossible for his anti-war machine to be accepted, Tesla's faith never wavered. Even when the Dove bade him farewell and told him he must leave his physical plane work, Tesla felt no sense of frustration or defeat, for he knew the physical activities would continue as usual through his many disciples.

He knew well the face of his Father, and his brushes with evil forces on the physical plane touched him but lightly. At the moment we are still faced with the same problems that faced Tesla, but the old order changeth swiftly.

After Tesla tried to get the various governments to accept the anti-war machine in 1935 and failed, he asked Arthur H. Matthews to continue working on the design and to experiment with certain improvements. He had assigned the work to Matthews in 1934 and it has been in his trust since that date. Matthews has operated an experimental workshop in Canada since 1904. It was in this laboratory, near Quebec, that he built the Tesla interplanetary communications set, in 1947.

Arthur Matthews was a boy in England and his father, an electrical engineer, was working there with Lord Kelvin, when he first met Tesla. Kelvin had become interested in Tesla's wonderful new discovery of wireless or radio, and had invited Tesla to come to England to discuss the subject. It was there that the lifelong friendship began between Tesla and the Matthews, father and son. The three worked together until the death of Mr. Matthews, the father, in 1915. Then Arthur Matthews carried on until Tesla left the physical plane in 1943, and has continued the activity since.

During his last years, after the farewell of the Dove, Tesla turned over a vast amount of material to Matthews in trust and confidence. He had in earlier years inspired Otis T. Carr to pursue 30 years of basic research leading to the present development of the Carr free-energy devices and the Carr spaceship. Apparently Tesla did not acquaint John J. O'Neill with any of these facts, because O'Neill claimed that Tesla had left a few papers in his safe and that these comprised the extent of his heritage.

In fact, when Tesla died in New York City on the night of January 7, 1943, it was generally assumed that his earthly work was finished. The forces of darkness rejoiced at news of his death which they considered most opportune. The world was at war and under pressure of this need the patents of Tesla were considered as royal plunder. The government agents moved in swiftly and seized all papers which Tesla had left in his safe, never suspecting that the incomparable genius had left them there merely to satisfy the idle curiosity of nosey people.

Later, after due inspection and after World War II, most of the papers were considered of such little value that they were turned over to the Tesla Institute in Belgrade, despite the fact that Tito was in power in that country. The Yugoslav Institute recently published, in English, a very impressive volume which they indicate is definitive, and which lists about 85 Tesla patents, together with reprints of some of his lectures and a brief story of his life.

However, Arthur Matthews is acquainted with at least 1,200 inventions, very important inventions, perfected by Tesla. He is only amused when he inspects recently published volumes, such as the Yugoslav book and another new American book, purporting to set forth the true facts about Tesla. These researchers have scraped the bottom of the barrel trying to turn up Tesla's inventions, but they all seem to stop when they reach No. 85, falling 1,115 short of the correct total.

Many top-flight scientists seek out Arthur Matthews these days in a belated attempt to "pump" him for information about Tesla's discoveries. But Arthur Matthews wisely keeps his own counsel; he also keeps the confidence and trust which Tesla bestowed upon him. However, the scientists do not go away empty-handed, even if they do depart with an empty head. Mr. Matthews gives to each and every one a sound piece of advice which he, himself, has tested over the years, and which he has found to be the ultimate goal for all seekers.

"Every time we wish to do something," he says, "we should go to God first for wisdom, because He is the Author of all science. Tesla was able to accomplish so much and see into the future because he understood God. From my own personal contacts with the space people, I find that their advancement is due to their faith and their obedience to Divine Law."

We might pause here and remember that the laggards lagged only because they had lost their faith in God and refused to serve the Light.

The scientists who visit Matthews usually arrive heavily burdened with many university degrees and much learning. but. as they confess, they somehow missed Tesla and now they would like to know something about him. Tucked under their arm is the new communist-issued volume on Tesla which they have just purchased in order to bone up on the subject of the great scientist who did his major work in the United States. But something is either wrong with them or wrong with the book, because the two cannot get together. So they trek all the way to Quebec, and far beyond Quebec, out into the deep countryside of lakes and forests. in order to seek out Matthews in the hope of getting some light on the subject of Tesla's theories. which they admit they cannot grasp.

Mr. Matthews receives them in his serene and cordial way. and then he tells them, as kindly as he can, "If you would understand Tesla, you must first attune your mind to God." Since the unfortunate scientists usually know less about God than they know about Tesla, the result is confusion worse confounded.

Since publication of *Return of the Dove* was first announced over a year ago, the forces of darkness, especially in the United States, have become very active in their efforts to suppress the truth about Tesla. Matthews and Carr have been ridiculed repeatedly, and often by the very scientists and government officials who sought their advice. The present author has received hundreds upon hundreds of letters praising her efforts, but she has received a few telling her she is just plain crazy. The writers do not explain why they think so, but they just think so. Oddly enough, these critical letters, so naive they might have been written by a somewhat retarded schoolboy, come only from men who call themselves experts and authorities.

They are experts, to be sure, but it must be clearly understood that they are experts in working for the dark forces only; they are authorities on the subject of evil; they are the chosen tools of the black magicians who roamed the astral plane freely and even the physical plane until just before the opening days of World War II, when they met their come-uppance from the Forces of Light.

It was at that time that the great Prince of the Archangels, Lord Michael, in one mighty herculean effort, led the Forces of Light against the forces of evil and put the last of the black magicians on this planet out of business permanently and forever. There has not been such a house-cleaning on this earth since the laggards came.

After He finished that mopping up operation Michael cleaned out a horrible astral center which had hovered over Africa since Lemurian days, releasing thousands and thousands of earthbound entities who had been trapped there for countless centuries. This astral cloud had so lowered the vibrations in Africa that the country became historically known as a land of darkness—the dark continent.

Michael's angelic legions were lined up, tier upon tier,

so that they formed a dome over the astral cloud, and as the trapped souls were cut free they floated upward, each one ballooning right into the arms of a waiting angel. They were carried swiftly away to Temples of the Violet Fire. and today these millions of disembodied ones are being healed, purified, and trained, so that they can be restored to civilization at some future date.

The entire astral cloud of contamination so dreadful it is impossible to imagine, was then dissolved by legions of angels firing it through and through with lightning-like bolts of Ray energy. The released matter, so long and so cruelly imprisoned, was carried back to the sun for repolarization.

But that was not all, for Michael then tackled His third great housecleaning job in the astral region over Siberia. where for countless centuries a Compound had been maintained for disembodied souls who had refused to serve the Light.

In the astral cloud over Africa the earthbound souls were all persons who had failed to develop much intelligence when in embodiment. They were so retarded in evolution and so attached to matter, that they simply had no desire to learn or to handle new experiences. They did not refuse to serve the Light, because they were not able to even generate enough energy to make a decision one way ōr the other. They had free will, and they could have freed themselves from bondage, received training, and then returned into incarnation. But they simply did not wish to be bothered.

But the tens of thousands of disembodied individuals who were held in the Compound were of an entirely different caliber. While in physical incarnation they had sat in high places. They had educational advantages and trained intellects. They had swayed large masses of people by their opinions and activities. They had positions as military leaders, theologians, fortune makers, doctors, scientists and teachers. But they were confirmed skeptics — ambitious, cunning, proud, and extremely expedient. They never missed an advantage, regardless of resultant harm to others. They were basically criminal but outwardly respectable. They were all tools of black magicians, devoting their lives on earth to serving the forces of darkness. They knew about the Forces of Light, but ridiculed all those who tried to serve the Light in a simple and practical manner, free from orthodox trappings.

Over the centuries, as these individuals shed their physical bodies, their vibrations magnetically drew them into the Compound. In order to spare the population needless suffering, these tyrants were not permitted to reincarnate. Neither were they permitted to mingle with other disembodied persons on the astral plane. If they decided through the exercise of their own free will to serve the Light, they knew they would be immediately freed from the Compound and could resume a normal existence. But so great was their rebellion that they remained bottled up and isolated as the years passed, their monotony broken only by the endless quarreling among themselves, and the arrival of newcomers.

Finally a sufficient number of disciples on earth became conscious of conditions in the Compound so that by combining their invocative strength they could do something about lifting some of the karma. They offered their assistance in making calls on behalf of the prisoners. If an individual in incarnation asks for help for another, whether embodied or disembodied, under Divine Law that help must be given.

But the assistance granted depends upon the amount of energy expended by the person who is making the request. A half-hearted request calls forth a half-hearted response.

That is why most people complain that their prayers are not answered. A sincere request is in effect a demand and it is not only the privilege, but the duty, of an evolving god to demand whatever he requires for his successful evolvement. A begging attitude or a servile approach to God will result in nothing, except possibly more trouble. God is a good God and He wants only perfection, only abundance, only beauty, only harmony for His children. The only demand that will penetrate to the higher spheres is a demand for these attributes. When a person demands harmony in his life and affairs, he immediately sets the Law into motion and is granted assistance by Masters and angels alike.

So much energy was expended by disciples in requesting help for those in the Compound that finally Lord Michael Himself was able to take action. The calls for help were continued over a period of years, until finally in 1957 the last prisoner left the Compound, using his free will to make the constructive choice to serve the Light. The Compound has now been demagnetized and dissolved and will not be set up again. Under the Aquarian system all disembodied persons are required to remain in Temples of the Violet Fire until their personal rebellions are transmuted.

The dissolution of the Compound will also have a refreshing and wholesome effect on the unhappy land of Siberia, and, in fact, on vibrations throughout Russia, and even throughout the world. The Compound was located in the area over Siberia because at one time, in long ages past, that physical territory was the focus for such extreme evil that Sanat Kumara ordered the land to be frozen. It is not

always necessary to submerge an evil land: a deep freeze
is just as effectual sometimes.

In this instance the angelic kingdom was called upon to
freeze the Siberian territory, and they did such a thorough
job in such a fast, efficient manner, that today bodies of
animals are being dug up from the ground in a frozen
state, and, in some instances, they still have grass in their
mouth. In other words, when the big frost came, they did
not even have time to swallow their last mouthful of food.
Incidentally, the land has now been ordered to be defrosted
and the polar ice caps melted in preparation for the Aquarian Age and new population movements. Scientists speak
of ice ages and assume that such catastrophes were accidents
of nature. But ice ages were planned, ordered affairs, designed to stop evil in its tracks.

It is Lord Michael who cooperated with Saint Germain in
the tremendous task of straightening the axis of the earth.
This work was handled entirely by the angelic kingdom, but
the great cosmic entities, Polaris and Magnus, governing the
North Star and South Star Rays, where these Rays meet
at the center of the earth, have cooperated in making the
axis project possible at this time.

Actually the long years of planetary housecleaning conducted by Lord Michael were preliminary to the axis project,
for it was necessary to lift the heavy karmic burden of the
earth and clear out much of the astral contamination before
the angelic host could work on the bent axis. Furthermore,
since it was the karmic burden that first caused the axis to
bend, there was assuredly no purpose in straightening it until
the weight of karma was considerably lessened.

Now that the axis is straightened and the Ray forces
can act on the planet in a direct rather than an eccentric

manner, changes will take place with incredible speed. These
changes will occur among disciples almost at once, because
disciples have long worked for the new Aquarian order.
They welcome change and are not frightened by mounting
evidence that the old order is being swept away. They understand the Divine Plan which the Hierarchy is trying to
precipitate and they want to serve as co-workers in that precipitation. They have supreme faith only in God and have
no faith whatever in man-made institutions wherein God is
not recognized as a co-worker. Therefore, they are not dis-
tracted by the glamour of militarism, politics, economics,
and churchianity, because they have not placed their trust
in these booby-traps.

Arthur H. Matthews clearly declared the depth of his
dedication to New Age developments when he advised seekers to go straight to God, as Tesla had done. Tesla did not
fear change even when it meant that his new inventions
would obsolete his earlier ones. Nor did he ever attempt
to harbor secrets concerning his discoveries. Arthur Matthews has pointed out that the lectures which Tesla gave in
London and in America between the years 1889 to 1894
contain all information that is needed to construct virtually
all devices patented by Tesla. These lectures have been collected and printed in book form, and have been available
at least in all major libraries throughout the western world
since the turn of the century. Yet hundreds of readers have
scanned them and passed them by as interesting but not
practical.

Mr. Matthews attributes this lack of realism to the darkness in which men's minds are immersed—the darkness of
materialism. He says that Tesla's lectures cannot be understood by those whose minds are not attuned to God. Mat-

thews has actually tested out this theory in the presence of top-flight scientists and engineers who visited him to inspect the Tesla set for interplanetary communication.

These men looked at the set; they asked questions which were frankly answered. Mr. Matthews even went beyond that point and gave several hints, but not one seeker could even guess at the underlying scientific principles which Tesla had discovered and which made the set possible.

Yet these same scientists and engineers and hundreds more of their kind are the very men who are called into government service and who are supported by the taxpayers. They are presumed to have sufficient intelligence to handle whatever scientific problems arise in the course of their work. Yet the greater part of their energy is expended in trying to maintain an attitude of secrecy so that the long-suffering taxpayers will not find out the cold scientific facts advanced by Tesla even before the year of 1900.

How many Americans know that Tesla designed the Sphere, a powerless aircraft that the Allies might have used to end World War I even before November, 1918; and that might have been used to launch an air age forty years ago which would have rivalled the jet age of 1958? And how many Americans know even today that Tesla had designed another aircraft far superior to the Sphere, and that he actually built a model of it in 1893?

And how many people in the world today realize that Tesla knew all about cosmic rays long before the turn of the century, and that in 1891 Tesla built a cosmic ray engine, a free-energy device, to utilize the rays, which, like God and electricity, are everywhere? Just as an electric generator by force or by some other action brings electricity into motion, so did Tesla's cosmic ray engine bring the rays into motion.

Tesla was the original discoverer of so-called radio waves and invented the wireless to utilize these waves. But Tesla knew that the operation of radio waves depended upon ground currents and induction; therefore they were earthbound and their action extremely limited. When Tesla designed the set for interplanetary communications, he therefore avoided the use of radio waves. The set will not receive on any frequency used on earth. The small model which Mr. Matthews built is designed to receive from spaceships which are at least 5,000 miles above the surface of the earth and not more than 30,000 miles distant.

Mr. Matthews believes that our entire electrical system as used here on earth will not work beyond 8,000 miles out in space. However, when he first contacted spaceships on the Tesla set, the space people told him that our radio waves did not reach much beyond 5,000 miles, and that it is impossible to send a message on the present Tesla set from a spaceship more than 35,000 miles distant. Mr. Matthews has since started construction of a new set which is expected to provide a wider range, and he is incorporating many of his own discoveries in it, although it follows the basic Tesla design.

The interplanetary communications set is, however, only an interesting gadget. Like the telephone, it requires someone on the other end to make conversation; otherwise, it is simply connected with the silence of space. The set has no commercial value whatsoever, as the space people have no time to engage in idle chit-chat, and they are assuredly not in the entertainment business. They use the set only when they have an important message to give to Mr. Matthews and do not wish to take the time to land on his property and speak to him personally.

They explained to him in the very first conversation, that they had contacted him on the set because of his great faith in Tesla, the Venusian they had brought to earth as a baby in 1856. They have, in recent years, made a world-wide survey to find out exactly what we have done with Tesla's inventions. They have also probed the depths of our hatred for each other, which is the main reason why most Tesla inventions have not been utilized, and they have reached the conclusion that, according to normal standards in this solar system, the entire population of the earth must be considered insane.

When the space people landed for a personal interview with Mr. Matthews they were primarily interested in stimulating renewed activity in the Tesla anti-war machine. They found the Canadian location of the Matthews property ideal for the landing of their ships. They had previously given Mr. Matthews details of spaceship construction, size, shape, and so forth, in talks on the Tesla set.

Mr. Matthews has described his place in detail in his letters, and it does sound so delightful that it probably reminded the space people of our lovely, flower-decked globe which we enjoyed before the laggards came.

"Our place was originally an old Quebec farm," Mr. Matthews writes. "I love trees, so I planted many thousands of them to offer shelter, to attract the birds, and for their beauty alone. My little electrical shack is just that—a small rough building surrounded by trees; just like a hen in her nest, and just large enough to hold me, a desk, bench, books and tools.

"Besides this small shack we have the barn—really a

barn—which we use for the larger stuff. But our real laboratory is the land, the open fields and bush: the mountain and the river. Here we study closely with God; it is wonderful what one can do when we walk with the Master!

"At one time we had a wonderful flower garden, but as the children grew up and got married off, and my lady and I traveled, we could not devote the necessary time to it: so at the moment we have a lovely garden of weeds, neck-high, but the flowers do shoot through the tangle. Besides, we have a lovely inside-the-house garden. You know—flower pots which do clutter up, and which keep me busy watering when their slave is away. Off-hand I cannot say how many flower pots there are, but they are plentiful!

"Anyhow, I use every bit of this property. In the winter I work in the old farmhouse which has stood here for over 200 years and which, like us, is old-fashioned. I have always been a tinker and always have something to fix for someone, from dolls to power plants. Then we must take time to listen to the wants and troubles of others, for there is always someone requiring help, which is our great joy to give, for this is our obligation to Him.

"In the early spring we start traveling, and most summers are spent this way, visiting and helping others. By faith I am a Christian Scientist, but let us always remember that Christ was and is the only true scientist.

"Mary Baker Eddy discovered a very wonderful thing in the Bible when she discovered Christian Science. Most people do not understand it, but even a slight study of her works does give one a better understanding of the Bible. I first obtained her works in 1937 and have found wonderful help through their study. It gives one a deeper sense of God and things outside our earth.

"You have, no doubt, noted the mention of spaceships in the Bible?

"I am a member of the Laymen's Movement for A Christian World. I am a Christian and don't care a hoot who knows it. I'm not a bit ashamed to display my belief in public. People who deny God are nuts.

"I have studied every branch of science, but I see pure science only in the work of God. I don't believe in pretense, bluff, bull or humbug. I never doubt anything until it is proved by demonstration and by every test to be impossible. I also believe that all things which man can think of are possible.

"In this work concerning Tesla we must expect the materialistic world to be against us. That is our Cross, but be of good courage, for God never fails those who have faith in Him. Having a true understanding of God we can do anything so long as we serve as witnesses for the Christ. We have the supreme power of God on our side in preparing the world for the return of the Christ, and I believe spaceships have a great deal to do with it. There is nothing impossible, for Christ is with us, and the spirit of Tesla is with us. All we need is the will and courage to continue our present efforts. God will provide the wisdom and point the way.

"You may use any material which I supply so long as it will be helpful in witnessing for the Christ, but I do not want any cheap publicity. As far as I can understand, the coming of the spaceships to earth ties in with the spiritual revival which seems to be worldwide in action, and the tone of several messages I have received recently on the Tesla set points that way, too.

"On my summer trips I take the Tesla set right along

with me in case the space people wish to send through any messages. We combine business and pleasure on our long trips, for I usually do some research. We travel slowly and stop along the way to serve and help, and to share our knowledge with others, for that is a practical way of applying Divine Law and is far better than preaching.

"We do all kinds of work on these trips. We sketch, write, paint, consult, draw, lecture, hold prayer meetings, and help wherever we can. Nothing is either too big or too small, from fixing a radio, knitting a sock, or building a transmission line. Of course, we have a wonderful time and there is nothing like having God on the tow!

"I just draw for pleasure. I'm no expert and never had a lesson. I sketch, paint with oil, water, and colored pencil, from life, just to rest on the trips.

"I have been on earth a long time, so require some rest. I drive slowly and never over three hundred miles a day, which is enough, considering that most of it is via Canada gravel. If I have any trouble I either fly or jump a train."

Mr. Matthews sent along some snapshots to us in the early days of our correspondence, so we knew that his description of his farmstead was indeed inadequate. But we were in no sense prepared for our first actual glimpse of the magnificent land of mountains and forests and open skies which greeted us on our first visit to this Canadian home.

It was autumn, and just at that moment of greatest loveliness when all Nature seems to hold its breath and say: "No, no, we cannot let this rapture fade. Let us hold this jewelled, this lighted moment forever! Let us breathe this wine-bright air; let us send forth our vision into the limitless blueness of space; let us dwell forever amid these jewel-tinted forests! Let us listen only to Wisdom spoken unto us by the Voice of Solitude!"

Then suddenly we were standing on historic ground— the great, sloping meadow that sweeps down from a forested mountain, aflame with autumn colors. "Here," said Mr. Matthews, "is where the ships land. This meadow, protected by the mountain at the back and the rise of ground at the front, forms a comfortable hollow in which the spaceships can nestle like birds."

He went on to explain that the first ship which came winging its way through the dark, moonless night, safe from prying eyes of the merely curious or the hostile, was a mother ship. "It was seven hundred feet in diameter," said Mr. Matthews, "three hundred feet high, with a center tube fifty feet in diameter. It held twenty-four small ships, each one from seventy-five to one hundred feet in diameter. None of the ships had windows as we know them, but the crew could obtain a full view on all sides by a device which somewhat resembles television. The ship was of Venusian origin."

Mr. Matthews emphasized the fact that all his contacts, both on the set and personally, had been with real, living, material persons, not spirits. He does not hold with mediumship or communication with the dead, for he believes that we can all be in contact with God—the only true Spirit— through the living Christ. He believes that all of us can receive comfort and other help from the Christ, and that only those who study spaceship information in the Bible and seek wisdom from God can ever understand the things of space.

Mr. Matthews has here touched upon a point which has proved to be an almost insurmountable handicap to many lifestreams who would otherwise go forward quickly into the Light, and take their place beside the other disciples in active service. The barrier which individuals place before themselves, and which keeps them immersed in psychism, is a tendency based upon morbid sentimentalism and the wrong use of the memory function.

During the past few years, since the public has become aware of visitors from outer space, the earth has been literally flooded with messages from so-called space people, most of which proved to be phoney.

Hundreds of mediums took advantage of the interest in space to pour out endless messages of meaningless drivel, purportedly coming from the space people themselves, or from disembodied relatives and friends of the eager listeners. These disembodied ones presumably knew all about spaceship activities, according to their story, which is ridiculous on the face of it. Disembodied entities until very recently, were confined to the astral plane as long as they had a tendency to waste their time in gossip, which is the proper term for the type of communication in which they indulged. A genuine space person avoids the astral plane as we would avoid a plague. A genuine space person knows that he is making the sacrifice of coming to the earth in order to abolish death on the planet—certainly not to encourage it.

Ordinary mediums who seek to contact the astral plane and the disembodied, are not used as channels by the space people, no matter what the mediums may say to the contrary. This entire psychic situation was running riot in 1956, but it cleared noticeably in 1957. Mediums today are no longer receiving exciting messages from the astral plane because they can no longer contact disembodied persons. The vibrations which mediums contact today come from thoughtforms on the physical or astral plane, or from astral shells. The whole psychic lure is waning. This is because of the drastic action taken on the Inner Planes by the Hierarchy in an effort to get the disembodied ready for reincarnation in the New Age.

In addition to the housecleaning by Lord Michael, the Aquarian Age fiat has gone forth which requires that the disembodied study, render service, and spend a certain portion of their time each day in the Temples of the Violet Fire, transmuting their karma and preparing for activity in the new civilization.

The unwholesome habit of embodied individuals seeking contact with dead relatives or friends must be ended if people are ever to restore normal contact with their Source. It must certainly be ended if death itself is to be abolished on this planet. Attempted communication with the dead is not only distracting to both the embodied and disembodied, but leads to a sense of smug satisfaction which prevents contact with the higher vibrations of the Forces of Light. There is nothing to be gained by seeking advice from a disembodied person; there is heaven to be gained by seeking advice from the Christ-Self within each beating heart.

Space people, or people from other planets and stars, are much more highly evolved than earth people. Otherwise, they would not be allowed to come to this planet, because we have trouble enough of our own without importing more from the outside. Therefore, space people, with their higher vibratory rate, fall into the same evolutionary category as our own Masters and Adepts who are members of our own Spiritual Hierarchy.

Tesla, being a Venusian, cannot be classed as a disembodied astral entity. He will not be found on the astral plane. If a medium makes a supposed contact with Tesla, the medium is only contacting a thoughtform hovering in the astral atmosphere—but not the real man—for psychics cannot reach vibrations beyond the astral plane. A person who is overshadowed by an Adept—either from this earth or from some other planet—is not in contact with the astral plane. Adepts do not work from that plane.

It has come to the attention of this author that certain mediums, much given to lower psychism, have claimed contact with Tesla. This is not correct and they have contacted only a thoughtform. Tesla can overshadow his disciples or can communicate telepathically if a definite purpose is being served for all humanity and for the Christ Forces. Moreover, he works only with those persons who are already affiliated with Hierarchial Ashrams established by the Forces of Light. No Adept who is genuine has any time to waste giving trivial messages to trivial people.

It is a well-known fact that members of the Hierarchy and also space people have spent considerable time contacting officials of all governments on the earth, and also scientists and church leaders. They felt duty-bound to do this, but having performed that duty, and having met only with hostility, they are now limiting their contacts to those individuals who can assist in some manner in carrying out the Divine Plan.

It has often been remarked in recent months that certain individuals who had excellent contacts with space people, now seemingly have lost contact. Exactly the same thing has happened with disciples who have, at certain times, been in touch with members of the Hierarchy for the express purpose of serving as an outpost of consciousness for an Ascended Being. In a case where an Ascended Master withdraws from contact with a disciple, or a space person ceases contact, the human being is always at fault. In some manner, the energy expended by the Adept has been misused by the one in human embodiment, and withdrawal is always the result.

This is not a sign of disfavor. It is a sign that the Adept knows that the burden of knowledge is more than the human can bear, and therefore the withdrawal is definitely a favor. Sometimes those who have lost contact with Ascended Masters or space people make the dreadful mistake of permitting pride to hold sway, and they pretend or fake contacts. This is a pathetic situation, and certainly calls for an application of the dictum that honesty is the best policy. No single individual has a monoply on the Divine Plan, and the teachings of the Ageless Wisdom are available to all. This is an age of freedom, and it is useless to pretend that special knowledge is granted only to special individuals. All knowledge is available to all, but it must be used to uplift all humanity, not to build a personal ivory tower of pride and prejudice.

The Divine Plan will emerge among the people—the ordinary man in the street, the housewife, the shop and office workers. It will most assuredly not emerge as a super-government, or as another church. It will not emerge among scientists who are slaves to the military; nor will it emerge among professors and teachers who are likewise enslaved by a barbaric educational system that is completely controlled by the forces of darkness. Therefore, the space people are only interested in contacting free souls; individuals who can speak, write and lecture without fear; persons who understand that those who snicker and sneer, those who shout and threaten, are merely tools for the dark forces.

The dark forces have been practicing their subtle tyranny for millions of years, but they have been especially successful since newspapers became commonplace. Newspaper editors and reporters readily respond to the lowest of human vibrations, for their business is the reporting of crime, war, and trouble of any sort. Good news is no news to a reporter. Their gullibility is the same today in their attitude toward spaceships, as it was in 1873 when a Boston newspaper published the following piece under the sensational title: *Beware the Inventor.*

"A man about 46 years of age, giving the name of Joshua Coppersmith, has been arrested in New York for attempting to extort funds from ignorant and superstitious people by exhibiting a device which he says will convey the human voice any distance over metallic wires, so that it will be heard by the listener at the other end.

"He calls the instrument a 'telephone' which is obviously intended to imitate the word 'telegraph', and win the confidence of those who know of the success of the latter instrument without understanding the principle on which it is based. Well informed people know that is is impossible to transmit the human voice over wires as may be done with dots and dashes and signals of the Morse Code, and that were it possible to do so, the thing would be of no practical value.

"The authorities who apprehended this criminal are to be congratulated, and it is to be hoped that his punishment will be prompt and fitting, that it may serve as an example to other conscienceless schemers who enrich themselves at the expense of their fellow creatures."

It was thought at one time that Mr. Matthews might bring the Tesla set for interplanetary communication to

New York and other cities and demonstrate it, but the space people informed him that such a demonstration would be useless at the present time. The doubters would still doubt, and even if they saw the machine and heard the messages they would still insist it was a trick of some sort. Apparently, there has not been much progress in these parts since the days of Joshua Coppersmith.

But there is another difficulty connected with bringing the Tesla set to New York. The set works on a very fine beam —finer than a hair, according to Tesla. The spaceships, flying at altitudes up to 25,000 miles, have worked out calculations whereby they can beam their signals to the set which is always in an exact location. The signal is not received if the set is moved even a few inches. Therefore, if the set is to operate in another city, it would be necessary to make prior arrangements with the space people, such as Mr. Matthews makes on his summer trips.

Furthermore, the space people do not warn Mr. Matthews when they wish to send their signals. He has rigged up an alarm on the set which rings if the spaceship is ready to send a message. If he is somewhere near the set he hears the alarm and answers.

It can readily be seen that the operation of the set is entirely in the hands of the space people. They have requested Mr. Matthews not to give out information on the construction of the set at this time. The reason is that this type of willing service only encourages laziness among engineers and scientists who are quite capable of building a set if they would apply themselves, and as Mr. Matthews advocates—if they would attune their minds to God, as Tesla did.

Mr. Matthews has explained one basic idea which is not clear in the minds of the average person today. He emphasizes the fact that every radio and television set is a Tesla set. Therefore, an individual cannot have a clear understanding of electronics unless he has a clear understanding of Tesla's basic principles.

Mr. Matthews goes on to say that "no one apart from Tesla has ever made anything new in the way of a radio or television set—except for changes in design. The circuits, coils, condensers, and all important parts are all part of Tesla's basic discovery. So regardless of brand names every set must be a Tesla set.

"However, the set for interplanetary communication is different both in the manner in which it operates, and because it is especially designed to receive signals from space. It is impossible to send ordinary radio waves through the upper layers above the earth. All such signals will bounce back to earth, as is well known to radio hams. Tesla knew this more than fifty years ago. He also knew that the space people would try to get in touch with us from their ships, so he devised this special machine which will receive their signals.

"Now due to the fact that the design was given to me by Tesla in confidence and in trust, to be used for the convenience of the space people when they approached the earth, I could not pass on this information to others without permission. The crew aboard the first space ship that landed on my property told me not to give out the information yet —which means that it can be made available at some time.

"Meanwhile the full directions for building the set can be found in the lectures which Tesla gave between the years of 1890 to 1896, and also in some other lectures which he gave in recent years. What the space people desire is that someone in the United States discover the secret contained in the lectures, build a set, and then give full credit to Tesla.

"The ''dull?' Russians are rapidly discovering the lost secrets of Tesla as they have demonstrated by producing the powerless aircraft Tesla invented for the United States at the close of World War I. But the Russians are giving Tesla full credit for the design.

"I do not know what Russia intends to do with the craft. Of course, the ship can carry the extra weight of bombs, and so forth, because there is no limit to the ground power plant, so it can be powered far beyond the ordinary plane. Besides the motor in the plane does not require any direct connection or fuel, so the craft is relieved of that weight. This machine was also reported in Tesla's old lectures, or at least the motor was described.

"The idea can also be adapted for both land and sea transportation. More than twenty years ago I suggested that it be used to power our trains, and I wrote a paper for the magazine *Railway Electrical Engineer*, but nothing came of it.

"You see how small are the minds of the so-called experts. Here is all this information lying about, wide open to the public, and yet the big-wigs have to spend their time having fun with their space rockets. A number of these experts in both the United States and Canada have been trying to pump me for free information. They are too lazy and too dull to grasp Tesla's principles, so they want me to do all the brain work for them. But meanwhile the Russians are doing their own brain work, giving all due credit to Tesla, and coming up with his discoveries applied to industry.

"The point is that Americans have never used the information that Tesla gave them so freely, and now they are trying to pump me for more—probably with a view to robbing Tesla, even further and making a few million for themselves. Nor does the pumping stop here. I have received letters from all over the world but they just do not have the right kind of bait to catch this fish. Money does not interest me, as it did not interest Tesla.

"Tesla was my lifelong friend and teacher. All I know concerning electrical engineering came from this wonderful man. He has always had first place in my thoughts, second only to God, and because of my faith in him all of my information concerning his discoveries and inventions is first hand. Many of his inventions, to my knowledge, have never been made public, and much of the confidential data which he gave me is not otherwise available. But until and unless these great experts who are riding herd over us today use the information which Tesla has made public, and give him full credit for it, it is useless to give them more.

"For instance, some American big-wig who read some excerpts from your book—*Return of the Dove*—wrote me a couple of letters. He seemed to be afraid that you, Mrs. Storm, would not do Tesla full and proper justice! On the other hand, he was looking for all the free information he thought he could pry out of me. You had not given him my address so he had gone to the trouble to work through a stooge in Glens Falls, and to try to get a line on me through my friends in New York. Finally, he traced me by way of my letters going into the United States to you!

"He said he had heard of my father, and that Tesla had recorded mention of him! But there is a great deal these people do not know. For why should Tesla have confided in people who went out of their way to rob and cheat him? Not one of his so-called friends went out of their way to help him, when help was most needed. But now, oh! now, since these very, very great friends of Tesla have heard of your wonderful work, and of *Return of the Dove,* they are trying to get into the limelight and pretend that they have been there all the time.

"But be of good courage as I know you will, and write as you think best, without regard for the opinions of anyone. Dear Margaret, let not your heart be troubled by these people. That was Christ's command: See that your heart be not troubled. All the troubles on earth can be cured in only one way, and that way is to obey God. So let us teach the truth to all mankind. That is our only aim. So be of good courage; teach the truth, and your faith will carry you on. We both know that the greatest force which can defend us against evil is still God.

"People have not been slow to write me about your work, and there is no question but that your forthcoming book has caused some of them to finally wake up. As this American big-wig wrote: 'The circle of friends of Tesla in the United States have worked devotedly toward the recognition of his accomplishments, etc., etc.'

"Well, if they are so devoted, then why have they been asleep for so long? Or is there something else behind their reaction to your work? It would appear that *Return of the Dove* is a thorn in their tender sides! They don't like it, because all scum fear the light!

"As recently as last night one of our top scientists spent several hours with me. He did his best to obtain information on how true radar works, as conceived by Tesla in 1890. Well, I told him that it works without the use of reflectors, poles, towers, and so forth, and that it contained the germ

THE ARTHUR H. MATTHEWS STORY . 211

of the idea that can explode all the atomic bombs on earth
before they can even leave their home.

"But what these small-minded experts cannot realize is
that Tesla designed radar as part of the anti-war machine.
What the Americans are trying to do is to copy the Tesla
system, of course, with no credit to him, but to use only
the radar part for a defense against attack. If they used the
entire anti-war machine, attack would be impossible and
world disarmament would become an immediate and per-
manent fact.

"This was known in 1935 when Tesla offered the anti-war
machine to various governments. The heads of the allied
governments then in power knew these facts and understood them. There was no excuse whatever for the second
World War. There is still no excuse for what is going on
today.

"For these facts are still known among the great experts, but they are carefully concealed from the taxpayers—
the little people who pay the bills for wars. A working model
of the anti-war machine will cost about two million dollars,
and it will include genuine radar—not the stuff the experts
are fooling around with. Look what a mess they have made
of it, trying to copy something from Tesla by stealing a
part of his work, instead of adopting the anti-war machine
outright.

"Millions are being spent on micro-wave towers for the
so-called Distant Early Warning (DEW) lines, when according to Tesla not one pole, reflector or tower is needed.
This is all utter waste. Even before the line was completed,
even while it was still being designed, it was known that it
would not be effective. Now the daily newspapers are coming out with a hint of the truth in headlines: Radar Defense

Is Full of Holes. The whole thing is just another busted bubble, with millions of dollars wasted.

"That is why I will follow Tesla's instructions to the end. We certainly do not want any of these fine experts messing around with the anti-war machine. I had several letters from Tesla during his last days and as the information he sent me was confidential I intend to keep it that way.

"From first-hand information I know that Tesla did not leave any important notes for the authorities to find. Apart from his letters Tesla had other ways of communicating with me. The clique of big-wigs in the United States does not like this. Neither do the authorities, as I have discovered. When will people wake up and find that they can have no secrets from God?

"Dear Lord, open Thou our eyes that we may see the wonderful things in Thy handiwork, in the Bible, in Tesla's work. That is what I tell the self-styled engineers and scientists who come from your country and mine, always in the hope of pumping me. I tell them all the same thing! Look with open eyes at Tesla's work. If you are a Christian in your inmost heart, if your intentions are good, you will find the answer, for it is very easy to see. But it is only by a close study of the Bible and by a sincere belief in God, that we can see clearly the truth in Tesla's work, and also in that of the Christ.

"I say to these engineers: Study carefully Tesla's patents and lectures. Note the simple way in which he talks. Study carefully the words of Jesus. Note the simple way in which He talks. You engineers have failed to discover the secret of one important thing—and there are many others. You are looking for the narrow radio beam, less than one degree.

Only Tesla knew how to make it. It is clearly stated in his lectures, yet the engineers cannot find it.

"I could build Tesla's anti-war machine at any time, and could blow up all the atomic and H-bombs in the world. But of what use would that be? It would only destroy. It would not serve God. It would not help mankind. Peace can never come by man-made means of destruction imposed upon humanity. So why try? Why bother? Peace can come only from the hearts of the people when their hearts are untroubled—when they really want to obey God and carry out His commands. The anti-war machine can be installed only when the people want it, in their hearts.

"Another big waste today is in the television field. Not one of those tall TV towers is required. TV can be transmitted to any part of the world without any form of pole or tower, and this has been known since the turn of the century. The public assumes that all of this equipment is needed, but it is utter waste and is just used in order to provide bigger money profits. Any excuse is good enough, and the public is impressed when it sees all those big towers going up.

"It is the same with the World Wireless System for electrical distribution which Tesla invented. No poles, towers or wires are required. No expensive surveying. No useless manufacturing.

"The Tesla anti-war machine follows the same principle. It requires no poles, no lines, or large reflectors mounted on towers. Neither does it require an army to maintain it. It does provide positive protection for any coast line or national border. It is not, in any sense, a fence. The whole thing depends upon the "peaks" which are, of course, invisible to the human eye. All electric currents of whatever frequency pass in the earth and can be made to 'peak' or bounce up above the earth at regular measured distances.

"So far as the sputniks and other orbiting devices are concerned, these could not be designed to drop destruction on us from above if the Tesla anti-war machine was functioning. In addition to the protecting wall of light, the machine can also be built with a ceiling. If Tesla's machine is adopted there is nothing that can affect it—nothing in the way of an A-bomb or H-bomb or any other bomb, even if it is transported on a missile, a rocket, or a sputnik.

"In the first place—and this is the important point—once Tesla's machine is set up, no form of bomb or high explosive can be made. In other words, if some nut tried to make a bomb and Tesla's machine was functioning, the bomb would explode right there, whether underground or in the air or any place else, and the nut would be blown to bits along with it.

"So along with the adoption of the Tesla idea no form of bomb or high explosive, such as an A-bomb or H-bomb would continue to exist. For instance, if the United States decided to adopt Tesla's idea, she would notify all other countries of the date on which the switch would be thrown, giving them time to dump all forms of high explosives. Then on a certain date she would throw the switch. After that date, if any bombs existed, they would automatically explode. Even though some way could be discovered to protect the bombs temporarily—and that seems impossible— the moment someone tried to use them they would blow up, killing the user.

"But just supposing it might be possible for someone to send a missile with an H-bomb over the country. Of what use would it be? Simply to destroy? Because if the Tesla anti-war machine was in use no one could enter the country. And after we saw the bomb coming, or even after it blew part of us up, we could still, from behind the wall of light, blow the enemy to bits and without the use of a single rocket.

"Rockets aimed at us would be useless, as would bombs in actuality, because anything would explode when it got within 200 miles of the wall, even if by some fantastic method it could be protected up to that point. So all these speculations really have no practical value, but they do help us to understand that Tesla thought of every possibility and prepared for every eventuality.

"Although Tesla himself loathed all deadly devices, nevertheless he knew that plenty of other people preferred war to God's peace. So when he designed the anti-war machine, he first worked out in detail all the possible weapons the machine might be called upon to destroy. He designed a jet-propelled airplane and an atomic bomb, the whole device radio-controlled, and able to cover a distance of 12,000 miles! And this was long ago. Tesla could easily look a hundred years into the future.

"In a letter which Tesla wrote to me in 1935, he said, speaking of his anti-war machine: 'My discovery ends the menace of airplanes, submarines, rockets or space machines, regardless of their height or speed. A century from now every nation will render itself immune from attack by my device.'

"I believe, as I believe in God, that the adoption of Tesla's machine will prevent war. Actually I have been fighting for Tesla since 1928, and have written hundreds of letters, newspaper and magazine articles about his inventions, so the world should know about this wonderful man."

Yes, indeed, the world should know about Tesla, but

the hundreds of letters received by Mr. Matthews and by the present author indicate clearly that most people are just finding out how to spell his name. Almost every letter received begins something like this: "I never heard of Nikola Tesla until I read your excerpts from *Return of the Dove*. Where can I find out more about this wonderful man?"

Well, no one will find out more about this wonderful man if the Silence Group has its way. Since the day that Tesla was brought to the earth from Venus he has been plagued by the Silence Group. This is a carefully organized super-secret group within the forces of darkness. It has functioned on this earth down through millions of years, directed by black magicians who were bent upon destroying humanity rather than permit the race to become merged with the Forces of Light. During nineteen million years Sanat Kumara and His Hierarchs have steadfastly defeated the forces of evil at every turn, and all without doing any damage to the delicately adjusted balance of free will, a balance which is the only spiritual guarantee of human evolution into the Light.

During the late '30's the last of the black magicians was caught during a moment when he had let down his guards, and he was removed from the planet. Prior to that time the Forces of Light had been catching up with the black magicians, one by one, and removing them. This was the last character of his kind. Capturing a black magician and all his evil links is not easy and it is very unlovely. Many disciples prefer not to talk about it, but in these tragic times it seems that the dear public should be able to bear up under some of these startling revelations, wake up to what is going on around them, and become aware of conditions which they are often unwittingly supporting to the hilt.

A black magician always operates in an astral body but he usually has a physical flesh body hidden away in a cave to serve as an anchorage for his contaminated energy. He usually steals this flesh body for he is too shrewd to incarnate, even if he could find parents, and besides he does not wish to be hampered by a physical body which he must tend and care for. He prefers to employ thousands of human tools who do not know that they are being used for his purposes. He can manipulate them, through their little egos, without their ever suspecting that they are being played for suckers.

Some of these human tools at the very top of the heap do know their boss, but they are virtually black adepts in their own right so secrets are safe with them. It is these wise guys and dolls at the top who form the Invisible Government or the Silence Group, which is still in control today on the physical plane only. Invisible, that is, to all but the Christ Forces.

Those heads remain very secluded, and, in turn, hand down directives to their stooges who are active in politics, churchianity, diplomacy, banking and economics, education, and in every line of commerce and industry which is in any sense associated with big business. Today they are especially active in connection with newspapers, magazines, television and radio, which they control through advertising. Because books do not carry advertising the dark forces have never been able to control the book field directly. However, they do control it in subtle ways through various book clubs, and through newspaper advertising, critics, and book shop sales.

The dark forces are very active in the field of medicine, and in connection with drugs, pharmaceutical products, vaccines, and even foods—particularly in foods such as candies, ice cream, bottled drinks, and, of course, in cigarettes, liquors and diversions such as movies. But in these commercial fields, their biggest control goes back to advertising. They use the weapon of fear induced through threats of economic boycott. They are also today very, very active in the utilities field, and in all the big industries connected with petroleum, steel, aluminum, and so forth. They are in complete control of all boom-and-bust cycles, even to spreading the rumor that these are caused by sun-spots!

The black magicians themselves operate and control their tools from the astral plane. Anyone can be a tool, and all of us have been tools at certain times, even though we may not have spent an entire embodiment working at it professionally, so to speak. After nineteen million years of this astral control, the last black magician has been taken and they will trouble the planet no more. But their tools are still functioning in a big way, totally unaware that the last boss has been liquidated. They are due to discover this soon: sometime after the news gets about that the axis of the earth is completely straightened. Then will the darkened minds of humanity begin to get a glimpse of the light.

However, the tools at best are only human, after all, and not always reliable, human nature being what it is. So the black magicians on the astral plane usually had a flesh body stored away somewhere on earth; stored away in a cave somewhere like a hibernating animal. Through this flesh body they could anchor their foul energy firmly in the earth and keep it anchored. The last black magician who was taken had a flesh body hidden away in a cave in western

Europe. The Forces of Light did not intend to remove him astrally and leave this focus of evil behind.

So finally They closed in on his hibernating flesh form and the angelic legions set to work. They found that this particular black magician had fangs which extended out from the face, and then far beyond that area the fangs continued in astral matter. This astral line carried a tremendous charge of evil force, and these lines cut deep into the earth, right through soil and rocks, and extended for miles around the globe. In other words, this character had a firm grip on the situation.

First the angels had to work from the ends of the astral fangs, and draw back into the body itself all the evil force which had been extended through the earth. When all this evil was drawn back into the flesh body the whole mass was transmuted with Violet Fire. Then the weary, liberated atoms were carried back to the sun for repolarization.

If this seems too fantastic to be true, let us glance briefly at the other side of the picture. In certain parts of the world are to be found deposits of diamonds, rubies, emeralds and other precious and semi-precious stones. How did they get there? At those points Adepts of the Christ Forces once lived. They anchored the energy of Light so firmly in the earth, in order to spiritualize the soil and raise the vibrations, that the Ray energy became concretized into lovely gems. Diamonds are concretized First Ray energy, rubies are concretized Sixth Ray energy, emeralds are Fifth Ray energy, and so on. Adepts leave behind them only beauty upon the earth and within the earth.

Naturally, those who are fighting the Forces of Light use similar methods of anchoring energy, but they anchor only ugliness, contamination and astral filth.

It is to be noted that the actual work of cutting away these lines of evil force was handled by the angelic kingdom. The angels took care of the astral cloud over Africa, the Compound over Siberia, and the angels have straightened the axis of the earth. Yet the very people who have been served by the Forces of Light through removal of these evil foci, and by the tremendous job of straightening the axis, are the ones who still feel that they can live without angelic help, and even without giving their Creator more than a passing how-do-you-do on Sunday morning.

These are the very people who are ready to kowtow every time the forces of darkness crack the whip. Most of them are considered nice people. Sometimes they are even pleasant, although they are more often tight-lipped and hostile, angry and rebellious. They sneer and snicker a great deal, too—especially when some clean-minded, open-hearted individual mentions space ships from Venus.

Now that all black magicians have been removed from the earth, the astral plane cleaned up, earthbound entities removed, the Compound emptied of refugees from evolution, and the idle disembodied rounded up and sent to etheric training centers, the picture begins to look brighter for that portion of humanity devoted to serving the Forces of Light.

But for the devotees of the dark forces, the sinister secretives, the greedy grabbers, the warmongers and all the lovers of blood and gore, the conniving politicians and diplomats, and the front pew-sitters in the whitened sepulchres of churchianity — for all these the picture could not look more gloomy. The Forces of Light are going to make sweeping changes on this planet within a very short time, and those who are not in accord with the Forces of Light are in for a very, very, very rough time. If anyone wishes to look with nostalgia over past history, he should take that backward glance right now, because history as we have known it is going to vanish like a dirty fog in a bright, hot sun.

It is a well-known fact that the Silence Group has been responsible for handing down directives to government officials, scientists and church leaders, which have frightened these spineless authorities into keeping all spaceship information from the public. These officials have deliberately hoarded all revealing references to spaceships and space people from other planets.

This hoarding has been directed by the Silence Group composed of top-flight black disciples who are now leaderless. Therefore, the whole Silence Group is due to collapse, carrying their thousands of manipulated human tools into a state of confusion and possibly panic. The various governments have indicated that they could not give out any information on flying saucers because the knowledge would cause panic among the masses.

If there is any panic it will start, not among the masses, but among those who have been imposing censorship on the press, on TV and radio, in particicular, and among those black disciples who have been acting through political, church and money channels. There is certainly no doubt in the minds of any thinking persons today about where censorship originates. Since the late '30's we have constructed a whole new rubber stamp language of gobbledegook consisting of words such as: secret, top secret, super top secret, super duper top secret.

Let no one think that the Silence Group has just got its second wind. It has been in active control for many, many centuries. Long ages ago, in the time of what we would call ancient civilizations, spaceships kept our planet under strict surveillance. People frequently observed these spaceships and many of the observations were recorded in the Bible. When Moses and the Israelites followed a cloud by day and a pillar of fire by night, they were following a spaceship. When the three Wise Men followed the Star of Bethlehem, they were following a natural spaceship or force-field directed by the Christ.

But the story then, as now, was readjusted so that it had the same old phoney ring that it has today. People are not seeing spaceships, so the tools of the dark forces claim. People are seeing stars, birds, weather balloons, kites, temperature inversions and hallucinations, but not spaceships. Never, never, never, quoth the black vultures, do people see spaceships.

But the space people, who have a telepathic record of every thought on earth, know for a fact that those in power in high places—in the military, in governments, in money marts, and in churchianity—do not want the man in the street, the little taxpayer, to know about spaceships.

If he did know about them, and if he had a grain of common sense left in his brain-washed head, he would look to the space people as his only hope, as his one salvation, and he would be looking in exactly the right direction. Little man, this is not the time to bow your head in abject servility; this is the time to raise your eyes to the skies and to your God!

Naturally those who are crazed with power-lust want nothing except more power. Dope addiction is said to be a mild affliction by comparison. The power boys are so deluded that, despite the fact that they are in full possession of flying saucer information, they still hope to somehow outwit the space people.

In this age of daily newspapers, radio and TV, they must carefully select and release only those bits of information which have been chosen by their great propaganda organization. These bits may contain ridicule, big whopping lies, delusions, or any other type of calculated deceit, but never, never, never the least hint of the truth.

And what if the newspapers and TV and radio stations refuse to go along with this imposed censorship? They will be taken care of in approved economic gangster fashion through advertisers who serve as tools for the dark forces.

But the big ball, the great big nineteen-million-year shindig, is all but over now. It might even be well for the gray flannel boys along Madison Avenue to begin to look toward conserving their wardrobes. It is just possible that in the coming shuffle they might lose their last pair of pants!

PART VIII

The Otis T. Carr Story

It was in November, 1957—that same glad November, decked with a sparkle and a twinkle, and with long, tall nights stretching upward to the stars—when Otis T. Carr of Baltimore, Maryland, announced that free energy and space flight had been once again made available to the inhabitants of this planet.

Carr, a disciple of Tesla, has come up with two new inventions. One is an electrical accumulator and the other a gravity motor, both utilizing the power of the sun and other forces of nature found in free abundance in the atmosphere. They are strictly free-energy devices, which Carr claims may be used to power anything from a hearing aid to a spaceship.

Although they are machines, just as surely as the Tesla

anti-war machine is a mechanical device, yet they follow the principles of nature so closely as to be almost organic in function. Like other New Age mechanisms, the Carr machines point the way to what may be expected from Ascended Master Saint Germain's scientific program for the Aquarian Age. The gap between organic and inorganic science is being closed rapidly, even in the minds of the laboratory experts who created the breach in the first place. The gap did not exist in actuality. It existed only in the minds of those who peered through very, very inadequate microscopes.

It was because of this delusion concerning the gap that science separated itself off from religion. The only religion that will bind one back to the Source, in the correct meaning of the word, is the science of man's evolution. The church that a man attends plays no part in his evolution, except perhaps to retard it. God is pure energy and He does not attend a church. He is also pure love, and He desires that His prodigal children return home to Him at the earliest possible moment. We can only go home to the Father's house when we have finished with our classroom work on this earth.

The entire Aquarian Age program is, therefore, dependant upon having an abundance of leisure time for evolutionary study. We must give up that ancient device of earning our living by the sweat of our brow, get busy with our homework, and make our Ascension.

Master Saint Germain is well aware that machines are necessary to accomplish the Aquarian program for all people everywhere. The homespun way of life may be quaint and even colorful, but is it dreadfully inefficient. There are ten billion souls who must be processed through this earth training center during the next two thousand years. There will not be time for anyone to sit around doing hand-embroidery in order to pass away the hours.

Actually the New Age machinery, much of it invented by Saint Germain Himself, is ready and waiting. But humanity is not ready to accept it. Therefore, in the interim period it is necessary for men like Carr and Matthews to invent machines which will carry the world peacefully through the transition period. Further, such inventions serve to anchor the New Age energies in physical matter, raising its vibrations and lifting karma, and that is a very important factor from the Hierarchial point of view. Adepts are not permitted to just hand out inventions to the human race, however desirable those inventions may be.

That is why men like Tesla, Matthews, and Carr, must serve as outposts of consciousness. They have human free will and can put forward inventions without imposing on the free will of others. It is up to humanity to accept or reject inventions which are offered in the open competitive market.

Carr has realized this fully, and has organized a solid business corporation under the normal conventions of the American free enterprise system. This is the system which prevails today, for good or for evil, and in order not to interfere with man's free will Carr has arranged his enterprise to fit into the established way of life.

It may not be tomorrow's way of life, but it exists today and we must accept it in good grace until change is indicated. Adjustments must proceed in an orderly manner, for it is the desire of the Hierarchy and the space people that the transition from the old age to the new be made without fear or panic, stress or strain. There is no need to talk of impending cataclysms, for with the straightening of the earth's exis in 1958, the greatest period of danger is over.

It was on a summer day in 1925 that Otis T. Carr was busy with his new duties as a package clerk in a large mid-town hotel in New York. He had just arrived in the city to study art, and he found employment in order to cover his tuition. First, he had felt impelled to come to New York. Upon arrival, he had felt impelled to apply for a job in a particular hotel. He was put to work at once and was just getting acquainted with his surroundings when Nikola Tesla wound his prophetic way through the subterranean passages of the lower basement and approached the new package clerk.

"When you finish your duties here," said Tesla with grave dignity, "go out and buy four pounds of unsalted peanuts and bring them to my suite." He handed the lad from Elkins, West Virginia, sufficient money to cover the purchase, plus a generous gratuity. The gratuity was part of the Tesla legend; to him the laborer was very, very worthy of his hire.

Otis was not surprised at the nature of the request because, as he had often been told, in New York one could expect anything to happen. It was not in the least like Elkins. The package clerk carried out the order and delivered the peanuts to Tesla. Meanwhile he had made a few inquiries among the other clerks, and he found that Tesla was a great scientist who fed peanuts to pigeons. He even took care of the sick and injured pigeons and kept many of them in baskets upstairs in his suite.

Upon making the delivery, young Carr was invited by Tesla to come in for a chat. This was the beginning of one of the most unusual and most fascinating stories of dis-cipleship that has yet come to light in modern times. Usually people look upon the training of a disciple as something extremely mystical and esoteric, something that takes place within a lamasery or secluded retreat, far from the haunts of men and pigeons. But in this instance—and it it certainly one of the most successful instances of discipleship on record—most of the training took place on the steps of the New York public library.

Day after day, in good weather and bad, young Carr carried peanuts to Tesla. And day after day, the elderly scientist and his young protege strolled slowly along certain streets where flocks of pigeons were wont to gather in anticipation of the scattered nutmeats. The pilgrimage usually ended on the steps of the library on the west side, facing Bryant Park. There the two sat side by side, with Tesla luring the birds to eat out of his hand, while he explained to young Carr the fascinating details of their mysterious intelligence.

Tesla is said to have talked but little in those years, but fortunately young Carr was not inhibited by any knowledge of this fact. He asked the great genius so many questions and listened with such rapt eagerness to every syllable, that Tesla soon gave him a nickname—The Sponge. This served as a little joke between two good friends, but actually the name was well chosen as Tesla realized when he selected it.

When the average disciple is in training, he gushes forth questions like a fountain in full play. It would seem to an observer that such an individual could not possibly absorb the answers, even if answers are forthcoming from a teacher. Usually they are not, for the wise teacher merely listens, and from time to time, when he can get in a word, he offers certain explanations. However, in all correct esoteric training, it is the God-Presence of the individual Who does the actual teaching—not a guru. The guru may be present, at the side of the disciple, but that is merely to provide a certain warmth of companionship. It is often much easier for a student to talk to a teacher than it is to hurl questions at empty space.

Esoteric training is based on certain scriptural phrases: Before you have asked, I have answered. Ask and you shall receive. Knock and it shall be opened unto you. Seek and you shall find. I am the Way, the Truth and the Light.

It is this attitude of seeking, questioning, asking, constant wonderment, that is the hallmark of the disciple. Direct answers from a teacher are not only unnecessary, but often confusing. It is absolutely necessary for the disciple to ask, for that is the spiritual Law. The Presence will do the answering when and if necessary. The Presence does not pour useless knowledge into the brain of a student. Only school teachers do that sort of thing. A disciple may ask a question and wait twenty-five or fifty years for an answer, but when the answer comes, as it surely will, it will flash into the mind at the exact moment when it is needed.

Therefore, when Tesla teasingly named young Carr "The Sponge," he indicated that he knew Carr was storing up knowledge that he could draw upon at any time in the future when he truly needed it. Assuredly he did not need to understand the workings of the universe in order to sit on the steps of the library with Tesla and toss peanuts to pigeons.

Tesla's correct attitude was proved again and again during the thirty years that followed the three-year period of Carr's training. Carr never saw Tesla again or had further contact with him after the third year. During the thirty subsequent years, Carr spent hours daily in his own little workshop, performing the thousands of experiments that led to final success with the gravity motor and electric propulsion system. There in the workshop he found that he could, at any time, dip into the reservoir of his photographic memory, and bring forth in total recall every needed thought concerning sine wave or coil winding or other Tesla applications and innovations.

Carr had no formal engineering training, nor had he any knowledge of esotericism before meeting Tesla. However, he was so inspired by the superman that he later steeped himself in philosophies of the east and the west, and ranged far and wide in his reading and studying, covering a vast field of knowledge. Like the martyred Bruno, Carr has come to be known as the academician without academy.

As he read and studied over the years, he always followed Tesla's example by going straight to the heart and brain of nature for his knowledge. He quickly discovered how to sort the absolutes from the mountains of dialectic chaff in the world's accumulated words and works. He never wasted precious time repeating what was proved.

As a result of his great perceptive guidance, it is estimated that Carr has advanced scientific achievement at least a century by concrete application of his free-energy discoveries. Like Tesla, he harbors no secrets about his inventions. He is more than happy to discuss them with anyone who will listen. Also, like Tesla, he has been unable thus far to sell them or even give them away. But that situation will change rapidly for both Carr and Tesla—probably in a matter of weeks now—as Saint Germain's new Aquarian program gets into full swing.

Carr, philosophically at least, is already allied with Ascended Master Saint Germain, inasmuch as Saint Germain had His last embodiment as Francis Bacon-at which time He wrote plays and sonnets under the pseudonym of William Shakespeare. Otis Carr has rooted his entire development in a total acceptance of Shakespeare's poetic dictum:

"There's a divinity that shapes our ends,
Rough-hew them how we will."

Carr is a man who is characterized by an attitude of constant gratefulness. He is not only grateful to God and to Tesla, but his gratitude extends back to Archimedes and forward to Einstein, for he feels that the application of certain scientific principles down through the ages, by countless discoverers and scientists, all contributed to his own inventions. This attitude is especially apparent in Carr's speech and writings. He stubbornly sticks to the plural form, we, in his narration of accomplishment.

When questioned about this he spoke of the total principles proved by the great men of history, and how each proof had entered into his final concept of the gravity motor and electrical accumulator. He acknowledges Archimedes' lever, Copernicus' constants, Galileo's acceleration, Newton's motions, Faraday's coil, Bacon's perrogatives, Edison's thermionics, Einstein's relativity, Franklin's static, Galvani's electrolysis, and Tesla's understanding of outer space; and the works of craftsmen like Fulton, Ford, and the Wright brothers, whose "follies, foibles, and infernal-machines" would never, it was said, perform the "fantasies" that are now commonplace.

Like Tesla, Carr desires that his inventions serve all humanity, not a privileged few. It is his wish that millions of individuals from all nations will have an opportunity to share in the development of the business as it unfolds. Aside from the fact that he is definitely opposed to any monopolistic practices, so common in big business, his corporate structure is not unlike that of other successful world producers.

The basic design for all his business stationery, brochures, booklets, and so forth, is not only interesting and original, but extremely-symbolic. His initials, OTC, are arranged so as to form the sign of Omega. Surmounting this is the White Dove—Tesla's Dove—in full, graceful flight. Below is the motto which reads: Peace and plenty through the application of free energy to supply all things to all people.

Carr has already met the same resistance from the forces of darkness that plagued Tesla, and, as usual, it comes through money channels and threats of economic boycott— this time in relation to newspaper advertising. In launching an announcement of his inventions Carr had a full-page advertisement prepared for insertion in a leading daily paper of Baltimore. The advertisement was paid for and accepted by the paper. Shortly thereafter it was cancelled by the newspaper and the money refunded. The newspaper had to cancel the advertising at the request of one of their big money-spenders who had metered power, not free energy, for sale to the public. Therefore, the people of Baltimore and vicinity were not even privileged to know that one of their own citizens had invented free-energy devices capable of powering everything from a hearing aid to a spaceship.

While the governments still deny the existence of flying saucers, and daily newspapers refuse to give outstanding news to their readers in the form of a paid advertisement, the uninformed public remains uninformed. They do not even know that the problem of space flight has been solved on this planet by an American citizen. They are not even told that it is now possible to power everything with free energy drawn from the atmosphere; that we need no longer be enslaved by petroleum, coal and old forms of fuel.

This is news of world importance, yet so strict is the gangster censorship imposed by the Silence Group, that newspapers founded for the purpose of giving news to the public dare not carry out their function, for to do so would mean running the risk of ruinous economic sanctions. However, Carr and his associates displayed no resentment over the refusal of the daily newspaper to carry the advertising. Instead, they placed page ads in small suburban weeklies which were overjoyed to have the sudden business windfall.

The result was not only amazing, but proved conclusively that the public wanted to be informed about Carr's inventions. From far and wide, letters of inquiry began to pour in. Hundreds of extra copies of the newspapers were requested to be sent to relatives and friends in distant states and countries. Requests for literature on the Carr machines reached huge proportions, and continued to soar day after day. Scores of people sent in small amounts of money—from a dollar to five dollars—as a down payment on stock that was not even offered for sale. Visitors began to arrive with requests for information on everything from vast power plants to spaceships.

Meanwhile Carr had offered to build and deliver space ships to governments wishing to send expeditions to the moon or elsewhere, but these offers were declined in favor of much more expensive rocket and missile programs.

This is a most interesting and intriguing development. The space people have stated that they will not permit military or tourist landings on the moon. The Hierarchy has announced that no individual in an unascended body can make a trip into outer space. If governments do not believe in the existence of flying saucers from outer space, then they cannot accept the fact that the space people have a station on the moon. Why, then, do they hesitate to use a Carr spaceship to go to the moon, and find out for themselves what is up there?

It seems obvious that they do know there is a space station on the moon. Undoubtedly, the space people have told them that they will not be permitted to land, and they know the space people mean business. In the meantime they can keep on playing with their rocket toys in order to fool the taxpayer, and give the impression that he is getting something big and grand for his money.

Carr is not planning to have a large spaceship ready for flight for at least a year. It is quite possible that he could make a trip to the moon and be permitted to land there. Inasmuch as he would be testing his own ship, the trip would have no military significance, and he is entirely in accord with the program set up by the space people. Also, by the time he has a ship of sufficient size ready for a voyage into outer space, it might be possible for him to make that trip too, especially if one or more space persons would agree to accompany him. But these conjectures are entirely unique and apply only to Carr.

What he can or cannot accomplish has nothing to do with the attitude of governments which first refuse to admit the possibility of spaceships from other planets and then refuse to try out a local model. Supposing it is not entirely successful on the trial run? It certainly could not be less successful than many of the rockets and satellites which the government is attempting to launch at the expense of the taxpayers.

Furthermore, a rocket leads but to destruction. A spaceship leads to the freedom of the cosmic lightways and opens a vast new universe to the wonderment of man.

Since Carr's free energy devices are designed to power anything from a hearing aid to a spaceship, it is clear why his advertising is refused by daily newspapers, and why the government refuses to even try a Carr spaceship on the national budget—just for size, at least. Carr's free-energy motors will power automobiles, for one thing; a development which would do away with the need for gasoline, and as an added advantage do away with smelly exhaust fumes.

For years, geologists and scientists have been bemoaning the fact that our natural fuels such as petroleum will soon be exhausted. They have painted grim word pictures of a shivering, stranded populace, hovering over a meager fire of sticks and twigs, and just about to perish for lack of fuel. Yet when Otis T. Carr announces free-energy motors the newspapers hasten to keep the whole thing hush-hush lest the people find out that they will not have to shiver after all.

There is still another reason why the Silence Group, operating through black disciples in the military and commercial business arenas, has decreed that Carr's inventions should be played down. Carr is obviously working on behalf of the Forces of Light and he is probably the first man in history who has had the courage to incorporate that theme in his paid newspaper advertising.

He is irrevocably against mistreatment of the atom, for well he knows that an atom is God's handiwork, and a tiny pulsing life. In the advertisement he states that his machines are natural machines; that they produce unlimited energy without fission, without fusion, and without violence of any

kind. They do not smash the atom. They do not split the
atom. They do not blast the atom.

He reminds his readers that his machines are profoundly
simple devices that collect and direct the free and boundless
energies of the sun "in the same way the sun's energies cause
the earth to spin and the rivers to flow, the bread to rise and
the plants to grow, and the great ocean tides to rise and
fall." He states that the accumulator uses the sun's force of
electro-magnetism by means of natural reproductive chemistry, and that the motor is powered entirely by the sun's
immutable pressure energy known as gravity.

He sums up not only his method but his philosophy as
follows:

> All energy is atomic
> The light from the sun
> The pull of gravity
> The fission of uranium
> The fusion of hydrogen
> All that moves
> Or grows, or glows
> Everywhere on earth
> And throughout the Universe.
> It is all atomic energy.
>
> Its utronic presence is everywhere,
> being even Nature itself.
>
> And held in plain view for all
> the time we know, it has yet
> remained Nature's closest secret.
>
> So, how to borrow of this energy
> from Nature, has been quite
> a problem.

When you *fight* Nature,
Nature *always* fights back.

If we try to share Nature's energy
by injuring Nature. we will only
injure ourselves accordingly.

Try to change the weather in one
place and you get storms. or floods.
or drought in another.

Crack or split the atom and you
get frightful devastation or
poisonous radiation.

And while you may blast a dog or
a man away into space. you will
never safely blast him back again.

We know the laws of Nature do not
change, so why waste the effort
and take the terrible risks?

There is only one right way.
The right way is the peaceful way.
And we have found the way!

Carr's architectural plans for a Space Research Institute
to be located at Space, Maryland, have been drawn up, and
preliminary construction activities are under way on a beautiful plot of land of about seventy acres, outside Baltimore.
The new postoffice will be called Space.

Space Research Institute is expected to become the world
center for activities connected with spaceships, interplanetary
travel, interplanetary communication, and a better way of
life through the utilization of natural solar energy devices.

The group of buildings incorporate new design motifs which should make them outstanding in architectural beauty.

The plans call for a huge, domed auditorium. The interior of the dome will be decorated by Salvador Dali, who is currently preparing a huge mural masterpiece to be enshrined there. The subject is the prophetic story of Ezekiel's vision, approached from the space-time cosmogeny. A total space concept is portrayed by four guardian cherubim. And over all hovers a portrait of the White Dove of Shamballa—Tesla's earth companion.

Although Space Research Institute will serve as headquarters for the Otis T. Carr Enterprises, he does not plan to mass-manufacture any of his devices. The institute, as its name implies, is strictly for research. There the group will design prototypes of machines which will then be turned over to other manufacturers to be produced in quantity. Mr. Carr has behind him the long history of Tesla's frustrated attempts to make the world a more comfortable place in which to live, and to give humanity countless hours of leisure time for study and evolutionary advancement. Therefore, his primary interest is not in becoming a manufacturer himself, but in the opportunity of all industry, the world over, to share in the ownership and distribution of products patterned after the basic prototypes.

Since Carr is a disciple of Tesla, and since Tesla refused to participate in the conniving, competitive commercial manipulations of his day, business men everywhere are eager to know how Carr, faced with problems almost identical to those of Tesla, plans to surmount the many obstacles which are certain to be placed in his way by the forces of darkness. The answer seems to be contained within the utilitarian functions of the inventions themselves. Once the public knows that the devices will provide a better way of life, it is up to the public to demand that the inventions be made available.

The OTC circular-foil spacecraft looks and operates like a flying saucer. The first experimental models will be anywhere from forty to a hundred feet in diameter, and will cost millions of dollars, as do first prototypes of any aircraft. However, one small model, ten feet in diameter will be constructed for special test purposes in actual usage.

Unlike conventional aircraft, the large space vehicles will soon be brought down to family size of about ten feet in diameter. They can be built to sell for less than the cost of a modern automobile, and are designed to take a family across town, across the nation, or around the world in absolute comfort and safety, and in a fraction of the time ever before possible. Carr expects to be ready during 1959 to start licensing manufacturers all over the world to mass-produce the OTC space vehicles in many sizes and styles for every transportation need.

It is Mr. Carr's sincere opinion that the introduction, manufacture, and use of the free-energy devices will bring more prosperity to more people in the United States and around the globe, than any single invention in the entire history of the world. He realizes that most of the world's problems today have their roots in hunger for more energy than is available.

"States and nations are already fighting over what is left of ordinary fuels and the available supplies of water to make electricity and irrigate the land," states Mr. Carr. "We have had many recent examples of our delicate balance of supply and demand, even in this great country. We've seen the rationing of gasoline and oil. We've seen the lights go dim in the Pacific Northwest.

"We've seen vast millions of burning desert acres barren only for lack of a little irrigation. And now even the oil men are beginning to squeeze the last drop out of every ton of shale.

"The power hunger is the same the world over, only it is more intense now. The most shocking recent example was the willingness of Egypt to close the Suez Canal and fight the world for a few kilowatts of electricity.

"Free-energy devices can change all this in a remarkably short space of time. Enough electric power and energy in the right places, and we will have undreamed of markets for every other kind of goods and materials and appliances our factories and shops can turn out.

"And so goes the simple formula: Give the world enough electrical energy, and you raise the world's standard of living. Raise the world's standard of living, and you raise the world's economy.

"The best way to get the total concept of what free energy means to the world today, is to suppose that the wheel were just now being discovered. Then visualize the free-energy motor putting the wheel into the air, into an entirely new dimension. Industry must realize that these devices will provide power for automobiles, trains, great ocean liners, and spaceships, as well as for such things as hearing aids, portable television sets, refrigerators, and will even furnish power, light, and heat for large cities or communities.

"Our free-energy devices will do all these things by perpetual space-forces of magnetism, gravity, and electro-magnetism—and these forces alone; forces which are free and available everywhere on the face of the earth and throughout the universe."

While the world is still groveling under the ancient edict that called for earning one's bread by the sweat of one's brow, the question of how free-energy devices will affect employment is a paramount one. But Mr. Carr feels that his inventions and discoveries truly represent the inception of a basic new industry, which for sheer size and scope might be properly compared with the steel, automobile and aircraft industries combined. He believes that pioneering in free energy will automatically introduce a new concept of employment practices and employee relationships.

Although the space people themselves have had no contact with Otis T. Carr and have had no direct hand in his work, it is safe to assume that they have been watching it carefully. In addition, Tesla and the Dove have assuredly directed it from the scientific department of Shamballa, making certain that it will fit into the Divine Plan at exactly the right moment. This, then, is the right moment.

The grave danger that might have turned the entire enterprise into a gargantuan war machine is now over, for with the straightening of the earth's axis completed, the Hierarchy and the space people will be able to neutralize major war efforts. There may be sporadic minor clashes, but even these may now be avoided. Lord Michael, Prince of the Archangels, has had such tremendous success in his housecleaning efforts, that the final physical plane adjustments are not likely to be too formidable.

It was that keen observer of Nature, now the Ascended Master Saint Germain, who, in a former embodiment as Francis Bacon, set the stage for the new civilization which He is building today. His basic plan for mankind was revealed in a simply prefatory remark in *Novum Organum*: "If man would conquer Nature, man must join with Nature."

Francis Bacon is an outstanding example of a man who successfully refused, through 70,000 years as a civilization-builder, to fight against Nature. As a result of this simple cooperative method, the floodgates of wisdom remained open to him. This resolute leader of humanity could look back down the corridors of the centuries with full continuity of consciousness, and review the events which had carried the whole human race to the threshold of the Aquarian Age.

Transmutation is the keynote of the Aquarian program for mankind. Any effort which man now makes to join Nature, helps to lift some of the heavy karma he has created by fighting Nature in the past.

Otis. T. Carr has recognized the true responsive Nature of the atom when it is treated as an Intelligence. "Essentially, what we have done is collect, arrange, adapt and orchestrate some of Nature's compositions into harmonious assemblage," he explains. "They are fashioned out of God's Creation. They are instruments of peace. Their music is for all the worlds of man."

We have come very, very far into the Light since the dark, uncertain days of 1955, when it seemed that the worst cataclysmic prophecies of Armageddon were about to be fulfilled. As Arthur H. Matthews so joyfully states: "Be of good courage, for we have God with us. And we have the spirit of Tesla with us."

Yes, indeed we have! All this, and the White Dove, too. We seem to hear the gentle rustle of white wings around us; we seem to hear the gentle vioce of Nikola enfolding us;

comforting us, assuring us that he still walks beside the one
who was obedient to his command: Go forth! Explore
space! There in the limitless azure skies is your rendezvous
with Destiny.

"The sea—the interminable sea—
Rolls on,
A fluid portion of Eternity.

"Wisdom—interminable wisdom—
Rolls on
To mark the course of Eternity.

"Jewels dropped at random
Are found, and their richness recognized
By children of Eternity;
And such children walk among the masses.
Unrecognized for a time.

"Many of your years past
A Gem was dropped
And found
And clasped close
By a youth, whom you now know.

"He is much loved here.

"And I send him again
A word, to lead him home.

"He knows me well.
And those who remember me, gently,
Call me Nick.

"Goodnight."

PART IX

Let There Be Light

On one occasion Tesla was presented with a medal, a symbol of gratitude, together with a paraphrase of Pope's lines on Newton:

"Nature and Nature's laws lay hid in night
God said, Let Tesla be, and all was light."

This was the Venusian, the superman, who arrived on this earth in a spaceship, as a tiny baby, and who grew to maturity to fulfill his great mission—that of assisting Ascended Master Saint Germain to set up the machinery for the new scientific civilization that will lift the Aquarian Age to heights of glory. Two thousand years earlier, Saint Germain, then Joseph, watched over the babe Jesus, while a radiant space vehicle, the Star of Bethlehem, hovered above the stable.

Few people on this planet today have any conception of

the herculean accomplishments of Tesla on behalf of the
Forces of Light. But on other planets in this solar system
and in systems beyond, the people are well aware that they
can extend the hand of friendship to us now, in this year of
1958, because of the mighty works of Tesla.

There are many earth people who will feel, even now, that
Tesla should have found a way to overcome the obstacles
placed in his path by the forces of darkness; that he should
have forced a showdown that would have thrust his inventions upon the world, regardless of the ignorance and ambi-
tions of a petty-minded opposition. But like the spaceman
that he was, Tesla knew that he could only encourage us;
he could not force his light upon us; he could only respect
our free will.

He was aware that humanity was plagued by the forces of
darkness. He well knew that people were unable to see the
significance of his role as a Lightbearer. He was never bit-
ter, never disappointed, when people failed to appreciate his
efforts. He would only smile his slow sweet smile in response to compassionate friends who felt they must offer
apologies for human arrogance, for human self-will, and
then he would quote in answer a favorite stanza from
Goethe's *Faust:*

> "The God that in my bosom lives
> Can move my deepest inmost soul
> Power to all my thoughts he gives
> But outside he has no control."

Well did Tesla know that each and every individual must
find his own Christ-center, must contact his own Source. For
the doctrine of vicarious atonement is a vicious one, an
escapist's dream. Each must transmute his own misqualified

energy; each must carve out and travel the razor-edged Path to the One. Tesla's inventions can make the journey easier— as can those of his disciples—Matthews and Carr. But only God can say to each pilgrim on the Path: Here is My gift of Violet Fire. Accept it. Use it. Transmute your past mistakes. Put your lower worlds in order. Then come home to Me!

There are those who will dispute the advantages of Tesla's inventions, and present developments made by Matthews. Carr and others who follow in Tesla's footsteps, arguing that machinery has nothing to do with discipleship. There are those who will say that we must not use a mechanistic approach, such as the anti-war machine, in trying to solve our problems; that we must use only Love and Understanding. But this attitude stems from the dreadful devoteeism generated under the mis-used influence of the Sixth Ray. Jesus was a practical man who lived in the workaday world: He made His Ascension by the application of scientific principles, which is the only method anyone can use. It is only the impractical mystic who views science as a handicap.

It is quite true that if men and women of goodwill could generate a sufficient amount of Love and Understanding. the course of history could be changed at once, but the change would still come about scientifically. For the energies generated in this way are simply collected by angelic forces, acting as accumulators, and then poured into certain specified areas of atomic matter, freeing it from low karmic vibrations and raising its frequency so it can function with greater freedom. There is nothing mystical in the process. There is nothing mystical about an angel.

When angels walked and talked with men, before the laggards came, they were accepted as a necessary adjunct to

successful human evolution, as indeed they are. They are
not any more mystical than trees, rocks, soil or rivers; they
are not one whit more mystical than the pigeons in the park
or Tesla's favorite Dove. It is the dark forces who have con-
jured up that phoney mystical story, so that people would
feel that they had to be practical in the materialistic meaning
of the word, and depend upon a job, a boss, a national ruler,
a military machine, instead of simply depending upon God
and His Adepts and His angels.

So let us not despise a mechanistic approach which will
allow us to lay down our weapons, and give us the leisure
time to develop the educated heart of Love, the enlightened
mind of Understanding. As the ancient maxim advises: "Do
not count the teeth of a camel which has been given to you
with love, but ride it with thanks in your hearts that you
have a vehicle which will carry you safely through the haz-
ards of the desert." Remember, too, that Tesla's anti-war
machine is simply a mechanistic version of the wall of light
built by Saint Germain's disciples through directed and controlled thought. But with this difference: Saint Germain's
wall of light must, like the Hierarchs Themselves, function
without interfering with man's free will. It would not be
occultly permissable for Adepts or disciples to build a wall of
light which would cause all bombs to explode, as Tesla's
anti-war machine will do. By taking human embodiment
Tesla could overcome that occult fiat to the extent that he
could counter with his human free will the destructive weapons fashioned by other human free wills.

That is why all Adepts in ascended bodies have to work
through disciples who are in physical incarnation. The disciple is perfectly free at all times to do or say anything, even
when the word or deed may actually work against the Forces

of Light. Of course in that case the disciple must carry the burden of the resultant karma. But a Master is not occultly permitted to warn the disciple against errors; if He did so He would interfere with the free will of the disciple, and deprive the disciple of learning through his own mistakes.

A Master working in the Light, never follows a disciple around, telling him what to do and what not to do. On the other hand, black adepts do nothing else, and they even enlist the aid of parents, teachers, doctors, newspaper writers and a thousand other tools to assist them in their nefarious practice of enslaving the human mind through dictatorship. This kind of tyranny exists in virtually every home today, and it is a well known fact that the forces of darkness are especially proud of the inroads they have made in destroying family love and harmony.

Masters of the Ageless Wisdom do not direct their disciples to follow certain lines of thought, or point out to them certain ideas which they should absorb. The disciple must at all times use his own discrimination, and must through his own efforts learn to handle only that type of energy which will increase his God-powers. Over the years many disciples have been sufficiently alert to apply ideas which they learned from Tesla, for disciples range far and wide in their search for the truth, striving to recognize it and greeting it with joy when they find it. The mystic or the devotee usually makes the mistake of searching for truth only in nice but innocuous books, respectable surroundings, and sanctimonious environments. Therefore, it has not occurred to many persons to look into the findings of an electrical scientist like Tesla, to confirm the Truths put forward by Ascended Master Saint Germain.

One of the most interesting examples of alert searching has come to light in a story reported by Elsie Bulow, and published in *Fate Magazine* in November, 1957. Mrs. Bulow had worked with the group of Saint Germain's disciples who originally built the protecting wall of light around North. Central and South America. Mrs. Bulow was well acquainted with the work of Tesla and as she explains, in a portion of her article quoted below from *Fate*, she knew his ideas could be used in a thoroughly practical manner even by an individual. She then demonstrated this in many ways. She told the author that in experimenting with the Tesla methods, she found the techniques to be identical with those taught by Saint Germain and other Hierarchs.

"When we lived in Illinois we had a little toy terrier named Midgie. When Midgie was nine months old she was ready for love. We were filled with consternation at the thought of all the dogs in the neighborhood congregating outside our door. What could we do?

"I was reminded of the scientist, Nikola Tesla. His scientific knowledge was four-dimensional. He believed in the spiritual nature of the universe and acted on the principle that all is governed by immutable law; that intelligence is present at every point in so-called space and can be acted upon through the power of thought. He astounded the scientific world by stating, over twenty years ago, that a wall of light, invisible and impregnable, could be built around a city. Its power to withstand any impact would be greater than that of any physical substance known to man, he said.

"Tesla was using thought dynamically to establish this wall of light from out of the very atmosphere in which we live, move, and have our being. He called this invisible substance intelligent energy which could be th ... into existence. He knew that thought was creative.

"Building this wall was not a supernatural feat for we were dealing with energy.

"I had already learned to draw this wall of light around myself. Therefore, it was not an impossibility to conceive of a wall of light around our home. We decided upon a wall of light to exclude all amorous male dogs, to repel any dog which touched its charged area.

"Everybody has an atmosphere, or electrical field, and the atmosphere in which we live is filled with invisible atoms. The center of these atoms is the intelligence which keeps the electrons revolving around it like the planets around the sun, in an orderly fashion, according to law. The pattern of the atoms changes with changing thoughts.

"With the above understanding . . . we visualized the wall of light around our house and its environs. We conceived of the outer surface as sending forth charges of electrical energy which would act as a repellent and result in completely discouraging all male dogs . . . . We watched from the window as the dogs came eagerly and confidently toward our home. There were a half dozen of them, all sizes.

"They came as far as the place where we had visualized and felt (accepted) the wall of light. There they stopped. They tried to come further but evidently could not and so circled the house in perplexity. Then, dog fashion, they lay down to await developments. But one by one, unable to approach one step nearer their heart's desire, they left the scene, not to return."

Mrs. Bulow also said she used the wall of light around her automobile at all times and it was demonstrated that she was saved from car accidents on more than one occa-

sion. As she stated in the article, she long ago learned to
draw the wall of light around herself. Later she lived in
Chicago for a period and there she found that she could
draw the wall of light about her on the coldest winter days,
and that she could walk through the biting winds blowing
from Lake Michigan, and yet remain comfortably warm.
On hot summer days she used it in a similar manner to
keep herself comfortably cool.

Most of Saint Germain's disciples can report similar personal experiences with the wall of light, which for individual use is visualized as a great tube of light, about twelve
feet high and nine feet in diameter. The light should be
visualized as cascading down around this tube like sunlight
flashing on snow. It is important to understand that in the
days before the laggards came to the earth, every person was
born equipped with this tube of light. The tube of light
afforded positive protection against accidents, disharmony of
any kind, and served an added purpose of constantly radiating forth pure energy which kept the surrounding atmosphere fragrant and refreshed. Therefore, wherever a human
being moved, he was rendering a constant service to his
Creator, by spreading radiant light.

Now, during the present Aquarian Age, all persons must
re-build this tube of light. In these early years of the new
era, the tube has been used only by interested disciples who
were eager to experiment with the technique. But as the age
advances, each and every person will be called to the ranks
of discipleship. That will be the only type of classroom work
on this planet. Those who cannot or will not serve the Light
on one or more of the Rays, and who refuse to take part
in new age techniques designed to banish disease, death and
disharmony, will be removed to a specially prepared planet

with low vibrations. There they can experiment with their own free will miscreations until such time as they are ready to qualify energy constructively.

In these latter days, since the axis of the earth is straightened, permitting the vibratory action on the planet to be rapidly increased in order to help individuals to reach the Ascension frequency, it would indeed be the part of wisdom to seriously construct and use the tube of light. Each individual should use it not only for himself, but for others.

It is usually not wise to inform the person who is being assisted, of the help that is being offered in silence: this knowledge often causes antagonism which defeats the whole effort, because the person who is being helped is, through his rebellion, accumulating karma more rapidly than it can be dispelled. In fact, the golden rule of the new golden age will be found in that one word—silence. People could halt half of the trouble in the world today if they would just stop chattering like monkeys in a tree and listen to the Voice of the Silence that speaks from the depths of each beating heart.

In addition to using the wall of light around yourself, it would indeed be wise for every mother and father to keep the wall of light constantly around their children. It can be used either to make a person invisible or for protection. It is even bulletproof. But if it serves as a protective device only, most people will feel that this is assuredly a sufficient reward. This is a mistake, for in dealing with God's laws it is extremely unwise to place any limitation on them.

That gambling attitude of—well, I'll take a chance; what have I got to lose; maybe it will work and if it does I'm that much ahead—is an attitude that might well carry one through a day at Hialeah or an evening at Las Vegas. But in building the tube of light one should begin by making an affirmation that is free from limitation.

"I place a wall of light around myself that keeps me invisible, invincible and invulnerable to everything that is unlike the Christ." is a free avowal. But it must not be left high and dry on the mental plane. for there it will prove sterile. Remember that most of the sorry individuals who were bottled up in the Compound for so long were. for the most part, intellectuals. It was their lack of feeling that prevented them from expressing love for the Light.

Therefore. when thinking the tube of light into manifestation, it is necessary to feel very deeply about the glory of serving the Light. There must be no feeling of personal glory, but rather a feeling that one is being. absorbed. body, mind and soul. back into the cosmic glory of God which we once knew when we emerged as White Fire Beings from the flaming heart of Alpha and Omega.

The wall of light or tube of light is formed of electronic substance which is the primal life substance released from the great Central Sun of the galaxy, the twin Flames of Alpha and Omega: so we. as individualized Sparks from the heart of that same sun, emerged in physical life surrounded by that protective God-substance. Since we lost contact with our Source, we must now regain the full realization of our divinity, and our efforts to re-form the tube of light around ourselves signifies that we are once more willing to serve the Light by using the electronic substance of light itself.

There is nothing mystical or mysterious about forming the tube of light, as Mrs. Bulow has so clearly shown. It is a strictly scientific matter, as practical and demonstrable as the multiplication tables. Of course, the individual, in his heart, must know that God-power is the only sustaining power in the universe. God is an invented name, and should not be used in building the tube of light if an individual feels that it has something to do with church-going. If that concept gets in the way it is better to simply realize that God manifests as Light, and in this galaxy, as the particular light from Alpha and Omega.

This electronic light is everywhere and is completely responsive to human thought. Thought is a rate of vibration which creates things. The tube of light which you build around yourself will take on the quality of your own thought. Therefore, if you think of the tube as being an invincible and invulnerable protection it will function as such, so long as you can keep your mind free from any doubt on the subject. If you doubt the value of the tube, it will simply disappear, because you have commanded it to do so by your own distrust.

The first step, therefore, is to command the electronic substance to surround you and remain permanently invulnerable to all that is not of the Light. The process of manifesting the tube is simple. It requires no money, no special equipment, no college degrees. It does, however, require a certain amount of practice, but five minutes three times a day is enough to start.

First of all, try to be alone and undisturbed if possible. In households where privacy is at a premium, it is perhaps best to utilize a few minutes before arising or after retiring. Make your physical body as relaxed and comfortable as possible, and then forget it. Focus your attention upon your own Inner Self, your Divine Presence within your own beating heart.

From this focus visualize a great white tube of electronic

light gathering about you. Make this tube about nine feet in diameter and see it extending about three feet beneath you and three feet above you. This tube, as seen in the ethers, is white and scintillating, like sunlight glistening on snow, and the electronic substance rushes continually over it, like the splashing of a brilliant waterfall, ever renewed, ever fresh, and yet ever flowing.

Needless to say, it is not well at the present time to discuss the tube of light in idle conversation. In a few years, when chaotic conditions have cleared, every child will be instructed in building the tube of light as part of his home training and school work.

Once the tube is built it is not advisable to leave it empty, with only you inside it. Visualize it filled at all times with the great surging flames of the Violet Fire of the seventh Ray. Visualize the Violet Light as permeating every atom in your four lower bodies—mental, etheric, emotional and physical. The etheric body substands every particle of the physical body and extends about two inches beyond the physical. The mental and emotional bodies are spherical in shape and form the aura surrounding the physical. The physical body is at the center of the entire sphere, much like the yolk at the center of an egg.

Visualize the Violet Fire penetrating every part of your aura, blazing in and through every atom, and transmuting all the misqualified energy which is lodged, in the form of astral debris, in every tiny chink between the electrons in each atom. In a short time you will notice an increasing sense of well-being, and a feeling of buoyancy. Meanwhile, of course, every effort should be made to cease misqualifying pure electronic energy as it leaves your heart.

In other words, refrain from getting mad at yourself and

the world around you; leave off all worry; cast out all fear. If your favorite worrying subject is lack of money, then use the thinking power that is wasted in worry in realizing that all supply is created by the Creator. This forms a magnetic focus for supply and it will flow in naturally; but remember that doubt will immediately cause demagnetization.

When your tube of light is blazing with the soothing, cooling, healing rays of Violet Fire, then further enhance it by filling it with a delightful perfume, such as the fragrance of lilacs in a spring rain. As a final touch add to the whole a joyous melody from your favorite music. Follow this practice diligently, day after day; focus your attention upon your Inner Self; cultivate an abiding faith in God, and you will find your outer world swinging into a wonderful new orbit of harmony.

Remember that if you need special help at any instant of the day or night to solve any problems, you should call on the angelic kingdom. You will get an immediate response, even though you may not recognize the energy form in which it comes to you. And when you gaze at the skies overhead on a clear night and you see an apparent star shoot suddenly through the heavens, know that it is a flight of cherubim speeding forth on some cosmic errand. Recognize them, acknowledge, and bless them, and you will receive their blessing in return.

In the very near future, as soon as the governments of the world are forced to release their information on spaceships, more and more of these vehicles will become visible in the skies. Remember that at present all spaceships and space people can use the tube of light at any time to make themselves invisible. As earth people themselves learn to form and use the tube of light they will develop a consciousness which will make them fit companions for space visitors.

At the present time, there will be no space travel permitted except for those persons who are using physical bodies vibrating at the Ascension frequency. In certain cases the space people may take visitors to other planets for some special purpose, although it is difficult to imagine what purpose would be served. Those individuals who have passed through the Ascension Initiation are free to come and go as they wish, but they travel only if they are serving Life by so doing.

Science is now attempting to solve the riddle of gravity, if it can be called a riddle. Gravity has no effect on a physical body or object vibrating at a high frequency. Otis T. Carr has solved the problem of gravity in designing his free-energy motors and his spaceships. There is no apparent reason why Carr's spaceships could not travel to distant planets and stars, but there is a very excellent occult reason why they cannot be used for that purpose at the present time unless they are piloted by individuals who have an Ascended body.

It is very possible that Carr himself might be permitted to travel in his own ships for test purposes, and because he has worked so closely with Tesla in designing the ships. But the average tourist is not going anywhere in outer space—not yet, for all unascended beings are held firmly within the orbit of the earth, not by gravity alone, but by the Rod of Spiritual Power.

Anyone who wished to learn about the Rod of Spiritual Power or the Rod of Initiation, as it is sometimes called, has certainly had every opportunity to study the subject

during the past century. Every writer on occult subjects
from Helena Petrovna Blavatsky down to Alice A. Bailey,
has had much to say on the Rod.

A Rod of Spiritual Power is assigned to each and every
planet or star, and is given into the keeping of an entity
known as the Lord of the Sphere. For the past nineteen
million years, the Lord of the World for planet earth, has
been Sanat Kumara of Venus. Only at the beginning of
1956 was He liberated from his self-imposed task, and now
Gautama, the former Buddha, is the new Lord of the
World.

The Rod for this planet has, therefore, been given into
the custody of Gautama. It is this Rod that keeps us all
firmly held to our classroom work until our evolutionary
lessons are completed. The Rod is used on many special occasions, however. It is always used during the formal cere-
monies of the Wesak Festival which takes place annually
during the time of the Taurus full mon. It is also used when
individuals undergo the higher initiations, when they are
touched by the Rod. When a person attains Adeptship, the
Rod is used in the initiation ceremony for magnetization
purposes, signifying that the individual is ascended and free.
Thereafter, the Rod cannot hold him within the earth's
orbit, and he may travel upon the cosmic lightways at times
when they are officially open.

All cosmic lightways or highways between planets and
stars are controlled magnetically by the various Rods of
Spiritual Power, one of which is on each sphere. The highways are normally closed to all interstellar traffic, but on
specific occasions they are formally opened in this galaxy
by entities from Alpha and Omega, and in other galaxies
by similar entities from their Central Sun.

The magnetic control functions automatically. The cosmic highways remain closed so long as the Rod on a planet is completely magnetized. If travelers desire to go to another planet, they must travel at a season when the planetary Rod is partially demagnetized in a manner which will permit properly qualified persons to leave the globe. On some occasions the Rod permits visitors to enter. On still other occasions the highways are open to traffic in either direction.

Frequently the cosmic highways leading to the earth are crowded with visitors from other planets and stars, and other galaxies, all in preparation for Saint Germain's great planetary triumph of restoration. Many of these cosmic visitors go direct to the Royal Teton Retreat in Wyoming, the spot where the First Root Race people established themselves as the first inhabitants on planet earth. The Royal Teton Retreat is the scene of much global activity, both within the mountain where a magnificent ampitheatre is maintained on the physical plane, and above the mountain where the etheric counterpart exists for those entities who work in subtle bodies.

In the Aquarian Age, it is expected that the various retreats around the world will be opened once again to the public. At present it is impossible for any visitor to gain admittance unless he has achieved at least minor initiatory status and has raised his vibrations to a point where he is seriously making an effort to advance to the Ascension frequency. In that case he is given every assistance by Adepts working on the various Rays.

In another great underground installation near the Royal Teton, is the collection of machinery which has been assembled for the New Age, and this will be released to the public as soon as present obstacles are removed. Saint Germain has been extremely active during the past century in preparing certain mechanisms which will assist people to rapidly raise their vibrations, once the New Age training can become part of the world educational system.

About twenty years ago Saint Germain perfected a device which he calls the Ascension chair. When an individual is mentally ready for the Ascension he may speed up the physical process by sitting in the chair while a Master, using White Magic methods, directs a flow of pure energy into the device. This acts upon the physical atoms of the body and raises the vibrations to the Ascension frequency in a matter of minutes.

The Ascension chair cannot be used by anyone who is below a certain mark in evolution, for if the individual is not ready the effect would be shattering to the physical body. The chair is mentioned here, however, because it is one more example of the many devices which will serve to advance Aquarian evolution, and which will lead to the end of death and taxes on this planet.

Although the Ascension chair perfected by Ascended Master Saint Germain is for the few, the masses have by no means been forgotten. The rejuvenation equipment which George Van Tassel is building at Giant Rock, California, is definitely designed to assist people physically to raise their atomic vibrations. As the New Age advances similar equipment will be in widespread use.

But the immediate need for individual assistance can be answered by the tube of light. All possible aid should be given at this time to help children and young people to not only build the tube of light, but to help them to understand something about the. tremendous evolutionary opportunities awaiting them.

This is a·very difficult period for children, because they are coming into a world filled with confused and bewildered adults who cannot find any sense of peace or security within their own hearts. Also, it must not be forgotten that hundreds of these children have been out of embodiment only a short time, having died during the violence of World War II. Their etheric memories of that period are still fresh and very disturbing. The United States is in an especially difficult situation so far as its young people are concerned, for thousands of those who formerly embodied in other nations have been attracted to rebirth in America.

However, it is cheering to know that at least one organization has been set up to assist these young people to become oriented in the space age as it dawns on the three Americas. This is the Junior Skywatch of the Americas. located in Washington, D. C. It was founded by Arnold Kruckman, a former newspaper writer and a friend of Nikola Tesla.

Mr. Kruckman has been interested in flying since its pioneer phases in the early days of the balloon. He originally helped to organize many of the pioneer flight groups, their membership drawn from those who owned balloons or who flew in them. At the same time these early pioneers were devoted to the new skyflier, the airplane. Mr. Kruckman finds that those who were interested in the rudimentary elements of flying that went into balloon activities, parallel those persons today who are interested in spaceships.

Mr. Kruckman was very fond of Nikola Tesla and utilized every opportunity to observe the unusual experiments which Tesla made in the field of aeronautics. At one time Mr. Kruckman wrote a series of articles about Tesla for the *New York World,* relating an instance when Tesla rented an armory in New Jersey and flew a dirigible in it, using only his will power to make the dirigible move through the armory. Mr. Kruckman also recalled a time when Tesla took an airplane to Marblehead, Massachusetts, and sent it out upon the water for a great distance, without any motive power except that which he himself supplied mentally.

Arnold Kruckman was a child prodigy and while still very young he performed brilliantly upon the violin, playing for the crowned heads of Europe. Later, as a teen-ager, he forsook the violin and took up writing and then journalism. He had a long friendship with Tesla, and for many years he wrote articles on flight for the *New York World* in the days when Tesla was about the only living man who had a comprehensive knowledge of the subject. It was in 1896 that Tesla built his first model plane in London.

Now Arnold Kruckman has grown to maturity, but his interest is still the same as it was in his teen-age days. He states, and rightly so, that the boys and girls in the Junior Skywatch of the Americas have a new light in their eyes: the work of sky scouting is new and it is real; the only boundary is the cosmos. Mr. Kruckman's organization answers a definite New Age need for young people. It forms an intriguing outlet for youthful energy, and provides a unique educational opportunity in a subject which is still not under the dull control of the school curriculum. It should be remembered that Einstein did not pursue his education until he received his doctorate. He escaped from the dreary classrooms at the earliest opportunity, and he stated that had he been imprisoned within those limiting walls only a few days longer, he would have given up mathematics forever, and turned to the violin as a more worthy instrument.

Now that Otis T. Carr's free-energy inventions have been announced, a vast new field of splendid far-flung wonderment opens up to the teen-agers. It is these young people who will refuse to be caught up in the outmoded power limitations that led to the past dull years of brutal human struggle. Mr. Carr has expressed his great concern for the young people of today, struggling for creative expression in the turbulent world in which they have been forced to live. He speaks as follows:

"Emotions were bursting their bonds wherever you'd go.

Crimes of passion and violence raged the globe.

Bored juveniles ignored all mandate of family or public authority and harassed their neighbors with deadly intent.

Already crowded asylums doubled and tripled their quotas to admit ever increasing numbers of the overstressed for treatment.

And still there seemed to be no good end in sight.

Those in greedy control of the mass of minds and materials still persisted in draining off all the wealth to feed their war machine.

Prices spiralled always higher while reserves of natural resources crept ever more swiftly toward wasted exhaustion.

The public media were splashed with these pressures of fear and hate. News of nations at each other's throats with boasts of bigger and ever more powerful weapons of devastation were coupled with loud threats, which if ever carried out could only result in the total annihilation of existing life on planet Earth.

Little wonder then that boundless joy came to the hearts of men when they learned that free energy and space flight had been returned to our beloved globe.

Soon will the spirit of Peace descend upon mankind.

Soon will the Dove return bearing the symbolic olive branch."

This, then, is our heritage, our divine and glorious destiny. Now in the glad years ahead, our New Age children will grow into the golden age of heaven on earth, with scarcely a memory of past darkness. This has been made possible because countless men and women, drawn from the farthest reaches of the galaxy, together with a certain White Dove, have chosen to steadfastly serve the Light.

There is more to be said, much more, and the story of the Light that ever lights the beating heart of mankind, will be continued in a second volume—*Flame of the Dove.*

SUGGESTED READING LIST

BAILEY. ALICE A.—

A Treatise on Cosmic Fire
A Treatise on White Magic
A Treatise on the Seven Rays
    Esoteric Psychology .... *Vol. I*
    Esoteric Psychology .... *Vol. II*
    Esoteric Astrology .... *Vol. III*
    Esoteric Healing .... *Vol. IV*
    Unfinished Autobiography

The above books (with the exception of *Unfinished Auto-biography*) together with many others presented by Alice A. Bailey, were dictated by Ascended Master Djwal Kul, from Shigatse, Tibet to New York City, via Master-to-disciple telepathy. Djwal Kul is a Second Ray Master, and directs the studies of many thousands of disciples throughout the world from a subsidiary ashram affiliated with the ashram maintained by Ascended Master Kuthumi, former Chohan of the Second Ray for many years, until July, 1958.

Last July Ascended Master Kuthumi and Ascended Master Jesus took over the official duties of the Office of the Christ and World Teacher. This is the first known instance in human history in which two Chohans were called forth by Cosmic Law to serve together in this high Office, indicating the great readiness of humanity to receive the illumination radiated forth by Christ's teachings.

Ascended Master Lanto, a well-beloved Teacher of Chinese origin. who was for long years in charge of the Retreat of the Royal Teton, Wyoming, has been appointed Chohan of the Second Ray to take over the work of Kuthumi. In turn, Ascended Master Confucius, the great Chinese philosopher and ruler, has once more drawn close to the humanity He so much loved in bygone ages, and has now entered the American scene as gracious Host to the thousands of Cosmic Guests and disciples who gather twice yearly for official meetings at the Royal Teton Retreat.

Ascended Master Djwal Kul, known to many as the Tibetan since He took His last embodiment in Tibet, is continuing His active work among Second Ray disciples all over the world.

Since the Ascended Masters will in coming years move more freely in the outer world, as They are rapidly accepted by the general public, it is very interesting to become acquainted with the history of those who have been our friends and neighbors during many lives.

Ascended Master Kuthumi, as Balthazzer, and Ascended Master Djwal Kul, as Casper, were two of the Wise Men who visited the babe Jesus. The third Wise Man, Melchoir, is now Ascended Master Morya.

BAUER, MARIA—Verulam Foundation, Los Angeles, Cal.

Foundations Unearthed

This is the story of the discovery of the vault containing all of Francis Bacon's private papers and writings. These are the documents which mysteriously disappeared from England when Bacon, in order to close his work there, arranged for his own funeral by borrowing a corpse destined for potter's field, and then attended the services disguised in widow's mourning veils. After seeing the grave close over the mortal remains of a supposed Francis Bacon, he made his way to Germany, and there re-activated the Rosicrucian Order; later he continued this type of work throughout Europe, consolidating groups of disciples and pouring the vital life of the Spirit into weary hearts.

Years later Francis Bacon made His Ascension from the Rakoczy Castle in Transylvania, the former home of the great Prince Rakoczy, Who is now the Ascended Being known as the Divine Director. Prince Rakoczy was for centuries the Teacher assigned to Francis Bacon, during that and many previous embodiments. So close was Their association and understanding that Teacher and chela merged in the minds of the public and to this day Francis Bacon is often referred to as the Master Rakoczy. He is, however, correctly identified as the Ascended Master Saint Germain, for He Himself selected the title of "sanctus germanus" or holy brother. For many years He has served as Chohan of the Seventh Ray, taking over that post from the beloved historical figure of ancient China, the Ascended Lady Master Kwan Yin. Although Saint Germain still retains His Chohanship, He was recently crowned as Lord of Civilization for the Aquarian cycle.

In *Foundations Unearthed*, Maria Bauer tells the inspiring story of the discovery of the vault containing Bacon's original papers. It still lies buried in Bruton Churchyard at Williamsburg, Virginia, where it was placed over 300 years ago by command of Bacon himself. The vault contains papers which reveal the Divine Plan for the Aquarian Age, and other valuable documents relating to the destiny of America.

Three centuries ago Francis Bacon preserved and for safety concealed this most treasured heritage of all times, for it is destined to serve as a guidepost for the American people in their hour of greatest spiritual hunger. Hiding behind the cloak of churchianity, vested money interests have thus far prevented the actual opening of the vault, depriving humanity of its rightful heritage which is so sorely needed now. Bacon predicted that the vault would be opened when "God, speaking through the voice of the people" would lead them to cry out against their overlords, demanding the buried treasure.

Foundations Unearthed is now out of print, but it is worth borrowing if you can search it out. However, some time in 1959, another book by Maria Bauer will be published, and it will incorporate all of the material presented in this first little volume. The new book will be much longer and much more thrilling, for it will cover two main themes—*The Birth of A New Age* and *Quest for Bruton Vault*. The full manuscript is as yet untitled.

BESANT, ANNIE—

The Self and Its Sheaths

A guide book for students who wish to take a backward glance through the early days of the Theosophical Movement, founded by Helena Petrovna Blavatsky at the behest of the Hierarchy. Although the turbulence and fiery zeal demonstrated by those pioneers in humanity's upliftment to the Light, have

no place in the calm and measured discipleship through which
Light consumes the darkness of today, it is nevertheless stimulating to look in on these embattled Servers at work.

Annie Besant, in a previous embodiment of historical moment, was the martyred Giordano Bruno, who was burned at
the stake in the year of 1600, by orders of churchianity's In-
quisitorial Court which pronounced him a confirmed heretic.

During that embodiment Bruno departed from his enforced
role as a Dominican monk and wandered over Europe and
England as an itinerant scholar. He contacted Francis Bacon
and many of Bacon's closest disciples and co-workers.

Recently Bruno again emerged in characterization, although
slightly disguised, in the literary marts of the land. He was
selected by author James Joyce for a special role in *Finnegan's
Wake*—that of Mr. Brown, a member of the firm of Brown
and Nolan, and again as Bruno Nolan.

In consciousness, Annie Besant continued the path of high
evolvement which she set as Bruno. All of her books, and
they are many, make splendid reading, even though our Aquarian Age disciples will not have to battle the turbulent sea of
hostility encountered by the stormy petrels of the Piscean days.
That good fight was fought by the valiant ones like Bruno and
Annie Besant.

BLAVATSKY, HELENA PETROVNA—

The Secret Doctrine
Isis Unveiled

In the outer world of discipleship, Helena Petrovna Blavatsky
has been aptly compared with the Rock of Gibralter. She can
only be described as one of Nature's mighty wonders. In this
last embodiment she emerged, or perhaps it might be better said
that she escaped, out of Russia and into the world. It was not
that any Blavatsky was unwelcome in the old Russia of the last
century—quite the contrary. Russia simply did not offer sufficient opportunities, amid its corruption and barbarism, for the
impetuous Helena to serve the Christ Forces openly and freely.
She felt cramped and awkward in that wasteland of frozen

evil, where even the very earth was tainted by the satanic forces which had made it a focus of darkness in ancient Lemurian times.

The entire globe became her abiding place physically; intellectually and spiritually she roamed the far-flung reaches of the universe. For long centuries, in embodiment after embodiment, she served the Forces of Light. In all history there have probably been few disciples who have enjoyed such a close working relationship with Ascended Masters and Cosmic Adepts. Madame Blavatsky was always the general-in-command of outer world strategy. She knew what support the Christ Forces needed for their outer world program, and she never failed to measure up to Their need.

Madame Blavatsky was the first tentative public relations agent appointed to serve as a bridge between the Hierarchy and the outer world. The Masters, even in those years of the last century were already preparing for the vast public program being directed today by Saint Germain. Ascended Master Djwal Kul handles outer world public relations for the Hierarchy, and today he works through a large staff of disciples who are employed in various jobs in the outer world. Most of them are trained writers, lecturers, teachers, artists, actors, or theatre craftsmen, and many of them are not aware that they are overshadowed by the Christ Forces.

But in the days of Madame Blavatsky this present streamlined set-up did not exist. The Masters were just getting the program organized, and Madame Blavatsky was the "girl Friday" who handled the hundreds of outer world office details. She was the ideal type for the job because all barriers, human as well as inhuman, removed themselves in the face of her executive advance. Naturally, in a public relations role, she had many dealings with printers. She was not exactly unreasonable; she was merely unyielding in her demands that "this must be finished at once for the Boss;" or in a tone of hushed confidence she would say: "The Boss wants us to do our very, very best on this work, and by the way, He was immensely pleased with your last printing job."

The harassed printers, bored by the endless daily grind, would

respond to her import-laden words as a dry sponge responds
to water. Thus refreshed, they would return merrily to their
type-setting, but only after making solicitous inquiries about
the well-being of the Boss, and complimenting Madame Blavatsky on her good fortune in working for an Employer Who
was obviously most generously endowed with every known
virtue. The printers little realized that Truth pressed close
upon them.

The famous document known as *The Secret Doctrine*, is
encyclopediac like Madame Blavatsky herself. Most of it was
dictated to her while she was residing in England. Portions
of it were supplied by various Adepts, including four Ray
Chohans and the Ascended Master Djwal Kul. However,
Madame Blavatsky did not hesitate to add her own findings,
her own deductions, if she felt that a bit of her own forthright
spirit would help to make Truth more refreshing to the public.

She drew freely on her own experiences as a lesser Initiate,
and on her personal visits with many Adepts, especially in India
and Tibet. In summation her work is brave and clear, and
for many years to come it will be required reading for every
disciple. It may not provide much Light on the particular Path
which modern disciples will follow under the new Aquarian
dispensation. But even the most astute sometimes find an
encyclopedia indispensable, and Madame Blavatsky provided,
through her writings, a complete index to human evolution as
it was understood in the Piscean cycle.

BULWER-LYTTON—

Zanoni

Zanoni is a book which should be read by every aspirant who
feels the compelling urge to ask that needless question: What
can I do personally to help the Forces of Light?

This book is classed as fiction, but that is only an editor's
way of saying that he does not have the courage to speak the
truth. Bulwer-Lytton has set forth facts as experienced by himself or other disciples who were his friends.

As an established author he served the Christ Forces by
writing this book. Disguised as fiction it was widely received

and is still much read and much discussed. It should be re-introduced to the young people of today, for despite its vintage it is still wholly enchanting.

CARR, OTIS T.—

Dimensions of Mystery

An heretofore unpublished document of scientific symbolism, revelatory of significant technological fundamentals for the Aquarian Age, *Dimensions of Mystery* offers an entirely new literary approach. It does not fall into any classification set up by Piscean Age editors. It definitely belongs in a free orbit where profundity of spirit can mingle socially with an insouciant charm.

Otis T. Carr is a Temple-Degree Frater of the Rosicrucian Order, whose Cosmic Illumination stems from the first personalities of this recorded age: Amenhotep IV and the beautiful Queen Nefertete.

This manuscript, which was written and first calligraphed by the hand of Otis T. Carr in 1952, has been previously restrained from public view pending the currently evolving readiness of observers to perceive the esoteric enlightenment that signifies a general preparation for transition into the new millennium.

Dimensions Of Mystery is an allegorical treatise of both historical and mystical aspect, which until now has been exposed to only seven persons in seven years.

Dimensions is an inspired testament to the true heritage of mankind as graven in the everlasting stone of the great Pyramid at Gizeh, and in the other six Temples of Posterity.

It makes delightful reading for everyone, but will be of especial significance to all true mystics, adepts, and other illuminati.

ELSOM, JOHN R.—

Lightning Over the Treasury Building

FRAZER FELIX and ELSA PETERS MORSE—

Tomorrow's Money

GEORGE, HENRY—Henry George School of Social Science.

Progress and Poverty

Here are three books, listed above, which will provide neo-phyte armchair economists with a feast beyond compare. How-ever, with the possible exception of *Progress and Poverty*, they are already as outmoded as the dinosaur so far as Aquarian Age disciples are concerned. Money as we know it in this year of 1958 is in the museum-piece stage on the Inner Planes. The black magicians and their teeming hordes of tools have held money completely captive for millions of years, irrespective of whether money was represented by gold, wampum or slaves from Africa.

Now all black magicians have been removed from the planet and cannot return. This is a Hierarchial decision and ir-revocable. The only remaining tools are those still in embodi-ment, and every minute of every hour of every day, their own discordant creations are closing more tightly around them. All tools, even the unwitting servers of darkness and ignorance, will destroy themselves during their present embodiment, and the rapidity of their self-destruction is being speeded up daily by the inflow of Cosmic Light.

This Cosmic Light, beamed upon the earth and its inhabitants from the heart of the Great Central Sun, causes extremely rapid fulfillment of the Law of the Circle which governs all life in the universe. Under the old order a crotchety individual could indulge for entire lifetimes in temper tantrums, emotional orgies, anger, hate, greed or lust, or any type of violence in-cluding murder. He could cycle in and out of embodiment time after time, and repeat all of his mistakes over and over again. Under the Law of the Circle his poisoned thoughtforms would travel to the periphery of the global atmosphere and back again before striking their fangs into him. Often he would be out of embodiment before the discord which he sowed returned. Of course his karma would be sitting there waiting for him when he did come back into embodiment, but by that time he was off on another destructive course of living, and it was mentally impossible for him to tie in present effects with causes which he had rooted in past centuries.

In order to rationalize these constantly recurring situations, millions of people turned to the easy way of blasphemy. They either profaned God because of their misfortunes or, if they were the more sanctimonious type, they raised their pious eyes to the ceiling cobwebs and spoke disconsolately of God's will. Official churchianity applauded loudly, because so long as their contributors shunted God out to the left field, there was a greater demand for on-the-spot services of professional prayer-mongers. For a small fee these agile performers could take the twinges out of the hinges of consciences that were creaking across the land like rusty gates.

Under their self-appointed power role, these paid professionals could officially forgive profanity and blasphemy, but they could not explain the hidden cause of such actions. They solved that problem by officially upholding as divine and insoluble all vagaries of a lucky or unlucky pattern of living, the outcome of which was more uncertain than a spinning roulette wheel.

From time to time, rumors that had to do with karma drifted through from the mysterious East. Outraged churchianity took care of that subject in a hurry, and in a way intended to make the listening sinners stop their ears and hold their tongues. The collection box was passed around with strict instructions to contribute to the poor heathens who were languishing in spicy lands like India, so ignorant that they had never heard of churchianity.

Under the new dispensation all of this has been changed. The inflowing Cosmic Light forces the closing of the Circle very rapidly. An individual who sows discord may feel the effects in his own body within an hour or two. This is of tremendous advantage to the disciple, for when he feels discord around him or within his lower bodies, he can transmute it instantly by visually blazing Violet Fire through it.

But the tools of darkness know nothing of these methods, and when their own discord closes around them they are helpless. In a short time disease grips them, and then death ensues. As

soon as they shed their physical body they are removed to
Temples of the Violet Fire to undergo purification. This purification must be satisfactorily completed before they will be
permitted to come back into embodiment.

This cleansing process will sweep through the entire economic
system on the planet in a very short time, because that is probably the most critical focus of remaining evil. Although war,
churchianity, crime and sex, are all foci of evil in themselves,
they have virtually lost their individual identities, and have
merged almost completely with the engulfing contamination
of the root of evil—money.

The secret of abundant money has been lost by the race of
man on this planet, because man has hidden it from himself in
a place he would never remember in his searchings. The secret
of money lies hidden in the law of gravity.

In the very near future man will discover that the force of
gravity can be safely utilized only if associated with levitation.
The free-energy spaceships now being built by Otis T. Carr
of Baltimore do not get off the ground by fighting against
gravity. Mr. Carr utilizes gravity to achieve the oppostie effect
—levitation. In order for a man to levitate or a craft to levitate
it is not necessary to do anything about gravity. It is not necessary to challenge gravity. Gravity can be left right where it is
—in its own negative forcefield. Any positive forcefield will
naturally float away from it.

Levitation is the exact opposite of precipitation in its effect.
In principle they are the same. Whatever is being levitated
goes up; whatever is being precipitated comes down, or is
attracted into the gravitational forcefield. We can therefore
precipitate abundance from the atmosphere, or we can, under
the Law of the new dispensation, attract to ourselves any
commodity such as money.

As a race we have completely forgotten how to levitate at
will, and yet at one time it was as simple for us as raising our
hand. But since the time of Newton we have become quite
gravity-conscious. Therefore, it is relatively easy for us to learn
to attract or precipitate.

It is easy, that is, if we clearly recognize that we are dealing with physics, and not with metaphysics. Precipitation and etherialization; gravitation and levitation, belong strictly to the high realm of pure science, and the individuals who would use these powers successfully must be pure in heart. This protection is a great divine blessing bestowed upon the race. If the impure in heart could levitate machines they would have landed rockets and warheads on the moon long ago.

Abundance of wealth will come about naturally under Law as the Space Age focuses the attention of the people on levitation of men and machines. Once levitation is accepted as possible, practical, and extremely desirable, the more familiar force of gravity will lose its hold upon the minds of men. The problem is in the mind, not in gravity itself. We must simply know and prove to ourselves that we can employ gravity at will, and that we can likewise levitate at will. The difficulty now is that we accept appearances. We see everyone around us walking on the earth by lifting only one foot at a time, so we unthinkingly do likewise. We see automobiles rolling along on four wheels and continue to manufacture them to operate in that clumsy, inefficient manner.

If we wish to change these things, we must simply refuse to accept appearances. We must then re-focus the beam of our attention. Actually it is much easier to lift two feet off the ground at the same time and levitate. It is easier to design an automobile to go over traffic, than to chug along, bumper-to-bumper, and swing in and out of traffic, mile after weary mile. In any case it is necessary to change the attention first. The result will follow naturally.

The change in our money system will come as soon as we take our attention away from the present diabolically engineered scheming, and follow natural, scientific methods of blessing money. That which is blessed grows and expands. As a race we will unite in freeing money from the imprisoning thought-forms which hold it captive. We will learn to etherialize all forms no longer needed, thus releasing the atoms and returning them to the universal storehouse.

The drastic change needed in our money system can be brought into manifestation with rapidity if we will thoughtfully

focus our attention on the third book listed in this series—
Progress and Poverty by Henry George. This economist was
one of the great men among the spiritual giants who have
appeared at opportune times upon the American scene. His
science of political economy is solidly rooted in one certain aspect of the Cosmic Law governing the service required of ele-
mental life held in manifested form. A form, whether it be a
human body or skyscraper or automobile, should be held in
manifestation only as long as it is being actively and creatively
used. But a form such as a planet is not subject to man's control, and is held in manifestation as long as it is being used as
a physical body by a planetary Logos.

All land and water on the surface of the planet therefore
belong to the universal storehouse of manifested natural resources. Man sins against the land when he lays personal claim
to it, holds it out of creative use, exploits it, or otherwise abuses
it. Henry George presented a system which, if followed, would
result in freeing all imprisoned and abused land and returning
it to the global supply of natural resources. Under his system
anyone may borrow the use of land for any constructive purpose
of production that will benefit mankind. But he states that
private ownership of land must not be permitted to continue. It
is an abuse which must be wiped out.

In his philosophy, written before the turn of the century,
he presents his reasons, in a calm, lucid manner. He always
tried to be a politely reasonable man. He hoped to win his
points with the gentle approach, for he could not bring himself
to believe that humanity was actually in love with its own foul-
ness. Yet at every turn he met with hostility and lack of acceptance. He was too valuable a man to waste on ingrates, so
he was permitted to withdraw from embodiment, leaving his
work for others to develop as a part of Saint Germain's program, until such a time as he may desire to again return to the
physical plane to take up New Age tasks.

Today we can be more forthright in our protests against
private ownership of land. Owning a piece of the physical body
of the planetary Logos, or a piece of land, is exactly the same
as owning a piece of the aggregate physical body of mankind,

or a captive slave. One is as bad as the other. The slaves have been extremely vocal about their situation and it has been alleviated in part. The good earth suffers in silence. But on the inner planes it is a silence which resounds like thunder. The storm is building up in intensity and will soon break over the usurious muddle which man pridefully calls his economic system.

Jesus had something to say about usury two thousand years ago. When He returns into outer activity as a World Teacher it is to be hoped He will not have to mention that subject. The least we can do for Him is to clean up the mess ourselves. Usury and private ownership of land are virtually synonomous today, and both must go.

Henry George knew all these things, for he carried over great memory sequences from a previous embodiment in Paris during the fateful years that preceded the French Revolution. At that time he was an active working disciple in the field of economics, although he served in another capacity at the Court of Versailles. It was during those years that Saint Germain tried to stem the tide of revolution in Europe and form the United States of Europe. At the same time He succeeded in establishing the United States of America, and it was His desire to have the entire western world peacefully organized into states held together by a common bond of understanding.

The plan of Saint Germain for a United States of Europe still remains to be carried out, but it will be successfully finalized during the next century, together with similar groupings in Asia and the Orient. Thus it can be seen that Saint Germain's United States of America is a pilot nation for the entire world.

To understand the system of political economy toward which the world is trending at the moment, we can find significant guideposts scattered all through the writings of Henry George. *Progress and Poverty* is his outstanding book because of its tremendous heart quality. The quality is there because he carried over the formulated science of political economy acquired during his years at the Court of Versailles.

When he wrote *Progress and Poverty* in the United States he was a lone worker, bringing forth cherished memories from the past. But in Paris he was part of a group of intellectuals who were spiritually oriented to their task by Saint Germain.

Their mission was a dangerous one politically and stood more to fail than to succeed at that particular time. But the men and women in the Versailles group had seen so many civilizations rise and fall that they were not concerned about that aspect. Had they not had that kind of experience in previous embodiments they would have been of no value to the group.

The Versailles group did not accomplish all that had been planned, but the one main objective did succeed and stands unshaken today—the United States of America, under the firm guardianship of Uncle Sam. Saint Germain was Samuel, the prophet, in a former embodiment, and in many incarnations had used that name. He therefore established the symbol of Himself as Uncle Sam, so that the nation which grew up around that symbol could always enjoy the protection of His guardianship.

France and America were firmly united in mutual assistance, for it was thought that when the new United States of America was launched, the French people would have the strength to lead Europe to its great destiny of unification. Russia was likewise to be included and Saint Germain was successful in placing Catherine the Great on the Russian throne. Had France continued on her path of destiny, Russia would likewise have succeeded. That plan was interrupted, but such interruptions are always temporary and hurtful only to those who refuse to follow a plan which will fit into the Divine Plan. For more than 150 years most of the energy which France and Russia have expended on their outer world work has been mis-used. Now they will have to start over again, for destiny cannot be avoided.

The Versailles group remained steadfast until the very end, hoping that Marie Antoinette would not succumb to the cloud of despair that hung over her. Saint Germain was untiring in His efforts to help her, but the task which she had so graciously accepted in happier days was more than she could cope with emotionally when she heard the ugly sound of the rabble at the palace gates.

Marie Antoinette became queen many years after the Versailles group had been organized during the reign of Louis

XV, and she had never really grasped the vision of the original
plan. It was the socially gifted Countess Jean DuBarry who
actually held the group together, both inside and outside the
palace, and during both reigns—Louis XV and XVI.

Countess DuBarry had the good sense to turn every opportunity to advantage to further whatever projects she might be
sponsoring at the moment. She possessed great personal beauty
and charm of manner plus an amazing ability to play any role
demanded, and play it to perfection. Her consummate skill as
an actress was so outstanding that she became historically identified as a courtesan, the role which she played year after year.
She was always on stage, always in character, and always willing to change roles a dozen times a day if necessary. And it
was indeed very necessary for those who expected to survive
court intrigue, scandal, lies and general blackmail. Survival
in itself was considered sufficient, and it required the gay
courage of a person like Countess DuBarry to accomplish
anything beyond that.

It was the Countess DuBarry who successfully and secretly
arranged for the cloistered meetings of the Versailles group
in an upstairs room near her quarters in the palace. Over a
period of many years these roundtable sessions were held and
detailed plans formulated for the new United States of Europe.
Documents were drafted and re-drafted, studied, discussed, and
submitted for general approval.

Downstairs in the palace reception rooms Countess DuBarry
played her gayest of roles while the meetings were in progress.
It was her task to keep everyone amused and interested so that
the long absences of certain key guests would not be noticed.
The work upstairs continued undisturbed and the final draft
of the necessary document was at last completed. It was
prepared in the palace by the most astute minds in Europe, but
it was essentially and basically for the humble, not for the
great.

It was a noble plan, prepared by those who were noble in
spirit, and it linked a free people to a free world. It was to be
a Declaration of Independence for all Europe, but it never

reached the eyes or ears or hearts of the very people it might have set free from limitations.

At the very end, when the people were crying for bread, Marie Antoinette was urged to give them more than bread— to give them the good earth itself and its abundance, for that is what the document would have provided. But Marie was a queen, carefully schooled in the ways of a queen. She knew nothing about the ways of a peasant mob. She was easily disturbed by their noise, their jeers, their uncleanliness. The document was beyond her scope of understanding. The people had asked for bread, and she had suggested cake. In utter confusion she attempted to flee from the scene of her great error.

Long years after the guillotine had taken its toll, and peace had settled over Paris once again, a clerk placed the document of the Versailles group in a proper file in the public library. Sometimes American visitors in Paris call to see it and to ponder over its quaint script. But the message is not quaint. It is still as fresh and bright as the high vision that Henry George brought with him into embodiment in America. The ideals which had been set forth when Henry George worked with the Versailles group remained so crystal-clear in his consciousness that his *Progress and Poverty* is almost a duplicate of the Versailles document.

LEADBEATER, C. W.—

The Chakras
Thoughtforms (In collaboration with Annie Besant)
Man, Visible and Invisible
Occult Chemistry (1951 Edition)
Man—Where, Whence and Whither

Here is a reading feast that includes some of the very choicest Piscean Age ingredients. Some of the statements in the two books on that most puzzling of subjects—man—may be confusing to the Aquarian disciple. But the reader should keep in mind one salient fact—when these great spiritual pioneers were plowing a path through a world atmosphere which reeked with the stuffy smugness of Victorianism, they were working

blind, trying to feel their way. If the furrow they plowed is
not quite straight it only means that Aquarian disciples must
smooth out the rough places. A reading of these books will
orient the alert disciple as to where to begin his work.

Remember that this globe and all inhabitants, both in embodiment and between embodiments, have been under planetary
Law until very recently. When spaceships began to be seen
frequently, and the attention of the people became focused
on things interplanetary, a new state of consciousness was born.
Nearly ten billion souls associated with evolution on this planet
must now get themselves into a state of mind wherein they can
freely accept, not only space visitors from other planets, but
also the complete freedom from limitations which Cosmic Law
will bring to this planet.

We can no longer accept death as a natural event here on
earth, because our new neighbors on other planets do not know
limitations such as disease, and death from disease. They do
change physical bodies from time to time, but the change is
completely under control of the individual. It is made for some
specific reason and is not regarded as a matter of distress for
anyone.

Likewise, we can no longer accept the scientific methods used
on this planet, and the long and costly experimental research
projects. It is an utter waste of time to spend years in a
laboratory trying to find an answer to a certain problem, when
a few minutes spent in communication with scientists on another
planet would result in the needed data. Those students who
would like to start some fascinating scientific explorations immediately, can do no better than get acquainted with Leadbeater's *Occult Chemistry*.

Leadbeater and Annie Besant worked in close collaboration
on the original volume which is out of print. But when the
Hindu disciple, C. Jinarajadasa, grew to maturity and became
head of the Theosophical Society, he revised *Occult Chemistry*
and brought it out in a large new edition in 1951.

There is a very interesting story connected with these two
men. The Leadbeater family originally lived in England, and
the father, a railroad builder, was called to South America to

supervise a new line which was being constructed in forested
territory inhabited only by wandering Indian tribes. There
were two sons in the family—Charles and a younger brother.
One day when the father planned to visit the construction site
for a couple of hours and then return directly to his home in a
nearby town, he took the two boys with him.

Shortly after they arrived the construction camp was attacked
by hostile Indians, and the younger boy was killed. Many years
passed and, back in England again, Charles completed his education and entered the ministry. He was assigned to a parish
and was regarded as highly successful in his chosen work. One
evening he happened to go to a lecture which was given in
London by Helena Petrovna Blavatsky. He sat listening in
spellbound attention, and when at the end of the lecture Madame
Blavatsky announced that she was leaving the following day for
India, Charles Leadbeater determined that he would accompany her, and her small group of disciples.

Within a matter of hours, Charles Leadbeater changed the
entire course of his life. He left everything—home, church,
family, friends, financial security, and even his native country.
With only his personal possessions and a completely new state
of consciousness, he joined the group for the long boat journey.
On the boat he had many conversations with Madame Blavatsky.
With this brief instruction he arrived in India and embarked
upon a new way of life that was almost the exact opposite of
the one he had so abruptly left behind.

He had been in India only a short time when he discovered
why he had made the journey. The parents of a small boy in
a distant village sent for him. They had discovered that their
little son had a certain destiny planned when he came into
incarnation, and he was to be placed in the care of Charles
Leadbeater in order to receive proper training. It was in this
manner that the little boy who was killed by the Indians in
South America, was restored to his older brother, Charles.

These days we are living through now are the most spiritually
exciting we have known on this globe for millions of years, particularly in America. In times past, about the only opportunities
that disciples had to get together in mutual recognition and

compare notes, was between embodiments or during sleeping hours when they met in their subtle bodies.

But now, since the beginning of this century, they are being gathered together again, and this time on the physical plane. Those who went out of embodiment, even recently, are returning to help establish Saint Germain's new Golden Age civilization. America is the heart center, and as the years pass, disciples who have served the Forces of Light down through long ages, will meet here in physical embodiment, but this time they will recognize each other's historical accomplishments.

It is around these historical accomplishments that the new history books will be written. All school children should bless this happy day when those frightful Piscean compilations of dates, dates, dates, and wars, wars, wars, can be tossed into the nearest trash basket. If book-burning fiestas should become the vogue, this is one time in history when they will be justified, and a bit of delicious fuel could be contributed in the form of many, many magazines, newspapers, and other periodicals which serve as shockers to jolt man's emotional body and force it to absorb more astral debris.

Luk, A. D. K.--

Law of Life (Book I)
Law of Life (Book II)

Here is the new textbook for the Aquarian Age, and it can be truly said that a book of this kind has never before been published. It is the Aquarian Age in essence, expressed in lucid words. Without a single quibble, it presents straight-forward rules for traveling the swift evolutionary road that will lead us all away from earth's classrooms to the distant stars. No longer will the student or seeking aspirant have time to spend laborious years in the pursuit of Truth. The pace will be swift and one-pointed in this Aquarian cycle, with all paths leading to the one glorious goal of the Ascension.

In this simple but magnificent work by A.D.K. Luk, the answers to life's problems stand clear and serene above the Piscean muddle of everyday living. With these two volumes

at hand, one can forget all yesterdays and step over into the
new Aquarian way of life with confidence and joy.

Specifically *Law of Life* presents unified teachings of Principles. No matter where you stand at the moment, and regardless of previous training, you can apply these unified teachings
without the slightest trepidition, because they are solidly rooted
in Principles; they are not tainted by personal opinions. Yet
they are vital and refreshing, and have the appealing warmth
of heart-quality that makes them a joy to read over and over.

The inner heart's search is for Truth, not fiction. The great
universal miracle of creation, the operation of the universe, and
the Principles which govern all, are Truth-in-Action. This is
the Truth that nourishes the eternal heart Flame.

Law of Life gives methods of practical application of laws
which cover every phase of daily living, in every walk of life.
These laws can be applied to adjust all your affairs of the day,
from the moment you waken in the morning until you sleep at
night. It is all there, to be applied to family and home life, to
business, health, and supply, to friends, to strangers, and to all
world events, from weather to politics.

Life's essentials are no longer a mystery, and a reading of
these two books will tell you why we are here, where we came
from, how we individualized, what we are meant to do, where
we are going and exactly what the *goal* is, and how we may attain it.

The *Real You* can be drawn forth into expression through
applying the laws of life, not at some particular moment or
hour of the day, but all day and every day. Latent talents and
powers from within can be drawn forth into outer activity, and
any task completed in joy and in triumph.

Law of Life is based on Retreat Work, formerly offered
only to those who gave up all outer world activity and devoted
their entire time to cloistered instruction supervised by Ascended
Masters. In the Aquarian Age the student will remain right
where he is—in home, family, business, nation—and yet receive
Retreat training. In other words, all persons will be students,
and the entire globe will constitute one vast classroom offering

Retreat studies. *Law of Life* is therefore a Retreat textbook, available for immediate use in the outer world.

It gives explanations of the Sacred Fire, of the actions of the Flame, of the word of Power—I AM. It explains the Presence, the use of the Transmuting Violet Flame, the organization of the Hierarchy, and the location of Retreats which are now used by students during their sleeping hours when their subtle bodies are freed from the physical.

Law of Life is a condensation of instruction given by Ascended Master Saint Germain and other Ascended Masters, covering potent points, vital information, and instruction never before published. Certain points of law which might have proved difficult to understand under the old dispensation are completely clarified.

The books will appeal to all readers—those who are just getting acquainted with this type of teaching, those who are sincerely desirous of stepping on the Path, and those who have traveled further along the way. Advanced disciples will not only discover a fresh approach to certain points, but will also find these books ideal to offer to those seekers who are in need of a constructive compilation of this sort.

Most home problems will vanish if these books are placed in the hands of parents and their children. In the Aquarian Age even very young children will seek to understand the eternal verities, and they will not be content with a partial answer. They will want the Truth.

MANN, THOMAS—

> *The Magic Mountain*
> *Joseph and His Brothers*

Keep these books in mind when you need another solid plank in the bridge between the old age and the new. For a while now we can still use the retrospective view so admirably expressed in *Joseph and His Brothers*. But as Joseph and all the other great figures of history cycle back into incarnation and achieve new heights of spiritual greatness, we will see them in-action-now and the past will fade from human memory. We will remember only the future, the goal which will complete our circle of evolution by uniting us to the only past worth grasping—our Source.

The Magic Mountain makes delightful reading at any time, but it belongs to a special group of books which tell in somewhat symbolical, yet extremely practical terms, the story of evolving man scaling his last mountain peak of consciousness —a peak that has for so long concealed from his view the effulgent glory of his Father's House.

Do not read this book until you have digested the paragraphs listed toward the end of this compilation, under the name of author James Ramsey Ullman.

MORGAN, CHARLES—Macmillan, New York and London

  Sparkenbroke
  The Fountain
  The River Line

Seek out a quiet spot and live with these books. Let their healing essence flow over you. Here is discipleship of the highest order expressed in books that reached best-seller popularity. *The River Line* was made into a play which had a short run in London, and as the writer seems to recall, it also laid an egg in New York. But that was not the fault of the play. It was presented in an era when theatregoers had acquired such jaded appetites that everything they consumed tasted like eggs, very scrambled and very stale.

Now that we have lived through dark days, and darker nights, of tawdry episode, let us relax and breathe the fresh, clean atmosphere created by the magic pen of Charles Morgan. Again, it should be kept in mind that the beating hearts of matters considered by this author are anchored in the last days of the Piscean age. The rugged path of discipleship revealed in these stories presents an appalling picture at times, with the suffering disciple in the full grip of every neurosis in medical annals.

The picture is correct, nevertheless, for a disciple achieves Mastership only by learning to master all situations he meets in the outer world. Sloshing through Piscean puddles he met with one abomination after another. If he was not exactly

serene and clear-headed at all times he can be forgiven for
his off-the-beam moments.

O'NEILL, JOHN J.—

Prodigal Genius

Here is the great story of the electrical age, founded by that
Venusian genius, Nikola Tesla, who volunteered to take embodiment on this planet in years when life here was not fit for
a pigeon, much less a man—and unspeakably putrid for a
gentleman and a scholar. However, he stayed with it physically
for 87 years, and then arranged to keep his eye on the situation
from a higher and more pleasant vantage point among the
Ascended Masters.

Tesla went out of embodiment in 1943, and O'Neill followed him a few years later. *Prodigal Genius* was published in
1944 and has served until now as the only substantial record
of Tesla's inventive achievements on this globe. However, in
1944, Kenneth Arnold had not yet made his famous sighting of
spaceships which led to the flying-saucer-conscious world of
today.

O'Neill probably knew nothing of Tesla's true origin, and
from his writings in *Prodigal Genius* it is quite apparent that
he had not even a slight suspicion that Tesla's great mission
was a voluntary one on behalf of the Forces of Light.

In *Return of the Dove*, this aspect of Tesla's role in the unfoldment of the Divine Plan, is made clear. The fact then
emerges that the relationship between Tesla and O'Neill was
that of Teacher and aspiring disciple, and it is likewise apparent
that the relationship had to be continued on the inner planes.
O'Neill had not yet achieved a clarity of consciousness and
freedom from limitations which would have enabled him to
remain in physical embodiment and receive teachings through
overshadowing.

The Aquarian Age civilization should reap rich benefits from
this association between Tesla and his eager pupil, when O'Neill
returns to the earth plane from his sojourn in the realms of
wisdom, and finds this happy planet to be once more a fertile
spot for the application of constructive endeavors.

PRINTZ, THOMAS—The Bridge to Freedom, Box 5, Flourtown, Pennsylvania.

> *The Seven Mighty Elohim Speak on the Seven Steps to Precipitation*
> *The Seven Beloved Archangels Speak*
> *Memoirs of Beloved Mary, Mother of Jesus*
> *The Archangel Michael, His Work and His Helpers*
> *The First Ray* (By Its Chohan, El Morya)
> *The Seventh Ray* (By Its Chohan, Saint Germain)
> *The Bridge to Freedom* (A monthly journal)

Thomas Printz is an American pseudonym used by El Morya, Chohan of the First Ray. He has recently presented several books through His publishing enterprise in Pennsylvania.

The monthly journal, which is edited by Thomas Printz, presents writings by the seven Ray Chohans, and by Their group leader, the Maha Chohan, formerly the historical personage known as Homer, who gave the Iliad and the Odyssey to the world.

ROCHAMBEAU—Congress of the United States of America

> *A Commemoration* (Prepared by authority of the American Congress and the Congressional Library by DeB. Randolph Keim.)
> *Rochambeau, Father and Son* (Translation published by Henry Holt and Company, New York. First part by Jean-Edmond Weelan; second part by the Vicomte de Rochambeau.)

In the pattern of swiftly changing world events that formulate the Aquarian program of the new Lord of Civilization, Ascended Master Saint Germain and His Twin-Ray, Portia, the Goddess of Justice, the name of Rochambeau will stand as a guiding beacon. This is a name to which our New Age school children will turn in love and confidence, as they struggle to separate Truth from that steaming bog of emotionalized fiction which our deluded educators dare to call history.

The history of a redeemed humanity is now being written —but not by those who love to wallow in blood and gore, and certainly not by those misguided free-willers who feel they are not really living it up unless they bathe daily in sweat and tears.

Return of the Dove is a swift historical review covering the past nineteen million years, and it will be a blessing to world consciousness if such a review can be accepted as a post-mortem to end all post-mortems. To continually dwell upon the sordid story of the past, and to continually hunger after juicy and rotten morsels of history, is not only useless but extremely dangerous. Such emotional and mental dawdling establishes a link with the lagging laggards who brought the reign of darkness to this planet. Remember that thousands of these dark force tools are still in embodiment, and still contaminating the air we breathe with their emanations of hate and greed.

Some fortunate disciples have enough light in their consciousness to just call quits with the past and transmute the etheric records which tie them to it. But the average person still craves for comprehension. He must have a clear, visual picture of the last nineteen million years, and then take a good understanding look at it before he can generate enough courage to transmute and sever all links which bind him to nostalgic memories.

Transmutation is achieved only through proper use of the Seventh Ray of the Violet Fire. This Ray swung into manifestation in 1675. Francis Bacon had been prepared through many, many embodiments for his present great historical role as Chohan of the Seventh Ray and Lord of Civilization. He has the task of housecleaning the globe of all laggards, and from this time on a laggard will be one who refuses to accept the Ascension story, personally demonstrated by Jesus. The planet must be completely cleared of laggards and all their accumulation of filth, during the next 2000 years.

The reason for the present over-population of the globe is because we are trying to accommodate about eighteen sub-races of three Root Races, on the planet. It simply cannot be done, and no Ascended Master would have attempted it. The abortive attempt was made by the free-willers who desired to take all matters concerning Creation away from God, and handle them in a high and mighty, and extremely brassy, pentagon manner.

Now that Ascended Master Saint Germain is back on the job in His role as Uncle Sam of America, the big global house-cleaning is in full swing. This is not just a surface dusting, for even the etheric records (which some call the akashic) are getting a thorough Violet Ray treatment. The etheric records of the world contain all the subconscious memories of all events on the globe, back to the beginning. The etheric body or the subconscious of each individual contains a similar record of all memories relating to that individual. Thus an individual is constantly adding to his own subconscious structure, and at the same time contributing to the global subconscious.

Before the laggards came these subconscious structures were perfect. After discord was introduced the etheric records had to accurately register all disharmony as well as harmony. Now Saint Germain is housecleaning certain etheric records with the aid of His disciples who, in former embodiments, were present when the etheric records were made.

For instance, until a few years ago there existed a complete etheric record of the beginning of the Revolutionary War. In the ethers, the first shot was still coming out of the gun barrel, and any historian who wished to write on the subject of the War could, by mentally reflecting on the theme, tie in with the etheric vibrations. He could pick up such an accurate vibrational picture that he might well feel that he was there on the original scene, firing the first shot.

In line with the Aquarian program, Ascended Master Saint Germain wished to remove all such discordant memories of great battle events, so that humanity might more easily forget war. Nearly all of the disciples who worked closely with Uncle Sam in the American and French revolutions, are back in embodiment. With the aid of Washington, Lafayette, Benjamin Franklin, Rochambeau and many others, Saint Germain has visited certain historic spots, and together the group has transmuted the discord in the original etheric records. Thus the cleansed Revolutionary records still stand, but they no longer give off a vibration of pain and discord. They do give off a true vibration of magnificent triumph, of glorious achievement, and of a cosmic victory gained by Ascended Masters working in collaboration with angels, elementals and men.

All history of the future will date approximately from the late Francis Bacon period, with flashbacks to those great scenes of Bacon's earlier triumphs as Joseph, gentle guardian of Mary and the babe Jesus; as Columbus, setting his face toward America, the heart-center of the globe; and as Uncle Sam, sitting in a secluded Boston garden, counselling with His disciples, pouring His great strength into Washington; and finally, when even that was not enough, calling upon the noble Rochambeau, the valiant disciple who could lead French troops into America to save the beating Heart of the world.

In 1940 George Washington, back in embodiment for the last time to assist Ascended Master Saint Germain in the Aquarian program, made his Ascension. The other great Revolutionary leader, Rochambeau, will continue to carry on outer world projects for Saint Germain. In 1907 the Congress of the United States of America compiled and published an impressive commemorative volume, honoring Rochambeau as leader of the French Auxiliary Forces in the War of Independence. At the same time a magnificent statue of Rochambeau was unveiled in Lafayette Park, near the White House, in Washington, D.C.

In 1936, just four years before Washington made his Ascension, a book was published in New York, entitled *Rochambeau, Father and Son.* The first part was published earlier in France, and the second part was originally written by Rochambeau's young son, who accompanied his father on the historical marches in America, and who had the foresight to keep a running diary of daily events. A foreword to *Rochambeau, Father and Son,* was written by Gilbert Chinard of John Hopkins University of Baltimore. It was in the area of Baltimore, south to Yorktown, Virginia, that Rochambeau marshalled his strongest forces and achieved his brilliant victories that enabled the Duc d'Enghien to say: "Thanks to you America is free."

It is to be hoped that all Americans in this great land, this heart-center of planet Earth, will remember those words, and repeat them in gratitude and in recognition of the magnificent comradeship shown by Saint Germain's stalwart disciples who went forward and prepared the way.

SAINT GERMAIN—Saint Germain Press, Chicago

Unveiled Mysteries
The Magic Presence
The I Am Discourses

These three outstanding books were dictated by Ascended Master Saint Germain to Godfre Ray King in the years of the early '30's. King, a former historical personage associated with Saint Germain's newly established United States of America, completed his discipleship in this embodiment and made his Ascension. The recording and publishing of these books rounded out his centuries of work on behalf of Saint Germain, and presented to readers a formulated concept of Principles through which Ascended Master Saint Germain's new Golden Age will rise to untold heights of glory.

SPAULDING, BAIRD T.—De Vorss & Company, 520 West 9th St.. Los Angeles 15, Calif.

Life and Teaching of the Masters of the Far East
(Five vols.)

In presenting his five-volume narrative on experiences during several years of living and learning among the Great Masters of the Himalayas, Mr. Spaulding has emphasized his personal belief in the Masters' abilities to demonstrate the workings of the profound laws of the Universe, which carry a promise that Man on Earth will soon inherit the illumination that will let him learn to transcend death and find the way to Eternal Life.

STEINER, RUDOLF—Anthroposophic Press, New York

Knowledge of the Higher World and Its Attainment

Rudolf Steiner was in many ways a great disciple, but he will be best remembered as an educator who wrote his own textbooks and then established schools in which his teachings could be presented, even in a world hostile to his basic concepts.

Many readers will find the followers of Steiner somewhat fanatical in their zeal, but only the most determined and emphatic servers were able to stand up against Piscean dogmatism.

So if you are inclined to the mistaken notion that Steiner was at heart an old-fashioned schoolmaster, just search through his early writings for one of his memorable statements. In effect he said that the dark forces were always on guard to prevent people from becoming too alert mentally. He predicted that in the twentieth century improved conditions in education would lead the forces of evil to use poisonous chemicals to make the populace stupid. He said that the people would even give their approval to mass-poisoning, for they would endorse and uphold fluoridation of the public water supply.

ULLMAN, JAMES RAMSEY—G. P. Putnam's Sons, New York
Tiger of the Snows

This is a fine example of a new age book designed to please the readers of popular sellers, and yet carry the high message that speaks only from the inner heart of a great solitude.

Author James Ramsey Ullman has given to the world some of the best books ever written on the subject of mountains and mortal men. In *Tiger of the Snows* he has presented the autobiography of Tenzing Norgay, the simple unlettered Sherpa who climbed his way to world fame by scaling Mount Everest with Edmund Hillary in the spring of 1953.

To the average reader the book has a warm, heart appeal not usually associated with so factual a story. But to disciples who understand the significance of two human beings standing atop Mount Everest, the successful pilgrimage to that high peak heralds the actual dawning of the new age on earth.

Great events have to be rooted in certain spots which serve as a magnetic focus. At the dawn of the Piscean Age the final triumph of the old and the great beginning of the new took place on Mount Calvary. It was not until around the time Everest was scaled, that a motion picture of *The Robe* portrayed a scene on the journey up the slopes of Calvary in which Jesus was shown as a Man tied to the end of a rope, and pulled forward and upward in this fashion by another man.

In 1953 a similar drama was re-enacted on the heights of Everest, but with a joyous, triumphal ending that sounded round the world by radio. The successful scaling of Everest by those particular men at that particular time was not a happenstance. It was a planned revelation and fulfillment of an ancient prophecy, as was the ascent of Calvary. If the rope was used in the original Calvary scene, the fact was apparently not recorded. But when *The Robe* was filmed, that was one of the never-to-be-forgotten scenes in the picture.

The release of the film was timed to make its impact on the consciousness of the public during the period when the Everest expedition was receiving widespread publicity and documentation. This penetration of world consciousness came about through energies which are released during great cosmic moments. A few years before the final successful achievement, the Ascended Master Djwal Kul had stated in His writings that the ancient prophecy was nearing fulfillment, and that the Hierarchy was watching with careful interest all plans to scale Mount Everest. He stated that when the peak was scaled, it would indicate that the hour had come when the human race had completed its last evolutionary ascent out of the densest aspect of materialism.

WOOD, ERNEST E.—E. P. Dutton & Co., Inc., New York
>   *Practical Yoga, Ancient and Modern*
>   *The Glorious Presence*

Professor Wood has authored these and many other books, all of which make inspiring and worthwhile reading. The writer is one of the great educators of the world, but his achievements in that field were confined largely to India. He labored there for thirty-nine years after becoming interested in colonial problems which were very close to his early life in England.

His years in India were colorful ones, for he had a flair for establishing lasting bonds of friendship wherever he went. He entered into the profundities of the very spirit of India, and emerged as an understanding student of their ancient philosophies, and also of Sanskrit. He handled the language so gracefully that he contributed to the English-speaking world one of the most acceptable of all translations of the Bhagavad Gita.

9 781564 599759